GLOBAL LATINAS

GLOBAL LATINAS

Latin America's emerging multinationals

Lourdes Casanova

First published 2009 by
PALGRAVE MACMILLAN

Palgrave Macmillan in the UK is an imprint of Macmillan Publishers Limited, registered in England, company number 785998, of Houndmills, Basingstoke, Hampshire RG21 6XS.

Palgrave Macmillan in the US is a division of St Martin's Press LLC, 175 Fifth Avenue, New York, NY 10010.

Palgrave Macmillan is the global academic imprint of the above companies and has companies and representatives throughout the world.

Palgrave® and Macmillan® are registered trademarks in the United States, the United Kingdom, Europe and other countries.

ISBN-13: 978–0–230–21996–0
ISBN-10: 0–230–21996–9

This book is printed on paper suitable for recycling and made from fully managed and sustained forest sources. Logging, pulping and manufacturing processes are expected to conform to the environmental regulations of the country of origin.

A catalogue record for this book is available from the British Library.

A catalog record for this book is available from the Library of Congress.

10   9   8   7   6   5   4   3   2   1
18   17   16   15   14   13   12   11   10   09

Printed and bound in Great Britain by
CPI Antony Rowe, Chippenham and Eastbourne

To Soumitra and Sara

CONTENTS

CONTENTS

FOREWORD

'THE NEXT GENERATION OF LATIN CHAMPIONS'
LUIS ALBERTO MORENO,
PRESIDENT, INTER-AMERICAN DEVELOPMENT BANK

One of the great unheralded stories of Latin America's recent economic recovery and one of its most hopeful offshoots is the rise
of the so-called 'Multilatinas' or 'Global Latinas', companies born in
the region with global aspirations and increasingly internationalized
business models. The emergence of these regional champions as world-
class competitors in manufacturing, natural resources, services and
even technology is undoubtedly a testament to the region's increased
economic maturity and its potential for successful insertion into the
globalized economy. Companies as diverse as Cemex, Vale, Tenaris
and Concha y Toro have carved profitable niches in the four corners
of the globe, bringing disruptive process and product innovations to
their sectors and giving established multinational corporations a run
for their money in their home markets and elsewhere.

To be sure, the recent success of the Global Latinas has been bol-
stered by high commodity prices and rapid economic growth in the
region and beyond. But these benevolent macrotrends are only part of
the story. In fact, one could argue, as Lourdes Casanova does convinc-
ingly in this important book, that it is adversity, rather than prosperity,
that has contributed most to these firms' ascent into global powerhouses. Much like the Darwinian struggle of organisms for fitness and
survival, these companies have endured such trials and negotiated
such obstacles as the boom-bust cycles that have characterized Latin
American economies, the lack of adequate access to long-term capital,
recurring crisis and major devaluations. These stumbling blocks, as well
as changing economic and regulatory frameworks, have contributed
to make them resourceful, nimble and opportunistic. At the same

time, family-ownership in some cases and partial or total government control in others have often enabled them to take the long view.

Governments in the region should continue working towards improving the conditions for the creation and growth of businesses at home, as well as bettering standards of corporate governance and fostering broader ownership of firms. They should take advantage of increased stability and prosperity in the region and work to nourish an environment to facilitate entrepreneurship, so that more companies can survive and prosper and more will thrive abroad. And both governments and corporations bear the responsibility for establishing the necessary conditions for achieving sustainable development with social equity: higher-quality education, better infrastructure, smarter regulatory regimes. I certainly look forward to the day when non-profit Global Latinas make headlines around the world.

The Inter-American Development Bank is proud to have partnered with INSEAD to support this notable book and looks forward to continuing to support countries, companies and foundations in Latin America in the creation of better, fairer, more sustainable business environments that can spawn the champions of the future.

PREFACE

This book builds on the research project entitled *Global Latinas – From Multilatinas to Global Latinas*, conducted in 2007–2008 under the supervision of the author, and funded by INSEAD and the Inter-American Development Bank. The study focused on the international expansion of Latin American multinational companies, in order to identify key success factors and the patterns and strategies utilized by these corporations to succeed beyond their home markets. The research project employed both empirical and case-based approaches, covering a total of 11 large and small companies from various sectors. This book goes beyond the research project to explore other Global Latinas and looks at relevant topics like country and corporate branding, corporate citizenship, leadership, privatization, national champions and trade agreements. All these issues influence the progress of the emerging multinationals from Latin America.

ACKNOWLEDGMENTS

A book is a long journey. This one started ten years ago with my MBA course about business in Latin America at INSEAD and at the Haas School of Business at the University of California at Berkeley. The accent in international management research had shifted to Asia in the 1990s and there was a definite vacuum in business education about Latin America and its firms. I spent the following decade developing case studies on successful firms from the region and fine-tuning courses on Latin American business, for both MBA students and executives. During 2007, I was the lead investigator in a research project, jointly undertaken by INSEAD and the Inter-American Development Bank, on emerging multinationals from Latin America. This book is the result of all of these efforts over the past ten years.

Every book is also the cumulative result of the efforts of many. A key contributor has been Matthew Fraser, senior research fellow at INSEAD and a co-author of the report on the joint research with the Inter-American Development Bank. My research has also benefited from the support of Henning Höber, Samantha Rullán and Anne Dumas, visiting researchers at INSEAD. This book would not have been possible without the generous support and collaboration of Carolyn Robert, senior trade and investment specialist at the Inter-American Development Bank and Orkestra, the Competitiveness Institute of the Basque Country. Thanks are also due to Yann Brenner from the Paris office of the Inter-American Development Bank, Andrea Goldstein from the OECD, Carlos Arruda from Brazilian business school Fundação Dom Cabral, Ramón Molina from Adolfo Ibáñez University in Chile and Hafiz Mirza and Anne Miroux from UNCTAD. The insights of the CEOs and executives of all companies interviewed for my research are gratefully acknowledged. The book has also benefited from the feedback of my colleagues from INSEAD's strategy department. Last but not least, my editors Morice Mendoza and Peter Bradley have played a key role in shaping the presentation of the ideas and results of my research.

I am very pleased with the end result, but realize that some oversights and errors may still remain in the text – they are my sole responsibility.

Finally, every book is also a personal journey – it is not always easy to separate the professional from the personal neatly. The book is dedicated to the two people with whom I have the pleasure of sharing my life journey: my husband Soumitra and daughter Sara. Without their encouragement, the book would not have been possible.

INTRODUCTION:
THE EMERGENCE OF THE GLOBAL LATINAS

> The new 'multi-Latinas' are aggressive, resourceful enterprises
> that are a developing byproduct of the market liberalization
> that swept Latin American economies in the 1990s.
>
> C. Krauss, 'Latin American companies make big
> US gains', *New York Times*, 2 May 2007

In the past few years, emerging-market companies have stormed onto
the world stage. Among them are a number of growing corporate giants
from Latin America. They are called the 'Global Latinas' – that is, Latin
American companies that have come on to the world stage and have
succeeded in the United States, European Union or Asia – and the
reasons for their dramatic appearance and the major potential they
represent are the subject of this book.

Suddenly, or so it appeared, companies such as Mexican cement producer Cemex or Brazilian iron ore giant Vale made the front pages
of the world's financial press with their huge billion-dollar acquisitions in Europe and North America. And in 2008, the leader of one
'Global Latina', Carlos Slim, the chief architect of the hugely successful Mexican mobile company, América Móvil, was named the
world's second-richest man, above Bill Gates and after Warren Buffett. Although at the time few knew much about these Latin American
super-companies, they had not appeared out of thin air. In the previous 20 years, they had gone through an extraordinary transformation
brought about by market liberalization and dynamic leadership.

Lorenzo Zambrano, for example, had taken Cemex – a company
founded by his grandfather in 1906 – from a small, local player in
Mexico to the third biggest company in the cement sector in the entire
world. How Cemex got there is a dramatic story that can be replicated
in many of the other thrusting new Global Latinas.

1

For a number of reasons, the Latinas developed compelling competitive advantages which have propelled them onto the world stage and enabled them to thrive. They are not 'lucky' third-world beneficiaries of an extraordinary period of high commodity prices. Even those firms that have benefited from the hike in oil and iron ore prices had already built carefully considered business models geared toward international expansion.

The new global firms in the region come from a diverse range of industries, from aircraft manufacturing all the way to fast food. This new business force from Latin America deserves its own study, as the conditions in the region and the leaders it has spawned have created something unique. This book is dedicated to chronicling their success stories.

A SHIFTING GLOBAL CONTEXT

In the, by now famous, 2003 report, *Dreaming with BRICs: The path to 2050*, Jim O'Neill at investment bank Goldman Sachs had predicted that four emerging economies would grow at a rapid pace and become a significant force in the global economy.[1] These were Brazil, Russia, India and China, from which the 'BRIC' acronym came. In 2007, well-respected economists such as Martin Wolf of the *Financial Times* were examining whether the emerging economies could keep the wheels of the global economy spinning around, even if the US economy slowed down.[2] Previously, it was always assumed that if the United States sneezed everyone else would catch a cold. But the success of the BRIC nations was so great that a new theory of 'de-coupling' had emerged, in which the new economies would continue to grow at a fast pace even if the developed nations went through a sluggish period. And Aloizio Mercadante, a senator for Brazilian president Lula da Silva's Partido dos Trabalhadores (PT, or Workers' Party), confidently declared to the *Financial Times* that Brazil would not 'catch a cold' if the US economy slowed down. He said, 'Now (July 2008) the US is in intensive care and we haven't even sneezed'.[3]

A fundamental shift in the global economy has been taking place over the last couple of decades. The axis of the world economy is shifting eastwards. China, in particular, has emerged as the principal driving force in Asia. The economic miracle taking place in China has enriched millions of people. One of the effects of this is an increased demand for food, including meat, leading to a rise in food prices.

China's industrial and construction sectors have also increased the demand for commodities such as copper, iron and oil, which again helped to push up prices in 2008. Some Chinese companies are becoming global powerhouses and making it to the 'Fortune Global 500' list in relatively large numbers. In one recent academic study, it has been argued that Chinese 'dragons' have introduced a devastating new competitive weapon into their arsenal: cost innovation.[4] In this theory, Chinese firms have found a way to drive costs down and deliver high-value goods, leaving little room for companies in developed countries to compete. One of the answers to this threat is for Western firms to learn the art of cost innovation – or join up with a Chinese partner. The implications of Asian competition for Latin America are immense. Chapter 6 examines this in detail.

India might be catching up. Since the 1980s, the Indian government has encouraged free-market growth. However, successive governments have failed to provide a first-class infrastructure to support the new businesses that have been growing at a rapid pace. In particular, the big stars in the information technology (IT) services sector such as Tata Consultancy Services (TCS), Infosys and Wipro have grown in spite of a poor infrastructure. Anyone who visits these companies in gridlocked Bangalore will soon see the problem.

Nonetheless, India, with state support for growth industries such as IT services (reducing taxation, for instance), and legions of newly qualified, English-speaking engineers spilling out from the country's excellent universities, such as the Indian Institute of Technology, has become a significant economic player on the world scene. In 2004, Professor C.K. Prahalad published his book, *The Fortune at the Bottom of the Pyramid*,[5] highlighting a debate on the potential value of large, low-income markets in emerging countries, provided the companies concerned shaped appropriate and often innovative business models to appeal to them. Naturally enough, local companies with a deep understanding of their local markets were better equipped to do so, a trend that has been just as pronounced in Latin America (see Chapter 4).

Prahalad argued that these were important innovations that Western firms should take note of if they wanted to prosper in new markets in the developing world. That argument has been won. The proof is to be found in the number of companies, such as IBM and Cisco, that have made India an important base for their business.

The rise of global firms from Latin America first attracted attention in the 1990s. But today we are entering a new phase as a significant number of companies have emerged from the region to join the ranks of the global giants. Ten Latin American companies – five from Brazil and five from Mexico – were listed in 2008's 'Fortune Global 500', representing one-seventh of the total number from emerging markets.[6]

In Boston Consulting Group's (BCG's) 2007 *100 New Global Challengers* list of top companies from the rapidly developing economies, there were 17 newcomers, of which five came from Latin America.[7] Latin American firms were at the heart of a new and exciting phenomenon that BCG had identified. The BCG 100 managed 'superior value creation', 'revved-up' revenues and more potent profits than their counterparts in the developed world. Overall, they accounted for 17.3 percent of real gross domestic product (GDP) worldwide, up from 15.7 percent in 2005. The report identified some key dimensions of these new global stars, citing Latin American companies as examples. For instance, as with the Mexican telecom América Móvil, some rolled out new business models to multiple markets. Or, as with the Brazilian cosmetics company Natura Cosméticos, others took their local brands global.

An Accenture report recognized the same seismic changes brought about by the booming economies in the developing world, identifying five models of global expansion for emerging-market companies: full-fledged globalizers, such as Mexican cement company Cemex; regional players that expand out of domestic markets to achieve scale, such as Mexican telecom América Móvil; global sourcers looking for raw materials, such as Brazilian oil company Petrobras; global sellers, such as Brazilian iron ore producer Vale; and multi-regional niche players, such as the Brazilian IT company Politec. As the above examples show, Global Latinas are to be found in each of these five categories.

Accenture's report noted that over US$3 trillion of foreign direct investment (FDI) had flowed into emerging markets in 2006, representing 26 percent of world FDI stock.[8] In Latin America, *América Economía* reported in 2007 that 334 of the top 500 Latin American corporations had revenues in excess of US$1 billion.[9] According to the Economic Commission for Latin America and the Caribbean (ECLAC), outward flows of FDI from Latin America had 'skyrocketed' to more than US$40 billion in 2006, an increase of 115 percent over the previous year.[10]

In spite of this phenomenal success, Latin America's image is still marred by its past history of intense economic instability. Most businesspeople remember vividly the collapse of the Mexican *peso*, for example, which happened in December 1994. Many also recall how the Argentinean economy sank into the abyss, following the unpegging of the Argentinean *peso* from the dollar in December 2001.

In the 1980s and 1990s, the region experimented with free-market economics, partly due to pressure from international bodies such as the International Monetary Fund (IMF). Governments in countries such as Chile, Brazil and Mexico made the region the world's laboratory in passing state assets into the hands of the market. Today, there is, in some countries, a backlash against the privatization model. However, what is not in question is that privatization has helped to create a number of highly successful Global Latinas, companies that have benefited from the injection of market dynamism.

OVERVIEW OF THE CHAPTERS OF THE BOOK

Leadership is key to the success of any company and the leaders of Global Latinas are a special breed of men and women. They are not CEOs of established companies of the developed world, they are creative world-leading multinationals in a continent that has put many hurdles in the path of business success. In Chapter 1, therefore, we examine the challenges and achievements of seven great business leaders who have each built their own Global Latina.

Global Latinas, to put it briefly, are companies (a) that have emerged from Latin America – the 'Latina' bit of the title – and (b) that have successfully made the transition to doing business in the developed world – the 'Global' part of the title. Three such examples are explored in Chapter 2, all Brazilian firms that started as state-owned 'national champions' and underwent a degree of privatization: mining company Vale; oil and gas company Petrobras; and aircraft manufacturer Embraer.

In Latin America, many businesses are state-owned or family-owned, even after the period of privatization in the 1990s. The Brazilian state, for example, retains the controlling stake in the oil and gas company Petrobras. So, while Petrobras has had an injection of market forces since it went partially private, the government retains a keen interest in it.

Many of Latin America's large companies are in the extractive industries, such as oil and iron, drawing on the region's natural resources. They have benefited from the price hike in the commodities market, helping them to finance their growth. Naturally, governments debate whether to cede control over the companies which manage critical resources and are a potentially plentiful source of revenue for the government. In Brazil and elsewhere, the trend is still toward private ownership or a public–private hybrid, such as Petrobras.

The fact that so many companies have been or are still state- or family-owned has created a unique legacy and set of characteristics. For example, state-owned Global Latinas have a better chance of negotiating complex and difficult contracts with other states. This, for instance, has benefited Petrobras as it secures partnership exploration deals across the world.

Being state-owned or family-owned also tends to mean that the board can act on a long-term basis, which is sometimes an advantage in terms of coherent strategic planning. The downside can be a certain financial conservatism.

The accession of Mexico to the North American Free Trade Agreement (NAFTA) in 1994 marked another important change in the region. It was at that time the largest trade bloc in the world opened up the wealthy markets in the United States and Canada to Mexican firms for the first time. Those Mexican firms first looked to their 'natural markets' in the United States, such as Texas and California, with their large Hispanic populations. But following the NAFTA accession, many Mexican firms drove into the US market in a more significant way, aiming to broaden out to all internal markets. Chapter 3 examines the rise of three Mexican firms, two of which – Cemex and baker Grupo Bimbo – have made a particular mark in the United States. The third, the mobile company América Móvil, built its empire largely in Latin America, though it does have business in the United States.

The ultimate star is Cemex, the Mexican building materials giant, which has grown fast in the last eight years after acquiring some of the leading companies in its sector in the United Kingdom, the United States and Australia, and successfully integrating them. In two decades, Cemex has been transformed from an emerging multinational into one of the three largest companies in the cement industry worldwide, achieving annual growth rates in sales of 22 percent from 1985 to 2006.[11]

There are now ten Global Latinas in the *Fortune 500*, though the numbers are not as large as those from Asia. Clearly, this is one of the reasons Global Latinas have not been noticed as a phenomenon to the same extent as 'tigers' or 'dragons' from India and China.

Chapter 4 explores the innovative business models developed by some of the new Global Latinas. As in other emerging markets, companies from the region have created remarkably successful business models under difficult circumstances. The region has gone through repeated periods of economic and political instability, followed by the sudden shock of free-market economics. The last policy also re-introduced competition from foreign multinationals, with which the local players had to contend or die. Global Latinas also had to devise goods and services tailored for the mass of low-income consumers. This chapter looks at eight companies that have developed impressive business models that have both enabled them to compete at a global level and distinguished them from Western firms.

Three of these have been local brands successfully rolled out across the world: Chilean winemaker, Viña Concha y Toro; Mexican brewer Grupo Modelo (which sells popular international beer brands such as Corona); and Brazilian natural cosmetics company Natura Cosméticos. As well as Cemex, the chapter includes another successful global manufacturing firm, Tenaris. Based in Argentina, Tenaris has gained an excellent reputation for its service as well as its high-tech standards in the production of seamless steel pipes for the oil and gas trade. Its model is rooted in a cross-border, multicultural background, which enables it to build highly successful international research teams. Mexican baker Grupo Bimbo's international success has been built on its mastery of the whole supply chain, from the making of the flour to the delivery of the goods. Finally, Brazil's rising IT services star, Politec, has a fast and agile model, which enables it to reinvent itself within a tough and ever-changing business environment.

Chapter 5 focuses on branding, the way some Latin American companies have started branding not just their products but also their country and even the region of Latin America. They want to go beyond stereotypes about Latin America, for it to be recognized for more than salsa, soccer and beautiful scenery. Policymakers have known for years that the region needs to develop strengths in new industries and services. Otherwise, it remains dependent on selling commodities, and is subject to the ups and downs of world price movements.

Led by companies such as Petrobras and a large number of ethanol producers, Brazil is in a good position to become a world leader in providing green energy. In an age when the need to fight global warming is paramount, this could pave the way for a new role for Latin America as a world leader on environmental issues, a new form of branding for the continent. Both of these topics are also covered in Chapter 5.

Brazil's banks are among the most sophisticated in the world in their use of technology, and this is reflected in the fact that three of them have rankings in the 'Fortune Global 500'. Around this has grown an IT services sector, which is as sophisticated as that in India or

Israel, although Brazil is certainly not widely known for its IT services companies. Perhaps the Brazilian government could do more to change this perception. In the meantime, some Latin American companies are developing impressive businesses in this field. One such, another Brazilian IT company, Politec, is discussed in Chapter 5.

Two restaurant chains are included, one specializing in fast food with a 'Guatemalan touch', the other providing high-end Peruvian cuisine. Both chains are examples of how successful Global Latinas can change the way their native countries – and even Latin America as a whole – are perceived globally.

Latin American firms have developed strengths because they have had to navigate turbulent waters, surviving major economic and political crises in their home markets. There are some parallels with India and China, where companies have also grown up in tough, demanding markets. Chapter 6 investigates the links between Latin America and Asia.

Japan has been investing in Latin America, in particular in Mexico and Brazil, for many decades and has been a source of new technology and skills in the region. However, the rapid growth of China (and India, to an extent) over the last couple of decades has triggered changes in the region. The staggering growth of Latin American trade with China in recent years brings with it both opportunities and threats. While cheap Chinese imports challenge local manufacturers and undercut Latin American goods in third markets, there are indications that the positive benefits of trade outweigh the negative. China is also becoming a major source of financing that Latin American companies can exploit to their own advantage. Global Latinas are learning that they have to bridge the gap with Asia to win globally.

Latin American governments have not always promoted their own successful businesses with the same vigor as governments in Asia. Politicians in Latin America are more suspicious of business and have not yet produced a regional trade agreement that could provide a stable framework to help companies take off. Indeed, there is much that Latin America can learn from Asia.

On the business side, a major challenge, almost unique to Latin America, is for the leaders of successful firms to demonstrate through their actions that they are a force for good. This is because Latin America is one of the most unequal regions in the world. Recent growth has appeared to create a rising middle-class in countries such as Mexico and Brazil. But the distribution of wealth is still weighted

toward the few at the top, leaving behind millions of impover-
ished people across the region. By their positive actions, be they
through their own charitable foundations or educational initiatives
such as company 'universities', Latin American businesses need to do
more to prove that the growth of businesses will be of benefit to the
majority. This important topic is explored in Chapter 7.

WHY GLOBAL LATINAS, WHY NOW?

From our present vantage point, the rise of the Global Latinas seems
to represent a significant departure. Previously, people used to wonder
why the region seemed to produce so few global players. Most economic analyses focused on underlying causes, such as protectionist
policies (import substitution and tariff barriers), captive local consumers, weak capital markets, low levels of research and development
investment, complex and unpredictable political environments, and
market domination by family-owned conglomerates.

Before we launch into the heart of the book – the recent rise of
the Global Latinas – it might be useful to look at the historical background: why the Global Latinas emerged and the underlying forces
driving their international strategies.

One key historical factor is the basic legal framework adopted by
Latin American governments. Unlike the United Kingdom or the
United States, for example, Latin America opted for the Napoleonic
system of civil law. This provided less protection for minority shareholders and creditors than in the Anglo-American and German legal
frameworks. The Napoleonic system has inhibited the growth of capital markets in Latin America historically; and even today they remain
small in relation to the size of regional economies. For similar reasons,
publicly traded companies have not always been attractive investments
because of the small 'floats' of traded shares.

As *The Economist* noted in 1997, 'This creates a vicious circle, in
which many entrepreneurs prefer not to issue public equity because
they think the market will undervalue their firms.'[12]

This legal framework that militated against public companies has
created a Latin American business environment that favored the
emergence of family-controlled companies, which tended to grow
through diversification. This could be seen as a strategic response
to foreign-exchange controls and import tariffs which frustrated any
internationalization strategies they might have tried to implement.

In other words, family-owned local companies expanded in their domestic markets because of structural obstacles to international expansion. For them, diversification was not so much a strategic drive as a risk-reduction strategy against economic and political volatility.

These factors, combined with widespread state protection, facilitated the emergence of the large-scale, family-owned conglomerate – and the socio-economic consequences it produces. In addition, family-owned companies in Latin America tended to have highly conservative corporate cultures, particularly regarding debt, whereas in Anglo-American capitalism debt is deployed to finance expansion. Most Latin American firms have had relatively low levels of debt in relation to total assets.

When not family-controlled, Latin American companies have often been state-owned and based largely in resources like oil, metals and gas – in other words, at the low end of the value chain.[13]

This is the broad historical backdrop against which Latin American firms tentatively began to emerge from their domestic markets to pursue internationalization strategies.

As the ECLAC observed in its 2006 study of 'trans-Latins',[14] the internationalization of the region's firms occurred in three successive phases. The first two phases – in the 1970s and in the 1980s – witnessed modest signs of internationalization. The third phase, in the 1990s, was characterized by more ambitious global expansion patterns.[15]

This book identifies a fourth phase, which began around 2002, when soaring commodity prices and high growth rates combined, along with strong demand from China, to foster a more aggressive global expansion by Latin American firms. Let us look at each of these phases in turn.

PHASES 1 AND 2 (1970–1990): LATINAS ENGAGING IN FOREIGN DIRECT INVESTMENT

In the 1970s, a number of Latin American multinationals were part of a significant foreign direct investment (FDI) wave from emerging economies. Most outward FDI flows from Latin America – often partnerships driven by market-seeking strategies, and sometimes to bypass tariffs – were 'South–South' investments, that is, emerging market to emerging market. Investment outflows were relatively modest during this period.

It was during this phase that regional 'multi-Latinas' first emerged, establishing operations in neighboring countries to exploit 'natural' markets (where there was a cultural affinity between the company's home nation and the new market) elsewhere in the region. The 'multi-Latina', a coinage from 'multinational', is the step before Global Latina, that is, a company operating in more than one country of Latin America, but not yet graduating to the world stage.

For the purposes of this book, 'natural markets'[16] as defined by the author display three criteria: geographical proximity; the same linguistic sphere; and common historical/cultural links. Just as Latin America has always been a 'natural market' for Spanish companies, so the Hispanic population of the United States provides one for Latin American firms. They can do business there with a high level of comfort and familiarity with consumer tastes and demands. Latin American companies frequently return the favor to their colonial 'founders', Spain or Portugal. These two countries are often an entry point to Europe for Latin American companies. Successful Global Latinas, having gone through the 'multi-Latina' phase, often move first into these 'natural markets' when they begin to internationalize.

This expansion came to an end in Phase 2 from 1982 to 1990, the period known as the 'lost decade'. Latin American countries, starting with Mexico, defaulted on their international debt, causing them to be isolated from the rest of the world and to undergo a major contraction of their economies.

PHASE 3 (1990–2002): THE 'WASHINGTON CONSENSUS' YEARS

The 1990s witnessed an upswing of both inward and outward FDI in the region, due to a number of converging factors. Politically, the set of policies known as the 'Washington Consensus'[17] brought sweeping economic liberalization, including privatization, in regulated industries such as telecoms, utilities, gas and steel. Encouraged by the IMF and World Bank, many Latin American governments abandoned their import-substitution policies and adopted more pro-market strategies.

Latin American economies were also moving swiftly toward integration into larger geographic spaces through liberalized trade treaties such as the NAFTA – between the United States, Canada and Mexico – signed in 1994 and put into effect the following year. Mercosur or Mercosul (Mercado Común del Sur) is a regional trade agreement signed in 1991 by the Treaty of Asunción (updated in 1994) by Argentina, Brazil, Paraguay and Uruguay. Venezuela joined in 2005, with the intention to promote the South American Free Trade Area. These agreements were preceded by other ones such as the trade bloc known as the Andean Community, signed in 1969 by Bolivia, Colombia, Ecuador and Peru. The continent lacks an overarching trade agreement framework.

It was not just local companies that benefited from this climate of economic liberalization in the 1990s; global multinational corporations were returning to Latin America.[18] Economic liberalization, combined with multinational-triggered rationalization of domestic industrial and service sectors, had a transforming impact on Latin American firms and, more generally, on the entire regional economy.

Latin American companies had an incentive to consolidate their position domestically and regionally by pursuing efficiencies, comparative advantages and foreign financing – and, inevitably, to expand their operations internationally. It was in this period of the 1990s that the Global Latinas – the subject of this book – emerged.

This third phase, however, lost momentum in the fallout from the 2000 stock-market collapse, fed by the contagious effect of the Asian and Russian crises of 1997–1998. Then there was the dot.com meltdown of March 2000 followed by the Argentine crisis in 2001–2002, after the unpegging of the Argentinean *peso* from the US dollar. The result was a sharp FDI downturn and an economic slowdown in the region, the so-called 'lost half-decade' between 1997 and 2002.[19]

But it is an ill wind that blows nobody some good. At this time of crisis, foreign multinational corporations operating in Latin America were avoiding risk and leaving the region. Their anxiety actually opened up opportunities for large-scale Latin American companies, which were able to consolidate their position in local and regional markets by buying up at rock-bottom price the assets of the foreign banks, oil companies and telecom players that were nervously withdrawing from the region. Some multi-Latinas were able to turn into Global Latinas as a result of these asset purchases.

PHASE 4 (2002 TO DATE): GOING GLOBAL

The key differentiator of this phase is the economic boom the continent has enjoyed since 2002. A sharp rise in commodity prices strengthened resource-based Latin American companies, whose strong cash position boosted regional economies – triggering a rebound for them. On the back of this cash position, levels of outward FDI from the region, especially in the form of large-scale asset acquisitions, went up dramatically.[20] Outward FDI from Latin America has been soaring since 2003, largely driven by a small number of major transactions, such as Mexican building materials giant Cemex's US$5.8 billion takeover of UK-based RMC Group in 2004, and the US$17.8 billion all-cash acquisition of Canadian nickel producer Inco by Brazilian mining colossus Vale in 2006.

A report from Chilean-based ECLAC[21] notes that while Latin America's FDI *outflows* have been soaring (US$43 billion in 2006), the region's share of FDI *inflows* has actually been declining (US$72.4 billion), as global investment shifts increasingly toward Asia (notably China and India). The same report says that, during the 1970s, Latin America represented 17 percent of total investment inflows. After fluctuations over three decades, by 1997, the region's share hit a new high of 16 percent of total investment flows, largely due to asset privatizations by many Latin American governments. In 2006, however, the region's share of global inward investment had fallen to 8 percent, after averaging 11 percent in previous years.

There were two main reasons for this decline: decreased investment by US corporations and a not-unrelated shift in investment patterns toward China.

EMERGENCE OF GLOBAL LATINAS

Although their origins go back to the early 1990s at least, the emergence to world prominence of Global Latinas has been facilitated by surging economic growth in Latin America, which has been driven by high commodity prices.[22]

From 2003 to 2007, while the growth rate for the entire region was roughly 5 percent, many individual Latin American countries were enjoying much higher GDP growth rates – more than 10 percent in Venezuela and 9 percent in Argentina. Although these rates did not match those recorded in Asia, they were still impressive for a region finally emerging from two decades of political and economic crisis and instability.[23]

At the end of 2007, most Latin American countries boasted current account surpluses, sound fiscal positions, growing foreign currency reserves, more flexible exchange-rate policies, low inflation and expanding credit. There is now talk of a burgeoning 'new middle class' throughout the region. *The Economist* summed it up succinctly in mid-2007: 'Adiós to poverty, hola to consumption'.[24]

Against this backdrop of economic boom at home, Global Latinas are making headlines as they expand their operations via bold
takeovers. In the fallout from these mega-deals, Global Latinas and
the executives who run them are becoming internationally famous.
In June 2005, a formerly unknown Guatemalan business executive,
Juan José Gutiérrez, made the cover of *Newsweek* for a special feature
on 'Super CEOs'. The magazine cited Gutiérrez, chief executive of the
Guatemala-based restaurant group Pollo Campero, as a business leader
who is 'sparking a revolution in corporate strategy'.

And in July 2007, news outlets worldwide feverishly reported that
the richest person in the world was a relatively unknown Mexican
business titan, Carlos Slim, founder of mobile telecom giant América
Móvil. But in 2008, Slim's personal fortune, pegged at US$67.8 billion,
gave him second place after Warren Buffett, dislodging Bill Gates from
his long reign atop the *Forbes* billionaire index.[25]

Cold numbers provide evidence of the macro-economic factors
driving the emergence of Global Latinas. Worldwide investment
flows were soaring in 2006, reaching US$1.3 trillion – a 38 percent
increase over the previous year. These flows continued to be dominated by multinationals from industrialized economies – US$857
billion-worth of investments in developed countries, and a record
high of US$379 billion invested by developed countries in emerging
markets. Significantly, FDI outflows *from* emerging countries reached
US$193 billion – remarkable growth over a timeline of a few decades.
Whereas in 1970 outward FDI from emerging markets was virtually
non-existent, by 2005 it had grown to nearly 16 percent of the total
flow. The most rapid growth has occurred since 2003.[26]

Brazil led the regional surge of FDI outflows from Latin America,
with US$28.2 billion in investment outflows of a total of more than
US$40 billion. The drivers for this phenomenal outward FDI growth
were primarily the mining sector, resource-based manufacturing
and telecommunications.

This trend marks a new phase of globalization, characterized by
outward investment flows in *two* directions simultaneously. First,
multinationals from developing countries – our Global Latinas – are
increasingly investing in other *emerging* markets – or 'South–South'
investment flows.

Second, multinationals from these same emerging economies are
conquering markets in the United States, Europe and elsewhere in the
industrialized world ('South–North' investments).

There is a direct link between increases in FDI outflows and overall economic conditions. FDI outflow from Latin America and the Caribbean increased during the economic boom in the mid-1990s, decreased during the downturn from 1997 to 2002, and then rebounded with the updraft that has created the most recent boom in the region.[27] But while Latin America's international investments increased after 2002–2003, they were no match for the outward investment patterns of developing corporations from Asia.[28]

Latin America's largest companies enjoy dominant positions in their home markets. Others have emerged as state-backed 'national champions' – state-sponsored firms protected from competition and benefiting from government support for exports, and the designated vehicles for national industrial policy objectives such as employment, economic growth and international prestige. Alongside these Latin American champions, however, a new breed of Global Latinas was emerging in a diverse range of sectors – Mexico's Grupo Bimbo in baked goods and América Móvil in mobile telecoms, Guatemala's Pollo Campero in fast food, Brazil's Politec in IT services, Chile's Viña Concha y Toro in wine and Brazil's Natura Cosméticos in cosmetics.

Indeed, Latin America's export basket has significantly diversified away from commodities, which have declined from 50 percent to less than 30 percent of total exports in the last two decades.[29]

Evidence of this growing diversity was provided in 2007 by *Latin Trade*'s 'Top 500 companies in Latin America' listings, which included a sector-by-sector ranking measured in terms of total trade. Although the largest sector was oil and gas, representing 30 percent of total sales of the top 500 companies in the region, service and manufacturing sectors were also significant, with respectable showings from retail (10 percent), telecoms (8 percent), food and beverage (6 percent), electricity (7 percent), steel (5 percent), chemical (3 percent) and automotive (6 percent). See the Appendix for more details on continental trends and individual company performance.

Latin Trade's 2007 ranking of firms in the region predicted for growth included Vale (mining), Embraer (aircraft), América Móvil (telecoms), Cemex (building materials), Grupo Bimbo (food) and Natura Cosméticos (cosmetics).[30]

The trend toward increased outward FDI from emerging economies is also reflected in the number of multinationals from emerging economies listed in *Fortune*'s 'Global 500', the ranking of the world's largest corporations by revenues – 68 in all (or 13 percent of the total 500). However, only ten Latin American companies[31] – five from Mexico and five from Brazil – made the list.

This number does not compare favorably with the 162 corporations from the United States, 38 from France, 33 from Britain, 16 from Canada and 9 from Spain. The score for the entire Latin American region was not only low compared with these industrialized countries, but also with other emerging countries, with 24 firms from China and 6 from India.

Whereas the joint revenue of the ten listed Latin American multinationals was US$341 billion, the 24 Chinese firms in the same 'Global 500' ranking produced total revenue of nearly US$840 billion. Furthermore, the number of Latin American firms in the 2008 *Fortune* 500 – that is, ten – has declined in the past 20 years. If we look at the Latin American firms in *Fortune*'s Global 500 of July 1987, we find 14 companies from a variety of countries and not just Brazil and Mexico (the only ones represented in 2007): Chile, Colombia, and Venezuela. If we exclude the three automotive companies from the United States (Chrysler, Ford and General Motors), the total number is 11, still one more than in 2007.[32]

All of which is to say that the rise of Global Latinas is still in its early phase and limited to a relatively small number of firms.

DRIVERS FOR INTERNATIONALIZATION

There is no shortage of analysis focusing on the factors that have constrained Latin American firms from expanding internationally, from becoming Global Latinas. As Jayant Sinha (2005)[33] observed, protected domestic firms, high tariffs, underdeveloped capital markets, inadequate levels of R&D, family-owned conglomerates with risk-averse cultures and a turbulent political and economic climate have all frustrated the emergence of globally oriented Latin American firms.

But a number of studies have attempted to explain why Latin American firms have pursued international strategies. As McKinsey's Pablo Haberer[34] noted in 2007, some of the same factors that had long held back Latin American firms suddenly became competitive advantages that could be strategically exploited. In a word, many Latin American firms, making a virtue of necessity, were forced to adopt *innovative* strategies as a matter of survival.

Latin American multinationals also faced commercial pressures in their domestic markets after liberalization reforms. When governments liberalized their economies in the late 1980s and in the 1990s, domestic firms could no longer count on the state protection which, in many countries, had been institutionalized through import-substitution policies. Liberalization policies also brought increased competition from foreign multinationals acquiring local industrial assets, often purchased from Latin American governments selling off state-owned companies to shore up their debt-heavy treasuries.

As Khanna and Palepu (2006)[35] have noted, competing with global multinationals in their own backyard was challenging for domestic firms, because foreign corporate giants had ready access to international capital markets, top-flight executive talent, powerful brands to leverage and leading-edge technology.

But as Dawar and Frost (1999)[36] have pointed out, Latin American entrepreneurs had 'contender' attitudes that drove them to upgrade and expand their operations to compete and survive. In a 'do or die' situation, they had to restructure, upgrade, acquire know-how and expand internationally. Indeed, as Andrea Goldstein has argued (2007),[37] those Latin American firms that succeeded were the ones that responded structurally to liberalization in order to develop competitive advantages.

Other macro factors served as a catalyst for Latin American firms to expand internationally. Starting in 1994, a thrust toward 'open regionalism' through trade treaties – notably NAFTA – opened up the US, Canada and other foreign markets to Mexican goods and services, as well as foreign imports.

In a similar move, Brazil, Argentina, Paraguay and Uruguay founded the Regional Trade Agreement, Mercosul/Mercosur (Mercado Común del Sur) in 1991, with the Treaty of Asunción. Its purpose was to promote the movement of goods, people and currency.

The World Economic Forum's *Latin American Competitiveness Review*[38] measured the impact of these strategies: from the early 1990s to 2006, Latin America's 'openness ratio', as the percentage of the economy (sectors) which is open to foreign investment and ownership, increased from roughly 12 percent to 21 percent of GDP. At the same time, merchandise exports from Latin America grew at an annual rate of 8.1 percent – about 3 percent faster than the world average.

These Latin American firms have also been opportunistic buyers of industrial assets when foreign multinationals have withdrawn from the region, due to unstable political and economic conditions. This shift in asset ownership has been dramatic. According to ECLAC (2006), foreign multinationals in 2000 accounted for 41 percent of revenues generated by the biggest 500 corporations in Latin America; but that figure had plunged to 25 percent by 2005.

Latin American firms moreover have proved more skilful at navigating domestic market and political environments, thanks, as you would expect, to their intimate knowledge of local consumer tastes and familiarity with institutional realities. In the final analysis, their home-turf experience competing head-to-head with foreign multinationals has proved to be a blessing in disguise for the Latinas. It has forced them to be innovative and to strengthen their operational capacities, M&A skills and brand management.

Besides macro-economic drivers, *firm-specific* factors are crucial indicators to understand the global expansion of Latin American firms. Companies tend to expand their activities in order to enhance (or protect) their profitability and capital value. Some multinational corporations pursue global growth to drive revenue, increase margins and enhance shareholder value through market access or asset acquisitions. Other multinationals expand globally to secure long-term access to raw materials. Taking Dunning's (1993)[39] conceptual framework, these dynamics can be expressed in terms of four broad motivations that determine investment behavior: market-seeking; efficiency-seeking; resource-seeking and asset-seeking (see Appendix for a company-by-company analysis based on these criteria).

Market-seeking strategies are the most common, though motivations for seeking market opportunities vary. They can be based on leveraging a successful brand, exploiting competitive advantage in market niches, or rolling out a business model. Many Latin American multinationals are primarily market-seekers. Since natural resources and labor are relatively plentiful and cheap at home, large-scale Latin American firms can devote their energies to seeking new markets. Often the prime market-seeking motivation is in their 'natural markets'. Mexican firms that expand into the US's Hispanic population are following this territorial logic.[40]

Efficiency-seeking is often characterized in terms of taking advantage of lower-cost labor in foreign countries. This strategy goes beyond low-cost input factors and also includes motives related to the efficiencies of vertical integration of production and service lines of business, particularly in *producer-driven* sectors such as electronics and automobiles. The Latin American manufacturing sector has been dominated by so-called *maquila* branch-plants – often assembly lines of US or Japanese industrial giants in sectors like automobiles – who achieve efficiencies in countries such as Mexico through access to relatively cheap labor.[41]

Similarly, all over the continent, from Manaus in Brazil to Costa Rica, we can find the so-called Free Trade Zones (FTZs), where multinationals from Asia, European Union and the United States have set up assembly plants to take advantage of cheap labor, low taxes and a lack of bureaucracy.

Resource-seeking global strategies are generally pursued by firms from countries – notably China – looking for access to natural resources such as oil and gas in order to fuel the engine of domestic industrial activity. Since Global Latinas come from countries with plentiful supplies of natural resources, they tend *not* to be motivated primarily by resource-seeking strategies. In some cases though – such as two Brazilian companies, Petrobras in oil and Vale in mining – Latin American companies have expanded to acquire reserves in foreign markets.

Asset-seeking, finally, is associated with research and development activities. Emerging-market companies can leapfrog into higher-value products and services by buying assets such as technologies, skills, R&D facilities, brand names and distribution networks. Many multinationals from Asia have chosen to expand globally in exactly this way.[42] Fewer global players have emerged from Latin America driven by asset-seeking strategies. But there are some. For example, the Brazilian IT services firm Politec gained expertise in iris-recognition technologies through its acquisition in 2000 of Washington-based Sinergy, a pioneer in the field. This has helped Politec strengthen its capabilities in the area of security systems and to enhance its reputation worldwide.

Petrobras also added to its considerable knowledge of deep-water exploration and production by joining in partnerships with other firms. For instance, in 2004 it joined Exxon and Colombian state-owned Ecopetrol in a major offshore exploration initiative in the Caribbean Sea.

In the above mentioned study, BCG expanded on these four conceptual models by outlining six strategic motivations: taking brands global; leveraging low-cost R&D talent; establishing category leadership in a particular niche; leveraging natural resources; rolling out business models; and acquiring resources. All apply in varying degree to Global Latinas.

I have also identified other motivations for international expansion with my co-authors in our report for the Inter-American Development Bank.[43] One is *competitive advantage-seeking*, where Latin American firms expand internationally to gain access to know-how and expertise.

Another is *access to cheaper capital*. For Latin American firms, a primary motivation driving this strategy is reduction of their cost of debt, due to lower country risk premiums that financing in foreign industrial countries – for example, a debt issuance in the United States or Spain can generate. The higher cost of debt capital in their domestic markets stems from more unfavorable national credit ratings (in Latin America, as of October 2007, only Mexico and Chile are investment grade[44]). This strategy has been facilitated by a global context of high liquidity levels and low interest rates.[45]

As the OECD observed in a 2007 study, 'A global appetite was stimulated among the enterprises by industrial and financial interests, that is, the quest to expand their markets and improve their risk profiles. Their hunger for new markets was combined with the financial need to reduce the cost of access to capital.'[46]

Beyond these motivations, it is important to emphasize that every firm also possesses its own specific characteristics in its own unique mix – leadership, innovation, technology utilization, organizational know-how, operational strengths and brand management – that are deployed as competitive advantages when pursuing internationalization strategies.

Every successful company, every Global Latina, is *sui generis*.

FIVE SUCCESS FACTORS

There are five characteristics that have contributed to help the Global Latinas get to where they are. Individually, they have much in common with other companies in other parts of the world, but, in combination, they make for the uniqueness of Global Latinas – and stand them in good stead as they expand globally.

1. *Long-term visionary leaders*. Historically, a large proportion of Latin American firms have been family enterprises, many of which had originally been developed as conglomerates, with their interests diversified across a wide area. In closed markets, the only growth was through diversification and, at the same time, this strategy helped to compensate them for the volatility they experienced in different industries during crises. In such circumstances, it was easier for family owners to develop their own firms with their own money. The relevant point here, however, is that it has meant that many emerging multinationals from the region have strong individuals at the helm. They are

used to seeing things in the long term, while keeping an eye on the quarterly pressures. At the same time they enjoy a long tenure.

There are, of course, exceptions. Many of the companies examined in this book are now listed on stock markets around the world. Nonetheless, many of the descendants of the original founding families still influence the companies they created. Lorenzo Zambrano, grandson of the founder of Cemex, is a case in point. Since he became CEO in 1985, he has steered the company from being a relatively small player to becoming a global giant. Chapter 1 profiles seven Latin American leaders who have put their stamp on their company's success. They have displayed impressive agility in regard to their decisions, focus, boldness, shrewdness and flexibility.

2. *A strong survival instinct*. Global Latinas have realized that the best defence is attack. For many years, Latin American companies have benefited from their governments' protectionist economic policies, notably import-substitution and export subsidies. This helped some of them to consolidate their positions in their home markets.

But once the winds of the free market were blowing across the region, these firms could no longer count on state protection. They had to survive as privatized, or partially privatized, entities, in direct competition with multinationals from the developed world. The multinationals had huge economic clout and experience and were encouraged by the new opportunities to build market share in Latin America; the Global Latinas had to survive and thrive in that tough context. América Móvil, for example, had to compete with Spanish telecoms giant Telefónica. Petrobras had to compete with both US oil giant Exxon Mobil and Spanish energy firm Repsol YPF. Embraer also lost the support it used to get from a military government, which disappeared as democracy took over in the mid-1980s. Embraer could not rely on big contracts from the military in Brazil or, as the Cold War ended in 1989, from the United States or elsewhere. Therefore, it had to fight in the civil aircraft market, against the likes of Canadian firm Bombardier. As will be seen later, Embraer (Chapter 2) and América Móvil (Chapter 3) did indeed fight back with flair and strategic cunning.

3. *Ability to navigate through turbulent waters*. Traditional theory states that successful companies have to have a country-specific and a firm-specific competitive advantage. We associate country- (or region-) specific advantages with, say, Silicon Valley in the United States. This is counter-intuitive. You would expect that emerging multinationals

would come from countries with no competitive advantage. However, 'being able to survive challenging economic times' turns out to be a major competitive advantage of these resilient companies.

Since 1980, Latin America has experienced major setbacks, from the debt crisis of the 1980s to the 'Tequila' or the 'Tango' effects of the 1990s, whether related to slowdowns in the world economy, a sudden crash of commodity prices or domestic crises springing from and/or followed by debt defaults and currency devaluations.

Global Latinas have also often had to survive a fast transition from state-ownership to privatization, accompanied by the onset of foreign competition. As will be seen, many of them have done so with great agility and panache.

Agility often includes being able to snap up bargains in tough times. América Móvil's leader Carlos Slim, for instance, has proven to be a master at finding bargain acquisitions during periods of economic instability, such as the post-2001 Argentinean economic turbulence. It has helped him create one of the most successful mobile firms in the region.

In an article in the *McKinsey Quarterly* in 2007, Haberer and Kohan described how Latinas make the best of a tough challenge in their own country and turn it to advantage when they venture overseas:

> One school of thought holds that emerging markets, such as those in Latin America, can provide an excellent springboard for global business. Its proponents, including ourselves, argue that factors such as demanding but price-sensitive customers, a challenging distribution infrastructure, and volatile political and economic environments, compel companies to develop distinctive capabilities that can serve them well abroad.[47]

4. *Internationalization as a way to balance risk in the home market*. Although this might seem contrary to conventional wisdom, internationalization for Global Latinas is seen by them both as a way to decrease exposure to risk and as a way to acquire knowledge and technology.

These companies tend to move first into 'natural markets' – usually neighboring countries in Latin America, then, in Europe, Spain or Portugal – as they expand internationally, a trend first identified by the author.[48]

By starting with markets where there is a cultural and linguistic affinity, the Latinas begin to build their model and test out the process of internationalization. 'Natural markets' share information flows which are critical for the internationalization.

But for the Latinas, expansion overseas is not just about acquiring knowledge; it can also be a real cushion against economic fluctuations at home, a theme explored extensively in Chapters 2, 3 and 4. Global Latinas have also had to learn to grow fast through acquisitions. This has enabled them to reach a global scale in a relatively short period of time. Again, Cemex is a good example of this. But so also are the Brazilian iron ore and metals group, Vale and the Mexican mobile company América Móvil. Their stories are covered in Chapters 2 and 3.

5. *Business model innovation.* Business strategists used to assume that innovation was largely related to products. While this remains important, there is a growing appreciation of the advantages companies can gain from innovations in their business model.

In 2006, Professor Gary Hamel discussed the value of such innovation in an article in the *Harvard Business Review*. He said, 'Innovation in management principles and processes can create long-lasting advantage and produce dramatic shifts in competitive position. Over the past 100 years, excellent management, more than any other kind of innovation, has allowed companies to cross new performance thresholds.'[49]

The Global Latinas have proved adept at developing unique business models that have given them significant advantage as they expand abroad.

No business exemplifies this point better than Mexican cement giant Cemex. It has created a business model which integrates acquisitions into the company quickly and efficiently. The result is that they have all delivered value to the company – and impressed the business world in the process.

Cemex's first major acquisitions were in Spain in 1992, symbolically on the 500th anniversary of Columbus's arrival in Latin America. General opinion in Spain was that a Mexican company could not take over a Spanish firm successfully. Today, no one makes such claims. Business writers applaud instead Cemex's business model which has applied technology to a commodity business, disseminated best practices worldwide, and promoted continuous organizational learning, as something for others to follow. It has created a system by which new acquisitions are integrated into the company quickly and efficiently. All this is part of what is now known as the 'Cemex Way', and is an example of successful business models grown in Latin American soil, explored further in Chapter 4.

Another example is Brazilian aircraft manufacturer Embraer, which has developed a highly original 'reverse outsourcing' model. Instead of providing components to 'Western' firms, Embraer imports the components it needs from top firms such as General Electric and Honeywell. It uses its own designers in Brazil to create the planes and assembles them there. In this way, it is able to keep costs down, as local engineers are cheaper to hire than in the West, and it retains greater flexibility than its competitors, who have to manufacture everything, from components to fuselages, themselves.

It is clever models like these that set the Global Latinas – and the would-be Latinas snapping at their heels, some of whom we also cover in this book – apart from other global companies and help to explain their success.

COMING BACK HOME: IS A NEW PHASE STARTING?

Latin America is today at a turning point. As a result of the boom years of 2002–2007, a number of businesses have grown overseas to a degree unimaginable in previous decades. Latin American companies have invested a large amount of money overseas and the scale of some of the acquisitions reflects this. However, as of 2008, the region has entered a new phase, where there is an economic slowdown in the United States – after the sub-prime crisis which started in July 2007 – and Europe, but, so far, a buoyant economic situation in emerging markets. This may encourage companies such as Bimbo and Cemex to focus more on their own Latin American markets, or other emerging markets around the world, rather than the developed world. A new South–South investment phase is starting.

The trade between nations in the emerging markets – the so-called South–South trade or E2E (emerging market to emerging market) – has been significant for some time. In 2006, 98 percent of outward flows of investment from the BRIC (Brazil, Russian, India, China) countries went to emerging markets.

In Latin America, much of Vale's iron and other metal products, for instance, have gone to China at very generous prices to the company. More Global Latinas may begin to see the urgency of establishing stronger positions in China, India and other emerging markets.

The other unknown factor will be the impact of the economic slowdown in the United States and Europe on Latin America. The obvious temptation for some might be to return to the era of state-ownership in the 1970s, when companies were more protected from global downturns.

Regardless of how turbulent the next few years turn out, Latin America has changed and Global Latinas have emerged. They will have to leverage their winning practices to thrive on the world stage. They will have to continue to learn to adapt to a dynamic and uncertain environment – something that they have embedded in their corporate DNA from their Latin roots. This book is not just about celebrating their success. This book also sets out to help the world understand the uniqueness of the Global Latinas – and to enable global executives to work with them and benefit from their unique strengths.

1

THE LEADERS OF GLOBAL LATINAS: LONG-TERM PLANNERS AND FLEXIBLE VISIONARIES

> From my position as a businessman I have always felt deep responsibility towards my country and have thus acted. Grupo Carso's philosophy, that I have applied in each and every one of the companies that form the group, includes a series of efficiency, austerity, honesty, modernization, reinvestment of profits and development among other principles, trying to always render the best service possible, promote job creation and strengthen the internal market.
>
> Carlos Slim, www.carlosslim.com, August 2008

It is beginning to dawn on the global media that some of the most outstanding business leaders in the world today come from Latin America. In this chapter, we look at seven who have propelled their companies into world status, into Global Latinas. Among the seven leaders are increasingly well-known figures, such as Mexican telecoms billionaire Carlos Slim, who was second on Forbes's rich list in 2007, and compatriot Lorenzo Zambrano, who transformed Mexican building-materials company Cemex into the third biggest player in the world in its sector.

Slim and Zambrano and María Asunción Aramburuzabala of Grupo Modelo are members of the Latin American elite. In Slim's case, his father emigrated from Lebanon to Mexico and built up a family fortune. Roger Agnelli, a tough negotiator with 20 years' experience in investment banking, steered the Brazilian iron ore company, Vale, into the global premier league. Like Slim, Zambrano and Aramburuzabala, Agnelli has won his spurs as a tough mergers and acquisitions (M&A) negotiator. In cases such as these, partial or total family ownership tends to keep company control in the hands of the family concerned, for better or for worse.

But not all leaders of Global Latinas come from old money. Latin America is still bedeviled by sharp disparities in wealth. Not enough people have felt the benefits of globalization and the impressive rise of outward and inward investment over the last decade. In this situation, it becomes ever more important that the region spawns top management personnel – capable of running global firms – from all kinds of backgrounds, and not just those fortunate enough to be born into upper-class families. Such a change is happening and is steering the region more in the direction of meritocracy rather than plutocracy, helping to spread wealth throughout society.

Three of the seven leaders profiled later in this section – Botelho, Acurio and Gabrielli – have risen on their own merits and, when put to the test, have proven to be world-class managers. For example, Maurício Botelho, a mechanical engineer who had never worked in the aviation sector, managed to pull aircraft manufacturer Embraer back from disaster; while Gastón Acurio, a Peruvian chef and entrepreneur, has built his own global restaurant chain.

Beneficiaries of inherited wealth or meritocrats, all seven of the leaders presented here have honed their management skills during times of tumult, ranging from internal economic crises of one kind or another to the sudden appearance of tough foreign competition after years of protection. Some, like Botelho, have held their nerve as they steered their ship through stormy seas; while others, like Slim, actually used moments of crisis to spot opportunities.

Above all, they are bold visionaries. José Sérgio Gabrielli of the Brazilian oil and gas giant, Petrobras, for instance, has planted the idea that his country will one day become the 'Saudi-Arabia of bio-fuels' – green fuel, built on sugarcane-based ethanol production. As the pressures to burn cleaner fuels in cars and factories accelerate, the Petrobras vision might help to put Brazil on the world map as one of the greatest contributors to world sustainability. In a completely different business, global restaurant entrepreneur Gastón Acurio has set his sights on helping to build a more positive image of Peru worldwide through the promotion of its cuisine.

One of the qualities Latin American business leaders are said to have is the ability to keep one eye on the next quarter and the other on the next 20 years. With this long-term view, they are often big dreamers with a passionate drive to develop their business empires. They are also more than able to navigate their companies through the often turbulent waters of the region's political instability and currency volatility. Since the 1980s, these leaders have also had to contend with the arrival of fierce competition from foreign multinationals, after the opening up of the region's economies.

Though they might not want to admit it, they all have something of the air of modern-day swashbucklers – who in some cases have reveled in the fact that, 500 years after the Spanish and Portuguese conquest of Latin America, their companies have gone back to Portugal and Spain as corporate raiders. Let's meet them.

GRUPO CARSO: CARLOS SLIM HELÚ

Fast and flexible opportunist

Carlos Slim Helú, the second richest man in the world, according to *Forbes*, with a net worth of US$68 billion, is a reluctant member of the billionaires' club. Unlike many of the globe's wealthiest people, Slim is not interested in amassing super yachts or second homes. Like entrepreneurs such as Rupert Murdoch or Warren Buffett, he lives and breathes business. In 2007, he told the *Financial Times* that 'creating companies with value' was more important to him than whether he was the richest man in the world.[1]

His unostentatious lifestyle is similar in some ways to Buffett's, who beat Slim to first place in *Forbes'* 2008 rich list.[2] Slim lives in a relatively modest home in Mexico, not the luxury mansion typical of other billionaires. When asked why he had not bought a bigger house, he said, 'What for? So that I can get lost in it? No, in my house I live with my children. It's a sociable space...'.[3]

His father, Julián Slim Haddad, seems to have had a big impact on the young Carlos, one of six children. Julián Slim migrated to Mexico from Lebanon in 1902 at the age of 14, to escape military conscription in the Ottoman armed forces. A decade later, with one of his brothers, he set up a dry goods store called La Estrella de Oriente (Eastern Star) in Mexico City. Four years later, he bought out his brother's stake and went on to develop the store. He also seized the opportunity to invest in real estate in downtown Mexico City during the 1910 revolution.[4] The ability to spot the right moment to buy distressed assets and act upon that vision is a talent his son Carlos would inherit, becoming indeed one of the key ingredients of his success.

By the time of Julián Slim's death in 1953, when Carlos was just 13, Julián had amassed considerable wealth in his adopted country. Carlos Slim calculates that his father's store in 1921 would be worth

US$7 million in today's values and his real estate portfolio would be worth a further US$28 million.[5]

Julián Slim taught his children the value of hard work and careful financial management, skills that Carlos would pass on to his three sons, who have taken up the reins of their father's much more considerable business empire. The impact of his father's death is captured in Carlos Slim's website autobiography: '...in 1953, Don Julián died suddenly, deeply affecting the Slim and Helú family; it was a sad and unexpected blow that left a noticeable mark in the home...'.[6]

Carlos is more of a strategic thinker than a technician, as befits someone who has built an empire that is so varied. Since the 1960s, he has amassed a range of businesses, from banking, insurance, supermarkets and retail outlets to restaurants, mining, cigarettes and cement, brought under the Grupo Carso umbrella in 1990, in addition to his telecommunications' companies, Telmex and América Móvil, for which he is best known. In spite of his long involvement in the telecoms industry, in which he has built up a near monopoly in Mexico and a considerable presence elsewhere in Latin America, he does not profess to be an expert on its technology. When asked a technical question at a press conference in March 2007, Slim politely said, 'Señorita, I have no idea what you are talking about.'[7]

But Carlos has a razor-sharp mind for market analysis and balance sheets. In his twenties he studied civil engineering at the National Autonomous University of Mexico (UNAM); he also taught algebra and linear programming (LP). LP is a mathematical discipline, often used to determine the way to achieve the best outcome, such as maximum profit or lowest cost. Slim has been a master of both.

Slim's no-frills style of business, passed on to his sons, keeps costs as low as possible. Personally austere in his tastes (he wears a cheap watch and uses a disposable lighter for his trademark cigars), Slim runs all his businesses with costs cut to the bone. *Fortune* magazine says, 'Telmex's net debt equals Ebitda (earnings before interest, taxes, depreciation and amortization), a statistic that's unheard of in its industry, where debt is typically three times cash-flow.'[8]

As already mentioned, Carlos inherited his father's knack for spotting a bargain. In the 1980s, when foreign investors fled Mexico following the debt default of 1982, Slim bought when the market was at its lowest. This placed him in a strong financial position in 1990 to make an offer when the Mexican government put the state-owned telephone company, Teléfonos de México (Telmex) up for sale. Slim bought 20.4 percent of the company for US$2 billion, in association with his new partners SBC (later the owner of AT&T) and France Télécom. He also managed to get what amounted to a virtual monopoly for Telmex in Mexico for seven years, something his competitors resented and used as a stick to beat him.

Later, in 2000, Slim again scooped up cheap telecoms assets – after the dotcom crash, as well as during the economic crisis in Argentina – to help develop his mobile business in Latin America. AT&T CEO Randall Stephenson, who worked in Mexico overseeing SBC's investments in the 1990s, recalled meeting Slim to discuss his business plans, *Fortune* reported,

> During a recent visit with Slim, Stephenson says he 'pulls out this piece of paper, and he keeps on folding and unfolding'. It was a handwritten table of all the major communications companies in the world. (Slim doesn't use computers.) In one column, he had listed all the companies he owns or controls. Elsewhere he listed the other players, along with their revenue and operating and net incomes. 'I took the sheet and made a comment about one of the companies, and he starts going through all the financial metrics for the company,' Stephenson says, grinning. 'He's got all that information in his head'.[9]

As Slim gets older – he is in his late sixties – and thinks more of his legacy (his wife died in 1999), he has been giving greater day-to-day management power to his sons, while focusing on philanthropic work. Some critics say he could and should have done more before. He replies that he did not have so much time then, as he was building his business. At any rate, he has recently decided to boost contributions to his companies' charitable foundations from US$4 billion to US$10 billion, one of which contributes to education, health and nutrition in Mexico, a country where more than half of the population lives in poverty.

It is striking how carefully Slim has built his business empire. Clearly no angel (he continues to be accused of exploiting his companies' near-monopolistic control of the telecoms sector, blocking innovation and competition in Mexico and over-charging for mobile usage), he has proved adept at seizing the opportunity to buy assets on the cheap, building new business models (in particular, the development of the Pay-As-You-Go market in mobile phones) and successfully managing the transference of his business empire to his sons. He seems also to have retained a clear focus on family, business and country and has not been tempted to take on a rootless existence among the rich global jet set. Some critics think that he could do far more to help Mexico fight widespread poverty. But they cannot accuse him of turning his back on the country that gave his father and his family a home from which to build their business empire.

CEMEX: LORENZO ZAMBRANO

Long-term visionary

When Lorenzo Zambrano was promoted to chief executive officer in 1985, after 18 years of quietly working for the company (in which his family still owned a large stake), Cemex's annual revenue was US$275 million. Just over two decades later it had shot up to US$18 billion. It had become a giant, a Global Latina.

The man behind the creation of one of Latin America's first truly global enterprises was born in Monterrey in 1945 into an upper-class Mexican family. His grandfather – also named Lorenzo Zambrano – founded Cementos Hidalgos in 1906; it was renamed Cemex following a merger with another Mexican firm in 1931.

In the mid-to-late 1960s, Zambrano, the grandson, studied mechanical engineering at the Tecnológico de Monterrey university, which has been compared to MIT in the United States.[10] Two years later, he studied for an MBA at Stanford Business School in California, which he said broadened his outlook, so much so that he encourages all of his managers to spend time outside their own countries: 'I learned that there are other ways of thinking – and also what the competition would look like later.'[11]

Zambrano has many other responsibilities, ranging from advisory or director positions on the boards of IBM, Citigroup, Allianz and Grupo Financiero Banamex. He is chairman of the board of his *alma mater*, the Tecnológico de Monterrey, and has found time to amass one of the biggest personal collections of Ferrari sport cars in the world.

In the main, this courtly, soft-spoken bachelor has been a hard-driving business leader who has steered Cemex with extraordinary skill. He has combined a careful attention to detail with a boldness and vision that have surprised many of his competitors. He has also made sure that his company adhered to world-class management standards and utilized IT to the full to maximize efficiencies and keep costs low, winning admiration the world over.

There is even a 'Cemex Way', similar to Hewlett-Packard's 'HP Way', which refers to the manner in which the company prepares for and then integrates a company during and after a merger. While some of these mergers were relatively small, others have been huge and would have challenged the best companies in the world. As will be seen in Chapter 3, Cemex has acquired major companies in the United States, Europe and Australia and boosted their profitability after integration.

Zambrano has been tested on many occasions in the toughest situations, and he has proven his mettle. At the very beginning of his tenure, Mexico was going through a major economic crisis, during the so-called '80s lost decade'; a stormier sea would have been hard to imagine. One of his first decisions was to divest the company of the assets it had acquired in hotels, mines and petrochemicals in order to focus on the production and selling of cement, its core product. This decision provided the foundation for the company's later success.

He also executed some important strategic acquisitions to strengthen the company's hold on the Mexican market – then experiencing an influx of foreign competition following the opening up of its borders to trade.

Then, in another blow in the early 1990s, the US government imposed an anti-dumping duty of 58 percent on cement imports from Mexico. This was the only time, Zambrano said, that 'he felt furious enough to cry'.[12] But the move, initiated by his North American competitors, did not hold Cemex back. With his eye on the historical irony of a Mexican firm successfully 'invading' Europe on the 500th anniversary of Columbus's discovery of Latin America, Zambrano executed one of his most audacious moves: the acquisition of two of Spain's largest cement companies. Not only was the integration a success, against the expectations of many, but profit margins at the new acquisitions soared from 7 percent to 21 percent.

Further bold moves continued, including the takeover of the US giant Southdown in 2000, the company that had led the anti-dumping case against Cemex in the 1990s. 'That was a bonus I really savored', Zambrano said afterwards.[13]

Zambrano now leads one of the largest cement companies in the world, employing 67,000 people in 50 countries; it is surpassed only by Lafarge of France and Holcim of Switzerland. Zambrano's skills were recognized when he was honored with the Stanford Graduate School of Business 'Excellence in Leadership Award' in May 2008.

Future challenges await him, such as transforming Cemex into a global brand. Zambrano says that he is not concerned about making

Cemex the biggest company in the world. But he does want to make it the best.[14] This attitude sums up his approach to management, honed over the last two decades.

VALE: ROGER AGNELLI

Innovative thinker

In 1997, a Brazilian-led consortium called Valepar, consisting of the local steel company Companhia Siderúrgica Nacional (CSN) backed by a number of banks, including Brazil's leading investment bank Bradesco, made a bid for 42 percent of the Brazilian iron ore company CVRD (known as Vale since 2007). This was the first part of a three-step privatization process, which lasted until 2002.

Roger Agnelli, an investment banker from Bradesco, was the Valepar consortium's lead adviser. Agnelli, who had worked for Bradesco for 20 years and had risen to head its capital-markets division, was reputed to be a highly successful M&A manager and negotiator. The stakes were high in the bid for almost half of Vale's equity and Agnelli did not let the consortium down. It won the bid at a cost of US$3.1 billion. In 2000, the Brazilian government listed some of its shares on the stock markets in Madrid and New York, and in 2002 sold the remaining publicly owned equity through a global equity offering.

In 2001, a power struggle ensued among the principal shareholders of the company; at that time, Agnelli was chairman of the board. The shareholders represented by Agnelli, including Bradesco, managed to wrest control from Benjamin Steinbruch, the combative chief executive of CSN. It was out of this struggle that Agnelli emerged as the new CEO and president of CVRD/Vale, at the relatively youthful age of 42.[15] Privatization was one of the leading factors that set Vale on its course to become a global behemoth focused ruthlessly on steel and its related products, rather than a diversified collection of assets including shipping, railroads and pulp and paper.

The second factor determining the fate of the company was Agnelli's appointment as its chief. By 2008, just seven years after he was brought in, Vale's market value jumped from US$8 billion to US$150 billion. Even Agnelli had not expected growth on this scale: his target for 2010 had been US$25 billion.[16]

Known by some as the 'iron man', Agnelli was a tough negotiator who believed that he brought to the mining industry some key management qualities from the world of investment banking, such as a sense of urgency and speed, a global perspective, strategic bent and a focus on financial performance.

In his view, he brought a fresh 'can-do' attitude to a traditionally conservative industry:

> The mining business was very traditional and closed to new ideas. Globalization pushes companies to be more efficient. The answer I used to get before I took over was, 'we are studying this issue'. As an investment banker, I was used to asking for results, as opposed to more studies. It was not enough for me to hear that nobody could beat us in iron ore, I wanted to see more organic growth.[17]

From the outset, he instilled a sense of urgency and a clear strategic direction. One of his most important decisions was to focus the business on metals and related products, including bauxite, copper and nickel, while shedding assets in unrelated areas such as pulp and paper.

The swelling coffers, boosted by the sales of the unrelated assets, gave Agnelli an enviable war chest with which to orchestrate new acquisitions. His most notable and dramatic was the US$17.8 billion cash purchase of the Canadian nickel producer Inco in 2006.

While suited to the swashbuckling world of M&A, Agnelli also kept his eyes fixed on costs and never missed a chance to make savings. In one early demonstration of his obsessive attention to detail, he challenged the practice (pointless as it turned out) of having two separate railroad-to-port systems for the company's operations in the northern and southern parts of Brazil. The company duly integrated the two systems and saved US$2 million in operating costs in the first year alone.[18]

In his drive to make Vale a one-stop global shop for steel, Agnelli has been described by some as a workaholic, who drives his people hard. Others claim that he is a consensus-builder.

Certainly, Agnelli is not just focused on the bottom line. He has also shown himself to be concerned about the welfare of communities affected by his company's operations.

For example, he has challenged the traditional notion that mines are best run in enclaves separate from the local community, which often results in a 'Wild West' atmosphere. In 2004, he seized the opportunity to build a model mine when CVRD/Vale set about installing the Sossego Copper Mine on a greenfield site in the Brazilian state of Paraná.

In a conversation with the author Antoine van Agtmael, Agnelli described his engineers' resistance to change:

> My engineers told me to forget this idea, that this was the equivalent of the Wild West. There was even a red light district with girls of ten years old, some suffering from leprosy. I went there and got the mayor to move this area. We brought in water and sewage treatment, a school, a police station and technical training. Soon the town almost tripled in size, to over 15,000 people. As modern miners we can't just be technicians. We need to listen to the community and be less arrogant.[19]

In a recent press interview, Agnelli described his approach: 'In the poorest regions, you have to factor in things like basic sanitation, education, security and health services, so in some way or another CVRD [Vale] is involved almost in a governmental level in the places we are present.'[20]

In April 2008, Agnelli was reported to be preparing to make a bid for the Anglo-Swiss mining giant Xstrata, which if successful would have catapulted the company to the top of the global premier league. It was estimated that Xstrata, a major player in nickel, copper and coal with operations in 18 countries, would command a US$90 billion price tag.[21] This time the deal fell through, but the fact that Agnelli considered an acquisition of this magnitude is proof that the dynamism and boldness that have marked his style of leadership are not on the wane.

EMBRAER: MAURÍCIO BOTELHO

Turnaround king

In 1997, just four years after 53-year-old mechanical engineer Maurício Botelho took the reins at Brazil's ailing airplane manufacturer Embraer, the company's finances went into the black after years of financial crisis. By the time he stepped down in 2007, it had become one of the top companies in the world, with an enviable niche in the regional jets market. The company that was down on its knees in 1994 was strong enough by then to expand into Portugal and China.

Botelho graduated from the University of Brazil in 1965 in mechanical engineering. After leaving university, Botelho's first job was building a sawmill in an isolated community on Marajó Island in northern Brazil. He later described the experience:

> We had to attend to the employees, their families and the surrounding communities. So we built a school. Children rowed their canoes on the river long distances to come to class. Seeing that was deeply touching. I learned that, if you give people an opportunity, they take it and blossom.[22]

He gained management experience from a Brazilian engineering company where he was responsible for project implementation and business development in power generation and transmission, steelmaking, mining and petrochemicals. His first leadership role, at Odebrecht Automação e Telecomunicações, took him into the world of process control and telecommunications systems implementation.

Lack of experience in the aviation sector was more than made up for by management skills and vision. Above all, Botelho introduced a sharper customer focus and made sure it stayed that way by building a new organizational model based on five profit centers, each focused on different markets.

In the past, the Brazilian military had used its influence (as one of the company's largest customers historically) to encourage the firm to build models it wanted to see developed, regardless of whether they were desired by the wider market – one of the reasons Embraer had been brought to near-bankruptcy by the early 1990s.

But Botelho was not the kind of man to lose his focus on customers. He is quoted as saying that, 'when you've got only 100 customers, you have to focus on what they want.'[23]

The first, critical step Botelho took at Embraer was to cut costs drastically, thereby stemming the flood of losses. In doing so, he had to lay off thousands of workers. Significantly, he did not ride roughshod over the trade unions. Rather, he negotiated a deal based on the promise that he personally would take a 10 percent pay cut and that he would create new jobs the moment the company was in a healthier state.

Like other leaders of global firms from Latin America, he was bold and prepared to commit the company to a high-risk strategy: to move into the regional jet market, even though Embraer's early attempts in pressurized planes had failed. However, according to Antoine van Agtmael, the decision to make the switch saved the company: 'Embraer's turnaround can be attributed to a single bold gamble, which in 1995 looked like a long shot. Engineering the transition from producing twin-engine turboprops to regional jets was a laughably audacious goal at that time.'[24]

Botelho had spotted the opening in this niche market and went head-to-head with Canadian company Bombardier to produce the regional jets the market wanted. This 'laughably audacious goal' paid off and by 1997, Embraer's ERJ-145 regional jets, which were lighter, cheaper and less expensive to operate than their rival's planes, accounted for 60 percent of its revenue.[25]

Botelho also supported a highly successful manufacturing strategy that gave the company greater flexibility over its rivals. This was the policy of 'reverse-outsourcing', in which Embraer contracted out the manufacture of many of its components to the likes of GE and Honeywell, while it assembled all the planes itself. This made it far more flexible than the vertically and horizontally integrated Bombardier, which did everything internally. Not only could Embraer get the best component-makers in the world to provide what it needed, but it could also speed up the flow of components when it had to increase orders. Bombardier did not have that flexibility.[26]

If Botelho is remembered for anything, it is for spotting the opportunity in the regional jets market while rival companies looked elsewhere. It was on the back of this 'audacious' decision, and Botelho's ability to drive the organization behind it, that Embraer recovered from near-death in such a short space of time.

PETROBRAS: JOSÉ SÉRGIO GABRIELLI

From professor to business leader

Before he became chief financial officer (CFO) of Brazil's oil and gas giant Petrobras, José Sérgio Gabrielli was an economist at the Federal University of Bahia in the Brazilian state of Salvador, where he was born.

Gabrielli had taken his master's degree at Bahia in 1987, with a dissertation on tax incentives and regional development, followed by a PhD at Boston University on the financing of state-owned companies in Brazil during the years 1975–1979. He rose to become deputy director of research and post-graduate studies at Bahia and wrote on subjects such as productive restructuring, labor markets and regional development.

In 2000–2001, Gabrielli was a visiting research scholar at the London School of Economics and Political Science. It was during this year that the Brazilian government injected new dynamism into Petrobras by selling 28.5 percent of the state-owned firm to the private market. It was also a time of difficulty for the company, as its plans to expand globally were marred by the impact of an economic downturn at home and a disastrous explosion at its offshore oil rigs in the Atlantic in March 2001.

In February 2003, when business conditions were a bit brighter, Gabrielli was appointed as CFO to Petrobras, following the election of President Lula da Silva. The decision to appoint the academic Gabrielli was not hugely popular, according to one press report.[27]

However, during his three years as CFO, Gabrielli managed the financial controls during a particular dynamic period of growth, which included the integration of a majority holding in Argentina's second biggest oil company bought just a year before, followed by investments in Mexico in 2003. In 2004, one year after appointing Gabrielli as CFO, the company also joined Exxon and Colombian state-owned Ecopetrol in a major offshore oil-exploration arrangement in the Caribbean, which consolidated Petrobras' reputation as an expert in deep-water exploration.

Gabrielli had proven his worth to Petrobras and was promoted to chairman of the executive board, chief executive and director of Petrobras in 2005.

He has since taken advantage of relatively benign global conditions of high oil and gas prices to expand the company's production and exploration operations across the globe. This bold and visionary approach earned him recognition from the *Financial Times* as one of the ten most significant people in the energy business in the world.[28]

Gabrielli has steered the company into a major deal with Brazil's former mother country, Portugal, by entering into an offshore oil-production and exploration deal with Portuguese companies Galp Energia and Partex. Petrobras also signed up to a joint bio-fuels production project with Norway's Statoil and a gas exploration project with Russia's Gazprom. In 2006, the company purchased a 50 percent stake in the Pasadena refinery in Texas. It is also looking for exploration opportunities in Africa.

While all of these bold moves, coupled with the company's expertise in deep-water exploration, have transformed Petrobras into one of the world's biggest integrated oil and gas companies, Gabrielli has also set a vision for Brazil to become the 'Saudi Arabia of bio-fuels' (ethanol and biodiesel).

In setting this vision for the company, Gabrielli is planning for the post-hydrocarbon age, when reserves have declined. Currently, Petrobras is heavily involved in Brazil's ethanol-distribution business. However, it has plans to enter into ethanol production.

Meanwhile, in 2007, Petrobras discovered a gigantic source of oil and gas in the Tupi oilfield in the Santos Oil Basin, in the South Atlantic ocean, some 300 kilometers south-east of São Paulo. It was, said Gabrielli, like buying a winning ticket at the lottery.[29] The field may contain 8 million barrels of light oil (more profitable because it is easier to refine).

Gabrielli has brought efficiency and strategic vision to Petrobras. He was primarily a thinker, who still has a professorial manner. But today, as he leads a Global Latina with a recent market capitalization of US$188 billion, he has proved himself to be a man of action as well.

ASTRID & GASTÓN: GASTÓN ACURIO

A master of branding

Peruvian chef and entrepreneur Gastón Acurio has, together with Astrid, his wife and fellow-chef, created a global brand based on the eclectic culinary traditions of Peru. Driven by his passion for the culinary diversity and cultural traditions of Peru, Acurio realized shrewdly that culinary excellence can be the basis of a successful global brand.

Just as Swiss companies have built global brand recognition in watches and chocolate and similar to Japanese and Korean companies who have created world-class technology companies by transforming raw materials into cars and cameras, Acurio has built global success on the insight that Peruvian cuisine was a resource of great value, that was essentially undiscovered by foreigners except those who happened to pass through Peru in visits. However, the great Peruvian kitchen, dusted and polished under the leadership of Acurio, has provided the conceptual basis for a great brand that has been successfully exported around the world.

In March 2006, Acurio set out his personal vision in a speech at the University of the Pacific in Lima. He said that Peru's greatness stemmed from the mix of people who had come there, contributing to the special blends and fusions or – *mestizaje* – that had 'captivated' international interest.

It is from the *mestizaje* where we Peruvians need to find our inspiration, not only to create wealth, but also to accept ourselves and love ourselves as a nation. Only then will we be able to find within ourselves all those ideas that will later be transformed into products and brands that will conquer the planet.[30]

Born in 1967, Acurio dropped out of law school in Lima to follow his passion for cooking. He studied at Le Cordon Bleu Hospitality College in Paris, which he attended with his wife. In 1994, armed with a capital of US$45,000 provided by family and friends ('without a lot of faith but with a lot of affection'[31]), the couple launched their first restaurant, offering Peruvian *haute cuisine* in what would later become the Astrid & Gastón chain, aimed at the premium market. Success in the home country was soon followed by successes in neighboring Colombia, Ecuador, Venezuela and Panama. Astrid & Gastón has made Peruvian *haute cuisine* come to be recognized as a leader side by side with European *haute cuisine*.

Since then, Acurio has developed numerous additional brands, each drawing on rich and specific Peruvian culinary traditions. While creating the fish-and-seafood chain Cebicherías, he drew inspiration from the traditional Peruvian seafood kitchen to create a fun and joyful atmosphere that could compete successfully with popular sushi bars in Mexico, Panama, Brazil, England and the United States. Driven by the desire to spread his Peruvian food-and-drink business across the world, Acurio continues to innovate with fresh ideas, such as a coffee chain called the Astrid & Gastón Café, and juice bars called Juguería. Like other larger-than-life chefs around the world, Acurio has also become a TV personality, with his own show in Peru.

He is passionate about promoting a positive image of Peru abroad and hopes that restaurant chains such as his will expand globally, not only raising demand for Peruvian food exports, but also improving the country's reputation, tarnished by its association with terrorism and dictatorship.

Acurio estimates that there are currently 500 Peruvian restaurants outside Peru. He would like to see that number grow dramatically.

What we would like to see is that number expand to 200,000 in the next 20 years. [This] is not impossible when you look at other cuisines that have taken off in the past. There are much more than

200,000 Mexican restaurants in the world and those restaurants increase the exports of products from Mexico.[32]

Acurio's ambitions for global success are still alive and undiminished.

GRUPO MODELO/TRESALIA: MARÍA ASUNCIÓN ARAMBURUZABALA LARREGUI

A leading Latina

If Latin America has a reputation for *machismo*, it may come as a surprise to learn that even that stereotype is being challenged. There are 'latinas' in the Global Latinas!

We could pick on several women breaking *el techo de cristal* – the glass ceiling – on the continent. Astrid y Gastón's Astrid Acurio, in Peru, for instance. Or there's the Brazilian Ana Maria Diniz, for another, who co-managed her family business for 11 years and then turned around Grupo Pão de Açúcar, transforming it into the largest retail group in Latin America with a US$5 billion turnover. She is one of the leading opinion-formers in Brazil. But we are focusing on María Asunción Aramburuzabala Larregui, who many consider to be the most powerful businesswoman in Mexico.

Born in 1963, Aramburuzabala went to the Instituto Tecnológico Autónomo de México (ITAM) in Mexico City, where she majored in accountancy. She is the grand-daughter of Felix Aramburuzabala, who was co-founder of the large Mexican brewery Grupo Modelo.

María Asunción's father Pablo was executive vice-president of Grupo Modelo. When he died in 1990, he left a widow and two daughters, María Asunción being only 27 at the time. The three women came under intense pressure from banks and major shareholders to sell out – as women without financial experience, they were deemed easy prey. The three set up a holding company with the bold name of 'Tresalia', from the Spanish '*tres alias*', meaning 'three allies'.

The women used Tresalia to hold on to their Grupo Modelo controlling shares and to diversify from brewing into growing markets such as media and telecoms. María Asunción, for instance, organized the sale of a non-controlling 50.2 percent stake in Grupo Modelo to US brewer Anheuser-Busch and used the proceeds from that deal to invest in Grupo Televisa, the largest media company in the Spanish-speaking world (and creator of that great Latin American cultural icon, the *telenovela* – see Chapter 5).

For the three women, corporate social responsibility (CSR) is a major concern. Their commitment to CSR has led them to focus on highly profitable investments that contribute to the economic and social development of Mexico.

The 45-year-old María Asunción is currently chairman of the board of Tresalia Capital and vice-chairman of Grupo Modelo. She was the first woman to become a board member of the Mexican Stock Exchange (2003–2006), as well as being the first woman chairman of the board of Siemens Mexico (2003–2006).

Aramburuzabala is keen to be a model for other *latinas* in Global Latinas, to show that the *techo de cristal* can be breached.

Moving forward

If the new great Latin American enterprises, the Global Latinas, come in all sectors, shapes and sizes, their leaders are not all from the same mold either. Of the leaders highlighted in this chapter, four have inherited wealth, while the rest have made it on their own terms. What has brought all through is strength of character and long-term vision. The period of these leaders' ascendancy in the continent has been a story of internal economic challenge and privatization, while the cold blast of world competition has made the Global Latinas win their spurs in 'interesting times'. Although reacting to the unique circumstances of their particular company, each leader has built strongly on the local culture, while having the vision to carry that local excellence on to a global stage. We could have picked many more than the seven presented here, but space limited our choice.

The leaders of Global Latinas have not only driven their firms to international success but also have played a crucial role in inspiring the next generation of leaders in Latin America. They are valuable role models inspiring a new group of leaders that are now emerging – from a diverse range of backgrounds and socioeconomic classes. The new leaders of Latin America are confident, ambitious and ready to play on the world stage.

2

BRAZIL'S 'NATIONAL CHAMPIONS': BEYOND PRIVATIZATION

> We will become one of the five largest (energy) inte-
> grated companies in the world and the preferred choice
> among stakeholders.
>
> José Sérgio Gabrielli, Chairman, Petrobras,
> Vision for 2020, 2007

Some three decades after Chile first experimented with privatization, led by the 'Chicago boys' of the Chicago School of Economics in the 1970s, the benefits of this policy remain as controversial as ever in Latin America. While the evidence suggests that the bulk of the privatizations in the continent as a whole have succeeded, there have been some significant failures which have helped to stoke up opposition to this free-market policy.

The three Brazilian global corporations covered in this chapter, Vale, Petrobras and Embraer, offer a clear example of the policy's success. It is true that they were protected by their status as 'national champions' – large national companies – before the 1990s, when they developed certain strengths and gained a hold over their home markets and resources that would prove critical in the aftermath of their move into the global market. But by becoming fully or partially private in more recent years, they have displayed a dynamism and will to expand and thrive on the world stage in a way that previously may not have seemed possible and merits them the title of 'Global Latinas'.

This chapter focuses on three 'national champions' from Brazil that have expanded internationally since the 1990s: the aircraft manufacturer Empresa Brasileira de Aeronáutica (Embraer), the oil and gas giant Petróleo Brasileiro (Petrobras) and the global mining company, Vale (previously known as the Companhia Vale do Rio Doce or CVRD).[1] Together, their combined market capitalization runs into the hundreds of billions of US dollars.[2] In only two decades, they have each earned a deserved reputation for excellence in their products and services as well as their management and leadership. More critically, they have carved out new markets, based on research and established partnerships with other enterprises across the world. They sought to expand overseas for a number of reasons (which will be discussed later) and by 2008, they had all established impressive strategic positions in global markets. Embraer's sales outside Brazil totalled 96.4 percent of its total sales, followed closely by Vale with 84 percent and then Petrobras with 21 percent. Vale ranked 60.6 on the Globalization Index produced by the Latin American magazine, *América Economía*, followed by Embraer at 48.0 and Petrobras at 39.2.[3]

Petrobras is a global oil giant with more than 100 production platforms, 16 refineries, 30,000 kilometers of ducts and more than 6000 gas stations in Brazil and abroad. Its main operations are in Latin America and the United States (Gulf of Mexico). It also has operations in Africa, Europe and the Middle East. In 2007, it earned US$87.5 billion in sales.[4] It is recognized across the world as an expert on ultra-deep-water drilling and was ranked 63rd in the 2008 '*Fortune* Global 500'.[5]

Embraer is one of the world's top aircraft manufacturers, specializing in small- to medium-sized jets. It competes for third place with the Canadian company Bombardier, beneath Airbus (European Union) and Boeing (US). According to *América Economía*, the company was ranked as the 79th largest corporation in Latin America in 2007, making US$5.6 billion in sales in 2007.[6]

Vale is a global mining giant with worldwide operations in nickel, copper, bauxite, manganese, potassium and other non-ferrous metals. Since its dramatic US$17.8 billion all-cash purchase of Canadian nickel producer Inco in 2006, Vale has become one of the world's biggest nickel producers. In 2008, it was ranked by *Fortune* as the world's 235th biggest corporation and the world's fifth largest mining company as measured by revenues.[7] According to *América Economía*, Vale was the fifth largest corporation in Latin America in 2007. In that year, it recorded sales of US$36.5 billion.[8]

In the 1990s, Latin America became the world's laboratory for privatization, representing a dramatic shift in regional policy that would benefit Brazil's 'national champions' – Vale, Embraer and Petrobras. During this period, the region accounted for 55 percent of total privatization revenues in the developing world.[9] The 1980s were dark years in terms of economic performance, marred by debt default, hyperinflation and stagnation. By the late 1980s, the prevailing view was that the region needed to swallow the tough medicine of economic liberalization to change things for the better.

This new thinking – known as the 'Washington Consensus' – called for wide-ranging reforms such as: fiscal discipline; tax reform; interest-rate liberalization; competitive exchange rates; trade liberalization; privatization of state enterprises (which accounted for 10 percent of GDP, on average, in Latin American countries in 1985); deregulation to abolish barriers to entry and exit; and secure property rights.

In this period, average tariffs fell from close to 50 percent in 1985 to around 10 percent in 1996, according to the Inter-American Development Bank (IDB).[10] It is not hard to see why the selling of state-owned enterprises (SOEs) appealed to many leaders in the region at the time. It increased state revenues; it helped them to balance budgets, to reduce government subsidies to failing public firms, to improve the efficiency and quality of public services and to attract foreign investment.

Privatization encompassed many sectors, including telecommunications, mining, energy, petroleum, finance, airlines, transportation and infrastructure. In Latin America and the Caribbean, it totaled US$151 billion during the 1990s. In Brazil, Mexico and Argentina, this broke down into US$72 billion, US$25 billion and US$23 billion respectively.[11]

This was the continent-wide context from which Brazil's 'national champions' emerged. While this chapter focuses on three Brazilian firms, similar stories have played out in other Latin countries also, such as with Ecopetrol in Colombia and Telmex in Mexico.

VALE: FROM STATE-OWNERSHIP TO ONE-STOP SHOP[12]

In the period of state-ownership between the 1940s and early 1990s, Vale, then known as CVRD, developed as an industrial conglomerate with wide interests in shipping, railroads and forestry, as well as mining. It benefited from being state-owned in a number of ways. First, in 1970, government policy forced the giant US Steel to enter into a joint venture with Vale after the North American company had discovered deposits of iron ore in Brazil's northern rainforest in the Carajás reserve in the state of Pará. It turned out to be the largest discovery in the world. Then, seven years later, US Steel walked away from the partnership altogether, leaving Vale holding the prize. State support manifested itself in other important ways. For example, a loan from the IDB in 1965 enabled the company to finance capital upgrades which included the construction of the Tubarão port in Espírito Santo, a state in southeastern Brazil; by 2007, it had become the largest iron ore port in the world.

During this phase, Vale also entered into important partnerships with foreign firms such as the Canadian Alcan and the Japanese Nippon Amazon Aluminium, giving Vale capacity in bauxite mining and aluminum refining. In the 1990s, the Brazilian government allowed Vale, still state-owned, to bid for newly privatized steel mills in order to integrate forward and consolidate its position as the dominant supplier of iron ore to the sector. The result was that the company gained a 57 percent share of the Brazilian market. Just prior to privatization, Vale also strengthened its position through new joint ventures, including a new pelletizing (compressing or molding of product into the shape of a pellet)[13] plant in Brazil with Korean-based Posco.

Privatization of Vale took place in three phases over the period 1995–2002. In the first phase, most foreign companies were kept out of the bidding process, ensuring that a strong Brazilian interest was retained. Two consortia bid for 42 percent of the company: the first consisted of the Brazilian conglomerate Votorantim Industrial and the British mining company Anglo-American; and the second consortium, called Valepar, comprised Brazilian steel producer Companhia Siderúrgica Nacional (CSN), with backing from Brazilian investment firms and international banks. As mentioned in the previous chapter, Valepar's lead advisor to the bid was Roger Agnelli, the head of capital markets at the Brazilian investment bank Bradesco, who in 2001 became the company's CEO. Valepar won the bid at a cost of US$3.1 billion. In 2000, during the second privatization phase, Vale gained access to the international financial markets through its listing on the new Madrid-based stock market, Latibex (which enables investors to buy Latin American stock in Euros) and the New York Stock Exchange. In the third and final phase, the government sold its remaining stake through a global equity offering.

From 1999 to 2000, Vale faced tough global competition in which giant mining firms such as the Australian BHP Billiton, and British companies Rio Tinto and Anglo-American had to consolidate in order to survive. In 2002, Vale rejected an offer from Anglo-American to merge, in order to pursue its own growth strategy.

Vale's first aim was to strengthen its hold on its domestic market, which it did by purchasing three Brazilian mining companies and jointly acquiring, with the Japanese conglomerate Mitsui, Caemi Mineração e Metalurgia – a Brazilian company with operations in iron ore, pellets, kaolin, bauxite and railroads. Caemi, accounting for 3 percent of the world's iron ore production, extended Vale's market position. By this point, Vale had amassed a 28 percent share of the global iron ore export market, higher than Rio Tinto and BHP Billiton. This was a period of economic uncertainty following the dot.com crash in March 2000, but Vale used the opportunity to buy assets at competitive prices from foreign firms wishing to leave Latin America.[14]

Recognizing that the global market was likely to continue booming, driven by the demand from rapidly developing countries such as China, Vale increased its capacity to produce and deliver iron ore by joining in partnerships with major international firms. For example, in 2006 Vale linked up with German steel giant ThyssenKrupp to create Companhia Siderúrgica do Atlântico as an export base to meet increased global demand for steel.[15]

Vale's Agnelli proved adept at negotiating price rises with steel mills in Asia. In 2005, he secured a 71.5 percent price hike for its iron ore, setting the price levels for the market and two years later, in negotiations with Chinese steel company Baosteel and other Chinese mills, got a further 9.5 percent increase.[16]

One of the biggest challenges facing Agnelli in 2001 was to strengthen Vale's global position. This was necessary in order to compete with its biggest international rivals. Vale also needed to reduce its dependence on iron ore, its business cycles, the Brazilian markets and country-specific risks. At that time, about 90 percent of its assets were located in Brazil and two-thirds of its value chain was linked to iron ore. The answer was to diversify its product range – becoming a 'one-stop shop' for the steel industry – as well as expanding its geographical reach. In this way, Vale would not be tied too strongly to the fortunes of the iron ore market, which was already experiencing slower growth.[17]

Critically, Agnelli shed the company's non-core assets in pulp, paper and forest products, fertilizers and so on, providing it with a sharp focus on non-ferrous metals and a bulging war-chest to use in an aggressive acquisitions strategy. The company began by taking a few small steps to expand its product base. For example, Vale joined with the Chilean state-owned mining company Codelco in November 2001 to explore for copper in Peru and Chile. It also signed a deal with Shanghai Baosteel, China's largest steelmaker, to supply 6 million tons of iron ore annually for 20 years.

Vale also moved into Africa during the 2003–2006 period, a continent regarded by Agnelli as one of the final frontiers for mining firms. Most firms are not willing to take the risk of investing in Africa, leaving adventurous Global Latinas such as Vale with greater opportunities. By 2006, Vale had subsidiaries in Gabon, Mozambique, Angola and South Africa. In one report, it was suggested that Vale might find cobalt, copper, gold, nickel, phosphates and platinum-group metals (PGMs) in Angola, where it is exploring through its subsidiary, Gervale. In Gabon, Vale has already explored for manganese through another subsidiary, CMTR. In South Africa, it might find manganese and iron ore.[18]

Given Petrobras' interest in Africa, Vale and Petrobras signed a deal to jointly explore opportunities in Mozambique's gas fields and electrical power generation. Agnelli referred to the deal as a 'very important strategic partnership'.[19] Indeed, the company regards the push into Africa, signaled by the move into Mozambique in 2004, as the beginning of its third phase of internationalization.[20] The first came during the period of state ownership and the second with Agnelli's appointment as CEO in 2001. Its fourth phase of internationalization is usually assumed to have started in 2006, with the Inco acquisition.

This boldest move of all took place in 2006, when Vale made a US$17.8 billion all-cash acquisition of the Canadian nickel producer, Inco. Inco was the largest nickel producer in the world and owned the largest global nickel reserve base.[21] The metal is used in stainless steel and special alloys. The Inco purchase was in line with the company's aim of strengthening its geographical reach and product range. In addition to the move into nickel, Vale strove for the final piece in the jigsaw and bought its way into the coal industry, an important material for steel producers. It achieved significant additional capacity in coal when it acquired the Australian-based AMCI Holdings in 2007. Prior to this purchase, Vale had a 25 percent stake in two Chinese coal companies. Now, in addition to AMCI, it also signed a contract to develop a large coal deposit in Mozambique.[22]

Vale, in its privatized form, has been boosted by the world price hike in commodities and Agnelli's skill as a negotiator has helped to ensure that the company got the best prices for its products. But its ability to finance expansion on the scale of the Inco deal was made possible by Agnelli's decision to sell non-core assets, coupled with the price boom. The state-owned period also laid a strong foundation for the company. In particular, it ensured that it had control of the huge Carajás reserve of high-grade iron ore, a supply which is expected to last for as long as 400 years.[23] Agnelli is close to achieving his goal of a 'one-stop shop' in which Vale can offer packaged deals to steel mills, based on its economies of scale.

PETROBRAS: BUILDING ON KNOWLEDGE[24]

The Brazilian government has chosen to retain a majority stake in Petrobras, due to the rent value of owning an oil and gas company, especially during a period of high energy prices. However, selling off a part of the company to private investors has enabled the semi-public company, founded in 1953, to benefit from market dynamism. At the same time, Petrobras retains significant advantages by having the Brazilian state behind it. This is particularly helpful when the company is in the position of having to negotiate with other governments for exploration rights.

Since the mid-1950s, Petrobras has developed a unique knowledge of ultra-deep water exploration, which provides it with a calling card when looking for new partners worldwide to explore off-shore sites. Like other Global Latinas, Petrobras has taken advantage of economic crises and market challenges to make strategic acquisitions and expand its asset portfolio. The company is regarded as one of the 'New Seven Sisters' of oil companies from the emerging economies and is a major contributor to Brazil's economic development.[25] In late 2007, the *Financial Times* named Petrobras chief executive José Sérgio Gabrielli as one of the top ten most important figures in the global energy industry (see Chapter 1).[26]

As with Vale, Petrobras has benefited from a significant increase in the price of commodities. In the last ten years, the price of oil has fluctuated from a low of just over US$9 per barrel in 1998 to more than US$138 per barrel as of June 2008. The investment bank Goldman Sachs, in May 2008, before the credit crunch bit even suggested that the price would increase to US$200 per barrel within six months, driven by demand from India and China.[27]

Two important discoveries of oil deposits in the Campos Basin in 1974 and of natural gas in the Santos Basin in 1999 have given Petrobras a comfortable resource position. The Brazilian government deregulated the oil sector in 1995 and opened the market to foreign competition. But between 1953 and 1995, Petrobras could build up its domestic position without having to worry about competition at home. Petrobras' monopoly was reaffirmed by Brazil's constitution in 1988, which ended the military dictatorship of nearly 25 years. During the 1990s, the government was preoccupied with trying to stem hyper-inflation and eventually controlled the problem with the 1994 'Real Plan'. This introduced a new currency, the *real*, stabilized the economy and encouraged foreign direct investment. But Petrobras was not significantly affected by any of the economic reforms until 2000, when President Cardoso organized the sale of a 28.5 percent stake in the company to private markets, including an ADR (American Depositary Shares) listing on the New York Stock Exchange. Although the state retained voting control, the sale transformed Petrobras into a more autonomous, market-driven corporation.[28] The election of the left-wing President Inácio Lula da Silva in 2002 did not usher in a return to price-control regimes and state regulation of fuel production, as some had feared it might. If anything, the government further loosened its grip. In particular, prices were no longer subject to government directives, though it still had power over the company's long-term debt and the Brazilian congress had to approve its budget. Overall, it seemed the government was encouraging greater autonomy.[29]

The Brazilian government's commitment to flexibility and to an element of market forces have provided the company with a strong basis for its internationalization strategy. Gabrielli, appointed CEO in 2005, has brought managerial skills and greater efficiencies to the company. Also, even though the company could finance its expansion with its own funds, generated by high energy prices, it insists on going to private sources for about 10 percent of its needs, in order to maintain good relations with financial markets.[30] Petrobras has launched an ambitious expansionary plan, backed by the promise of US$112 billion in capital spending over five years, covering oil and gas exploration, production, refining and gas infrastructure, as well as new downstream activities in petrochemicals and biofuels. As with other energy majors, Petrobras aims to share the risk of oil and gas exploration with international partners. So far it has amassed an impressive number of partnerships with major firms such as the French Total and US companies, Exxon-Mobil, Chevron Texaco and Devon.

The biggest factor underpinning Petrobras' successful internationalization is its expertise in deep-water oil exploration and production, which goes back to 1986, when the company created the 'Technological Innovation and Advanced Development in Deep and Ultra-Deep Water Program (PROCAP)', to study exploration and production in deep waters to a depth of 2000–3000 meters.[31]

Petrobras experienced three phases of internationalization. The first occurred during its period of full state ownership between 1972 and

2000, when the company established a subsidiary called Braspetro to manage its overseas exploration activities. The government of the time wanted to preserve the company's reserves in Brazil in order to promote self-sufficiency and therefore encouraged Petrobras to develop external resources as well. Also, it was a period of high oil prices, encouraging the company to take advantage of the temporary boom.

Early disappointments in Iraq and Iran in the early 1970s, however, refocused the company on its 'natural market' in Latin America. But apart from investments in Colombia in the 1980s, Petrobras did not enter the region in strength until the 1990s, after the Brazilian economy had started to recover from the economic crisis of the previous decade. For example, Petrobras took advantage of the privatization of Bolivia's gas industry to carve out a significant position for itself, becoming a partner in the Bolivia–Brazil gas pipeline project between 1997 and 2000. In this phase, Petrobras also invested in Argentina and Ecuador. This period of global expansion came to an end in the late 1990s, due to the combination of a major economic slowdown in Latin America (caused initially by the economic crisis in Asia in 1997 and Russia in 1998, and a subsequent devaluation of the Brazilian *real* in 1999) and the plummeting of the price of oil in world markets.

In the second phase of internationalization, during the years 2000–2006, Petrobras had first to navigate the turbulent waters of economic recession until 2002. In fact, it was in this phase that the company executed some strategic acquisitions in Argentina, then being rocked by a catastrophic currency and banking crisis, out of which Petrobras emerged as a major Brazilian multinational company for the first time, as the then president of the company, Francisco Gros, has pointed out.[32]

In this period, the company had to manage the evolution to a partially privatized ('semi-public') company, as well as taking on a new international mission. As regards the latter, Petrobras had set up the International Business Area (IBA) to manage assets and operations outside Brazil (as before), but this time the IBA was also charged with driving global growth. In addition, it was responsible for refining, pipeline transportation and retail distribution. At the same time, Latin America in general was affected by the global dot.com crash, while, closer to home, Argentina went through a major economic crisis during 2001 and 2002, in which it defaulted on debts of US$144 billion and suffered a currency crisis and collapse in its banking sector. As if all that was not stormy enough, the leaders of Petrobras had to deal with a major explosion and subsequent oil spill at one of its oil rigs in the Atlantic Ocean in March 2001. In this second phase, Brazil also opened up to foreign oil firms as part of its economic liberalization and dropped the goal of energy self-sufficiency.

In 2001–2002, Petrobras made some key investments in Argentina at the height of the latter's economic troubles. For example, it conducted an asset-swap deal with Spanish oil company, Repsol-YPF, including the receipt of Argentine-based Eg3, which included a network of more than 700 service stations and refining assets. But the biggest move came in 2002, when Petrobras paid approximately US$3.5 billion for controlling a 58.6 percent stake in Argentina's second-largest oil giant, Pecom Energía, which was part of the family-owned Pérez Companc conglomerate.[33]

One of the talents of Global Latinas in difficult times is for buying up assets from foreign firms, which prefer to withdraw from a country rather than sit out the downturn. Petrobras did just that in a classic move in which it bought another Argentinean oil and gas company, Petrolera Sante Fe, from US-based Devon Energy Company for US$90 million in 2002.[34]

Following the Pecom Energía deal, Petrobras controlled upstream assets in three Latin American countries – Ecuador, Peru and Venezuela. At the time, the company believed this expansion would help it off-set the risk of being dependent on exploration and production in one country.[35] Since then, the company has also developed its interests in the Gulf of Mexico region. For example, in 2003 it sealed a partner-ship deal with Japanese-based Teikoku Oil and Mexican-based Diavaz to explore and produce onshore gas. One year later, it entered into a major off-shore exploration initiative in the Caribbean Sea with Exxon and Colombian state-owned Ecopetrol.[36]

But by far its biggest legacy from this period is the position it has created for itself in Argentina. Petrobras was able to build on this and by 2007 ended up operating an extensive network of retail stations that have a 13.8 percent share of the Argentinean national gasoline and diesel market and 11 percent of the lubricants market. It also has extensive interests in Argentinean gas pipelines and electricity genera-tion. In 2006, Petrobras was selling nearly 1.5 million tons of ethane, propane, butane and natural gasoline in Argentina.[37]

Nothing reveals Petrobras' ability to ride a storm than its invest-ments in Venezuela and Bolivia, both of which have governments that have initiated nationalization programs. Petrobras retained its natural gas interests in Bolivia, despite President Evo Morales's nationalization of the industry in 2006, although it had to renegotiate its agreement with the government, giving the latter a greater share.[38] Anxiety about the political changes in these countries worried Royal Dutch Shell, which decided to withdraw from other parts of the continent, such as Paraguay and Uruguay. Petrobras bought Shell's operations in those countries for US$140 million, plus gas stations in Colombia.[39] This deal gave Petrobras 261 more gas stations.

The third phase of Petrobras' global expansion started in 2006, when it focused on new growth markets and the emerging biofuel opportunities. The company has balanced its exploration and production portfolio between initiatives in the Gulf of Mexico and Europe, on the one hand, and promising initiatives in Africa, on the other. In Europe, Petrobras became involved in a deep-water project off the Portuguese coast with Galp Energia and Partex in 2007.[40] As with Cemex's entry into the Spanish market in 1992, Petrobras' move into Portugal is another reminder of how the balance has changed, with emerging countries such as these investing in the home markets of their former colonial masters.

Petrobras sees Angola, also a former Portuguese colony, as a 'natural market' and has been operating there since 1979, four years after Angolan independence. It has also developed off-shore exploration partnerships in Nigeria and plans to invest US$1.9 billion in two joint ventures with Chevron Texaco and Total. Petrobras plans to supply ethanol as well as crude oil to the Nigerian market. In 2001 and 2004, Petrobras signed deep-water exploration deals with Tanzania's national oil company, Tanzania Petroleum Development Corporation, and purchased a stake in a similar exploration project in Senegal from Italian company Edison Spa in 2004. It has interests in Libya and Mozambique as well, which include a project to produce biodiesel from the *Jatropha* succulent plant.[41]

One vision held by the company's CEO José Sérgio Gabrielli is to export 4.75 billion liters of ethanol annually by 2012 (see Chapters 3 and 4 for more detail).

Petrobras has had many benefits from its history of complete or partial state ownership. For example, in its past as a classic Brazilian 'national champion', it used monopoly rents to finance its expansion elsewhere. It was also the Brazilian government's desire to push for self-sufficiency that propelled Petrobras into seeking new markets in Latin America. In addition, having the Brazilian government as a majority shareholder has given the company 'leadership continuity', enabling it to plan for the long term, as well as strengthening its hand when negotiating for exploration rights with foreign governments. On the other hand, the state involvement has made the company financially conservative, compelling it to use its internal funds for expansion rather than seeking finance from the markets. The current price hike in energy prices has definitely boosted its recent fortunes and its ability to negotiate offshore exploration deals in Africa and elsewhere owes much to the company's historic expert knowledge of deep-water exploration and production.

The company now stands at a crossroads. On the one hand, it could become one of the largest ethanol producers in the world. On the other, a huge oil find in Tupi in 2007 is set to propel Petrobras into a new era as a major player in oil and gas. It also means that Brazil is on the cusp of becoming a key oil-producing nation, with the ability to set the world agenda, as Venezuela has for many years. The profit that may accrue from the Tupi discovery has also sparked a debate about the merits of re-nationalization.[42] Whatever happens, Petrobras will be greatly affected by the new oil discovery in the giant Tupi oilfield in the Santos Oil Basin. It may contain as much as 8 billion barrels of oil and natural gas, an amount that would boost the country's reserves by 62 percent. It is not only plentiful but it is also light oil, offering enormous cost advantages in refining. CEO Gabrielli predicts the company could start producing from this deep-water field in five to six years.[43]

EMBRAER: FROM NEAR-DEATH TO RESURRECTION[44]

The story of the Brazilian aircraft manufacturer Embraer demonstrates the power of placing a state-owned enterprise (SOE) into private hands. During its long experience as an SOE (1969–1994) Embraer did well, provided the orders kept coming in from the Brazilian military or other governments elsewhere. But as soon as orders began to decline in the late 1980s and early 1990s, owing to an unfortunate confluence of circumstances, there was little else for the company to fall back on. As the Brazilian government was not in a position to keep Embraer afloat as it sustained heavy losses, it was eventually put on the market. Its biggest weakness at the time was that it lacked sufficient customer focus. Its new life as a private company helped it to survive and has set it on a new and healthy course as a global supplier of regional jets.

Before privatization, Embraer developed a market niche for small jet planes for the civilian and military markets. The civilian aircrafts were technologically innovative and well-suited to the difficult flying environments prevalent in the Third World at that time. For example, Embraer's turbofan model was not as fast as jet models but it had wider wings, enabling it to land on small runways. It also used less fuel.[45] Its military planes were deliberately less sophisticated than some rival models and could be produced in low-cost countries such as Egypt under license for the British and French air forces.[46] In this state-owned phase, Embraer, well protected by the state, developed some important capabilities that would stand it in good stead when it became a private firm. In particular, it chose to develop the capability and skills required to design its planes, produce the fuselage and assemble the final product, relying on the delivery of components from outside suppliers. For example, more than half of the components for the 19-seat non-pressurized, twin-engine Bandeirante turbo-prop plane were imported.[47] The state helped Embraer in a number of ways in this period, apart from being one of its biggest customers. Embraer provided its customers with alternate financing through Brazil's state-owned development bank, BNDES, and benefited from export subsidies through FINEX (Fundo de Financiamento à Exportação), a scheme administered by Banco do Brasil. Suppliers were compelled to provide Embraer with kit to assemble final products in Brazil. If they did not comply, Embraer, with its links to the Brazilian state, could threaten them with a steep increase in import duties. In this way, the company gained access to important know-how. For example, Embraer has been the sole subcontractor to design and produce outboard flaps for the McDonnell Douglas MD-11 since the 1980s.[48]

The company was built on a 'triple alliance': foreign corporations, who acted as joint venture partners; local entrepreneurs who invested in the company; and, last but not least, the Brazilian state. Embraer's early focus on the export market enabled the company to offset development costs through longer production runs and encouraged customers to bring new ideas to inspire technical improvements. It also ensured that Embraer had to work to exacting standards.

However, in the late 1980s and early 1990s, this delicate house of cards collapsed and the company fell into a tailspin. There was a fatal pincer movement: a declining home market and a dwindling export market. As a result of the Latin American debt crisis in the 1980s and the end of military rule, Embraer lost one of its critical props, support from the military. The new democratically elected government, facing staggering inflationary pressures, was less able and willing to help the company with export subsidies and placed fewer orders for aircraft. A global recession in the late 1980s also made matters worse, private equity as a source of funding started to dry up and the government was unwilling to fill the investment void.

On top of this list of woes, the winding up of the Cold War, the end of the Iran–Iraq war and the reduction in intensity of violence in Angola all contributed to a smaller order-book for Embraer. As if that was not bad enough, the 1990s saw a major product flop. Embraer had invested time and money into producing, with the Argentinean company Fábrica Militar de Aviones (FAMA), the high-tech pressurized CBA-123 plane. The project had appealed to the Brazilian government as a way to help cement diplomatic ties between Argentina and Brazil and it appealed to engineers at Embraer because it was a technical challenge. But no one had ensured that there was a sufficient market to justify the investment.[49] And there was not.

During this period, the company's annual revenue sank from US$700 million in 1989 to US$177 million in 1994. In that year, it made losses of US$310 million. In 1992, the government had put Embraer on its list of SOEs targeted for sale. After six failed attempts, a consortium including US investors paid US$89 million in 1994 for a 45 percent stake. The Brazilian government assisted with the debt, provided some capital and kept a 6.8 percent 'golden share', which gave it veto power over such areas as a change of control and the corporate mission. Foreign ownership was limited to 40 percent and there was a six-month moratorium imposed on any future lay-offs. The company had already reduced staff numbers from 13,000 to 6100 during the early 1990s in order to stem huge annual losses.

It was into this scenario that Embraer began its life as a private company and that a mechanical engineer called Maurício Botelho, with no specific experience in the aviation industry, but a lot of experience in turning companies around, walked into the company's HQ to begin his rescue operation.

In ten years, Embraer went from annual losses of US$310 million in 1993–1994 to a net profit of US$291 million in 2005. The turnaround in the company's fortunes was directed by Botelho as CEO.

The situation he inherited was bleak. The company's backlog of orders only amounted to US$200 million. Botelho persuaded the board and the trade union representatives at the company to support his drive to improve productivity as a first step in the recovery plan. He secured agreement from the workers' union representatives to make further cuts to the workforce, as well as accept a 50 percent drop in overtime hours. He promised to rebuild staff numbers when the company had turned itself around, a promise he was able to honor three years later when he increased the workforce numbers to 11,000. To help push through the cost-cutting negotiations, Botelho agreed to take personally the 10 percent pay cut which was then being imposed on others in the company.

Getting managers and workers behind his plans was the first critical step taken by Botelho. He was then able to introduce a whole raft of organizational changes to upgrade performance and efficiency. For example, the company invested heavily in information technology systems, instigated a flatter hierarchy, promoted Total Quality Management (TQM) and introduced a system of performance feedback.

On top of the organizational changes, Botehlo made several key moves to bring Embraer to its present healthy state. By far the most important move was the decision taken in 1995 to stake its future on a growing niche market for medium-sized regional jets. American Airlines and other carriers needed comfortable planes to ferry people across an increasing number of short regional routes, known as the 'spokes' of the wheel of major airport hubs. Montreal-based Bombardier had already started to fill this market space with its Canadair jet CRJ-200, which was launched in 1992 and immediately secured US$4 billion in orders for Bombardier. Embraer's only foray into the production of pressurized planes[50] had been with the disastrous CBA-123.

It was brave for Embraer to move from its comfort zone of twin-engine turboprops to more hi-tech pressurized models. But its weakness also provided a key advantage. As it had never produced such jets before, it did not have a previous model to reconfigure. It could, therefore, start with a blank sheet. In contrast, Bombardier had reconfigured one of its existing larger jets to make the CRJ-200. As a result, the design was not as perfect as it could have been. In fact, it was heavier than it needed to be, had outdated systems and unnecessary operating features.

Having to start from scratch, Embraer was able to take onboard customer suggestions at the design stage. The company could also use the computer-aided design and manufacturing systems it had purchased for the ill-fated CBA-123 project and put them to better use in this new product sector, in which there was a clear market demand.

The 70-seat ERJ-145, which Embraer launched in 1996, was 2 tons lighter, US$3 million cheaper and 15 percent less expensive to operate than the Bombardier model. Embraer sold 300 of the new planes in three years and by 1997 the ERJ-145 represented 60 percent of the company's revenue. A year later, the company's accounts were back in the black, after 11 consecutive years in the red.

Behind the great success was an efficient manufacturing model that was highly unusual for an emerging-market company, in that it had reversed the normal outsourcing model (see Chapter 4).

Crucially, Botelho exorcized the company's past demons by creating a more customer-focused ethos. He did so by setting up five profit centers based on region and geography, light aircraft and government sales. An 'entrepreneur' was put in charge of each division and was given full responsibility to develop and improve customer relations.[51]

As the new millennium approached, Embraer's position was strong. In October 1999, a consortium of French aerospace companies, including Aerospatiale/Matra, Dassault, Thomson-CSF and SNECMA, acquired 20 percent of the company's equity, reducing the Brazilian owners' stake to 69 percent. The following year, Embraer listed its shares on the New York Stock Exchange. A few months previously it had announced the launch of a new family of larger regional jets known as E-jets, aimed at the US market. Swiss-based Crossair's 200 aircraft order, the largest ever for regional jets, was worth US$4.9 billion to Embraer. In 2003, Jet Blue also went on to order 100 of the new 100-seat Embraer 190 jet, in a contract worth US$3 billion.[52]

The terrorist attack on the Twin Towers in New York on 11 September 2001 reinforced the view that Embraer could not afford to become over-dependent on the US market. Therefore, as the demand for air travel declined in the United States in the immediate aftermath of the tragedy in New York, Embraer focused its global plans on Asia and Europe. To date, its move into Europe has been limited to the purchase of a former Portuguese state-owned services and maintenance company, OGMA (Oficinas Gerais de Material Aeronáutico). Embraer successfully won the bid in 2003, with the European company EADS and the Portuguese government each maintaining small stakes in the new company. Embraer is developing OGMA primarily as a service center for its clients, though it has a small manufacturing capability. One of the attractions of the purchase was the fact that the company produced helicopters, an area Embraer wished to move into. With a relatively expensive workforce, however, it needs to find significant process innovation in order to make manufacturing more cost-effective.[53]

Since 2000, Embraer has made efforts to move into the high-potential Chinese market. In the six years between setting up an office in Beijing and the winning of a significant order in 2006,

Embraer developed important ties with Chinese government officials and found joint venture partners. Significantly, Embraer has proved willing to agree to transfer technology to its Chinese partners, one of the key elements in winning over the Chinese government. In 2002, Embraer finally established an assembly line for regional jets, gaining Chinese state approval for the production of ERJ-145s. In 2003, it was able to form a joint venture with two Chinese companies controlled by the Aviation of Industries China (known as AVIC I and II). The joint venture is called Harbin Embraer Aircraft Industry (HEAI), and is based in Harbin, 900 kilometers north of Beijing. Embraer negotiated a 51 percent stake in the joint venture, which was designed to have the capacity to produce 24 aircraft per year. The first ever Embraer plane produced outside of Brazil was flown in China in 2003. In August 2006, Embraer secured its first major Chinese deal, with the sale of 100 aircraft to Hainan Airlines Company for US$2.7 billion.[54]

In 2007, Botelho was succeeded by Frederico Fleury Curado. The company is still on a journey from state-owned 'national champion' to private multinational. Its teething troubles in China – known as a difficult market to break in to – attest to the fact that it will need time, skill and patience to build up its position in new-growth markets. As a Brazilian multinational, Embraer has found it hard to deal with some of the local idiosyncrasies it has encountered in China. Clearly, as other companies have also discovered, succeeding in China takes a great deal of time, experience and patience. Embraer needs to be prepared to dig deep into its pockets to hold out in markets such as China until such time as it gets the return on its investment. It inherited useful knowledge about design, and about export markets, from its previous existence as a state-owned 'national champion'. Its importance to the Brazilian state has continued to bring it benefits even after privatization. For example, public-sector institutions such as the National Bank for Economic and Social Development (BNDES) contributed 22 percent of the development costs of the first ERJ family of jets and 100 percent for the AL-X light-attack jet fighter.[55] Embraer is also fortunate to be based in a technology cluster, in the components and electronics industries, in the Paraíbas Valley, where it can tap into the latest knowledge and capability. In addition to these factors, Embraer's new leadership has instigated efficiency improvements, enhanced its 'reverse-outsourcing' model and taken some tough but ultimately successful decisions to specialize in the regional jets space.

From national champions to Global Latinas

The three Brazilian companies covered in this chapter are among the largest Latin multinationals, measured in terms of their sales outside of their home countries. Petrobras and Vale rank as numbers two and four respectively and Embraer is a very respectable number 22.[56] They have all displayed a strong survival instinct. In Embraer's case, it was a matter of corporate life or death, and it managed to pull out of a very tough situation. In Vale's case, it has not only avoided becoming a take-over target but instead has grown quickly through rapid acquisitions, one of which was the huge Inco deal. All three have had good, long-term leaders driving them forward. Their internationalization programs have been fuelled by the desire to offset the risk of being over-dependent on the Brazilian market and to avoid the risk of economic or political instability. Embraer has further to go, but has started to make inroads into China, with the first glimmerings of success.

Both Vale and Petrobras have stepped into tough, risky markets in Africa, believing that this is a new frontier for their industries. Being hardy companies used to negotiating tough terrain, they have been able to make significant investments in Africa, putting them ahead of their Western rivals.

Being partially state-owned 'national champions' has helped all three consolidate their domestic markets and build important competitive advantage. It continues to color their present fortunes. Embraer, for example, still receives financing from public-sector sources and the Brazilian state remains in control of Petrobras. The future for all three is exciting. Petrobras has the opportunity to embrace the rising demand for ethanol, Vale will continue to develop as a one-stop-shop mining company and Embraer faces challenges in Asia and Europe. Privatization has helped transform the three national champions into Global Latinas with a bright future in the world.

They have each found successful routes to support their internationalization strategies. Vale has transformed itself into a modern global mining company. As it moves ahead, it is in a strong position for future growth. There are, of course, many unknown factors. What will happen if commodity prices begin to decline? What moves will Vale's major global competitors make to further consolidate? Whatever new issues it faces, Vale will tackle them from a strong position.

Petrobras has become an agile energy company, using its technological expertise and soaring profits (again buoyed by high commodity prices) to extend its global reach. Its semi-public status has been helpful, especially when negotiating with foreign governments for exploration rights. Many big questions face the energy industry in general, which will be just as relevant to Petrobras. How long will global reserves of oil and gas last? Will the price of oil eventually dip and what will happen to the profitability of extracting oil from hard-to-reach sources such as deep-water sites? What impact will climate change have on the industry? In one future scenario, Dr William Nuttall, an energy expert based at the Judge Business School at the University of Cambridge, suggests that the advanced nations will lead a global effort to regulate the trade in fossil fuels in order to limit the amount of greenhouse gases pumped into the atmosphere.[57] Petrobras has already put itself in a strong position to deal with such pressures, with its bet on the future attractiveness of sugarcane-based ethanol as a viable alternative to fossil fuels. This Brazilian Global Latina could become one of the world's major producers of ethanol and be ready for the time when oil really does run out.

Embraer has transformed itself from a state-owned 'champion' to a world-leading exporter of planes. It has shared the risks by growing through partnerships, joint venture agreements and a few critical acquisitions, all of which have helped Embraer offset its development costs and reduce risks. Looking to the future, it has a potentially huge market in China. This will help it reduce its dependency on the United States. But there are many uncertainties. It requires a great deal of time, patience and skill to negotiate a way through the Chinese market. Will Embraer be able to do this before its stamina for the significant investment it is making wanes? What will be the effect of the economic slowdown in the United States? Can Embraer develop greater inroads into other emerging markets?

The answers to these questions, and others, have yet to be fully revealed. But there is little doubt that this troika of Global Latinas from Brazil has steered its way through some tough times and undergone radical transformation boldly and creatively, making them global companies to reckon with. They have also shown the way for other SOEs which have been either fully or partially privatized over the last years. Latin America has demonstrated that national champions can become successful Global Latinas.

3

THE GLOBAL MEXICANS: BETTING ON THE US?

What has globalization meant for us? To summarize a long, complex process, we have harnessed the forces of globalization to transform a Mexican-based company with a few international operations into one of the largest global companies in our industry.

Lorenzo Zambrano, Chairman and CEO, Cemex,
Speech at Stanford University, 23 January 2002

In this chapter, the focus is on Mexico, a star creator of Global Latinas. We look at the country's route to economic strength, despite some rocky times in the past decades and examine the impact on Mexico of its participation in NAFTA. Finally, we look in detail at three of the country's most innovative Global Latinas: Cemex, Grupo Bimbo and América Móvil.

Mexico has produced some of the biggest companies in Latin America.[1] Six of the ten biggest Latin American firms are based there and it is home to almost one-fifth of the top 500 companies in the region.[2] The journey from the era of economic protection to the current liberalized environment has not been an easy one for today's Mexican Global Latinas. They have had to survive some very testing times, caused by the boom-and-bust economic cycles of the 1980s and 1990s. World economic conditions forced the Mexican government to devalue an overinflated *peso* in 1982, fuelling high rates of inflation. In the same year, the government had to default on its international debts, ushering in a period of extreme economic stagnation in which GDP grew at an average rate of 0.1 percent per year. By the end of the 1980s, the Mexican economy had started to recover, at which point the government began to implement its policies of denationalization and deregulation of the economy. But in 1994, disaster struck again, this time in the form of the collapse of the *peso*, which crashed under the weight of US$160 billion in foreign debt.

In the 1980s, more than 80 percent of the state's assets were divested, including Telmex, the telecoms sister of América Móvil. Local Mexican companies, accustomed to import-substitution policies and other forms of protection, had to weather the sharp winds of competition. The crowning glory of the government's liberalization policy in this period was its decision to join the North American Free Trade Agreement in 1994. This opened up the vast US and Canadian markets to Mexican companies, including the 'natural markets' of Hispanics in states such as Texas and California. The total Hispanic population in the United States in 2007 was 45 million, two-thirds of Mexican descent, and Hispanics represented 15 percent of the total US population. The main beneficiaries of this new trade agreement were not just North American corporations but also large-scale Mexican firms like Cemex and Bimbo, which had become competitive enough to thrive in the US and other global markets.

NAFTA was groundbreaking in the sense that it was the first free-trade agreement that joined advanced economies (US and Canada) to a developing one (Mexico). As part of the agreement, the three countries committed themselves to lowering their tariff walls for most goods. Mexico had the highest tariff barriers at the time and therefore made the most dramatic change. It reduced its tariffs on US and Canadian goods from 12 percent to 1.3 percent in the period 1993–2001. The United States dropped its tariffs from 2 percent to 0.2 percent in the same period.[3]

NAFTA: A SUCCESS FOR MEXICO?

Fifteen years on, most analysts agree that there have been significant benefits, though Mexico may not be able to depend so much on NAFTA membership to generate economic growth in the future. It now faces competition from China, which became the United States's second-biggest trade partner, displacing Mexico, in 2003. Mexico will have to improve the competitiveness of its economy through further liberalizing reforms to maintain momentum. But NAFTA has helped to stabilize the Mexican economy, remarkable when one considers that Mexico experienced two major economic crises between 1982 and 1994.

Mexico recovered far more quickly after the 'tequila crisis' of 1994 (after accession to NAFTA) than it did in 1982; but both crises involved currency devaluations. And much of the country's speedy recovery was due to the credibility Mexico had gained as a result of being part of NAFTA. For instance, in both crises investment levels fell by roughly the same proportion. An IMF study published in 2004 noted the way in which investment had recovered after both crises:

> Although investment fell by roughly similar proportions following the two crises, there was a stark difference in the recovery of investment. After the 1982 crisis, investment did not return to its pre-crisis level before 1991. In contrast, the recovery in investment was much faster in the crisis of 1994–95, as investment was back to its pre-crisis level by the third quarter of 1997.[4]

There were clear differences in the way the Mexican government responded to the crises in both periods. In the post-1982 scenario, it raised tariffs to 100 percent and imposed strict licensing agreements on all imports. In 1994–1995, however, the Mexican government respected its NAFTA obligations and continued to reform the economy. Being part of NAFTA also encouraged the United States to offer much-needed financial support in 1994. In particular, the Clinton administration extended a US$50 billion line of credit to Mexico. With this help, the Mexican government managed to get inflation under control, and by 2003 was enjoying the lowest and most stable inflation rates in its modern history.[5]

NAFTA boosted trade. Mexico's exports to the United States and Canada more than doubled in dollar terms between 1993 and 2002 and its trade (imports and exports) with them increased from 25 percent of its GDP in 1993 to 51 percent in 2000.[6] NAFTA also boosted investment flows into Mexico. For instance, FDI from the United States into Mexico increased from US$12 billion over 1991–1993 to roughly US$54 billion in the 2000–2002 period.[7]

Overall, some researchers have concluded that Mexico's participation in NAFTA led to an increase of about 70 percent in FDI flows.[8] Its GDP growth rose from an annual average of 2 percent in 1980–1993 to an annual average of roughly 4 percent in 1996–2002. Even more impressively, the average growth rate of investment in Mexico rose almost eightfold during the period 1996–2002.[9]

There are some downsides to Mexico's membership of NAFTA, however. Being dependent on trade with the United States has made

Mexico vulnerable to an economic downturn there. Since 2001, growth has slowed down in the industrial sector in the United States, which has had an impact on Mexican exports. There is also increased competition from China (following China's accession to membership of the World Trade Organization in 2001), which has been carving out its own share of the US market (see Chapter 6 for more on the impact of trade with China on Latin America). There is also the possibility that other states in Latin America might get a greater share of the US market through bilateral free-trade agreements.

According to the International Monetary Fund, Mexico needs to implement long-awaited reforms to improve its economic position for the next period of growth and cannot rely forever on NAFTA. For example, Mexico needs to improve the infrastructure underpinning its electricity generation, to deregulate the telecommunications industry and to end some of its labor-market rigidities. The IMF report notes that, for Mexico, 'Addressing these challenges will be central to recovering the growth momentum experienced in the latter part of the 1990s from membership in NAFTA.'[10]

As a result of NAFTA, Mexican firms were the first in the region to begin internationalizing their operations. A 2006 United Nations report said,

> The urgency increased with the 1994 financial crisis, as Mexican firms had to alter their defensive strategies and seriously rethink their corporate strategies to adapt to the new conditions. Thus it was that, from an almost non-existent base, Mexican companies began to invest outside the country, hesitantly at first and then with great enthusiasm.[11]

By 2006, Mexico had a stock of outward FDI totalling US$35 billion, about nine times as much as in 1994, the report added. In 2007, the United States imported goods and services from Mexico to the value of US$136 billion, over twice as much as in 1994; and in the same year, the value of goods and services imported into the United States from Mexico totalled US$210 billion, more than four times as much as in 1994.[12]

The United States did make some efforts to extend the scope of NAFTA to other countries in Latin America and the Caribbean, with the exception of Cuba, through the proposed Free Trade Agreement of the Americas (FTAA). However, the enticing possibility of widening a NAFTA-style agreement to the whole region and thus boosting the continent's trade with the United States was dashed in 2005 when members of the other main regional trade agreement, Mercosur (which includes Brazil, Argentina, Paraguay and Uruguay) disagreed with the United States over tariff reductions. Mercosur wanted greater tariff reductions in the United States in key areas such as agriculture and industrial goods. So, for the time being, that opportunity has been lost. The result has been to tie Mexico's economy more closely to that of the United States, while other countries in the region have continued to develop alternative trading partners.[13]

We next turn our attention to three Global Latinas that have emerged from Mexico: Cemex, América Móvil and Bimbo. All of them have benefited from NAFTA and the geographical proximity to the United States. However, these are only partial explanations for their successes. Their global expansion has been built on innovative business models, visionary leadership, aggressive ambition and excellent execution. They are truly world-class companies.

CEMEX: THE 'NÚMERO UNO' GLOBAL LATINA

Cemex is the tenth largest corporation in Latin America, with a US$2.9 billion profit (operating income) in 2007 on annual revenue of US$21.6 billion.[14] According to the 2008 ranking of 'Fortune Global 500', it is the 389th largest corporation in the world. It employs 67,000 people in 50 countries and has made itself the third largest company in its sector worldwide.[15] In 2005, a United Nations report stated that: ' "Cementos Mexicanos" (Cemex) is the only Mexican-based company that can be said to be a major multinational at the global level, given the percentage of its sales generated outside the country and the degree of geographical coverage its operations have attained.'[16]

How did a Mexican cement company, set up in 1906, near Monterrey in northern Mexico, grow to such dizzying heights in the last two decades? It did so, not by diversifying into other business areas, like a conglomerate, and as many traditional firms have done in the region. Instead, Cemex focused on its core business – cement and then building materials – and drove growth in global markets through a rapidly executed acquisitions strategy across two decades.

In 1992, Cemex CEO Lorenzo Zambrano (profiled in Chapter 1) engineered a hugely symbolic victory in Spain, on the 500th anniversary of the Spanish arrival in the New World. Zambrano, who at that time had been the company's CEO for just seven years, managed to acquire and integrate two giant Spanish cement companies (and went on to make them considerably more profitable). The idea that a Mexican company could muster the financing, the will and the management capability necessary to acquire a First World set of companies and integrate them was barely imaginable at the time. Old notions that a company from the Third World could not operate at the top level persisted and Zambrano relished the fact that he could prove such doubters wrong.[17]

Cemex's managers used to pore over every detail of a prospective acquisition. In 1992, they lacked the time and had to act fast. Zambrano plunged in – and won. This marked the beginning of a string of dramatic acquisitions in First World countries that sealed Cemex's growing reputation for managerial skill and brilliance. Strong leadership, fast growth through acquisitions, strong survival instincts, business model innovation and the ability to navigate turbulent waters: Cemex had them all. Its story remains an important one, not just for those who would like to copy its management techniques, but for its wider significance as a trail-blazer. Cemex has proven that a Latin American firm can stride the business stage as a colossus – utilizing its own talents hewn in a tough local market – and win. Others will follow, but Cemex will always be remembered as the pioneer.

From its beginnings in the first quarter of the 20th century to the late 1970s, Cementos Mexicanos or Cemex (as it was known after a merger in 1933) grew through acquisitions in its domestic market, protected by import-substitution industrialization policies of tariff protection.

Cemex has retained its character as a family firm, even though it has been listed on the Mexican Stock Exchange since 1976. The Zambrano family maintained its hold on the company through shareholdings and board positions. Cemex in the 1970s also became a conglomerate, with interests far afield in hotels, mining and petrochemicals.[18] None of this fitted it particularly well for the imminent challenge of the 1980s.

As the founder's grandson, another Lorenzo Zambrano, stepped up to the plate as CEO in 1985, the company was ill-prepared for the opening up of the Mexican economy. Cemex was over-reliant on its domestic market, then rocked by ferocious economic storms, and over-burdened with a disparate set of business commitments. For the first time, the biggest cement corporations in the world, Lafarge and Holcim, were prowling for market share and, by the end of the 1980s, the latter had carved out a 25 percent slice of the Mexican market.[19]

It was at this juncture that leadership made the difference. Zambrano made two decisions that were to have a major impact on the company. One was to ensure that Cemex strengthened its position in its home market, as the foundation stone for all other moves. The other was to rid itself of its conglomerate baggage. In the late 1980s, the company solidified its domestic position with the acquisition of two of Mexico's largest cement companies. By 2006, Mexico accounted for 20 percent of Cemex's total revenues and as much as 32 percent of its profits.[20] In Mexico, there is a consumer market for cement, because so many people are involved in building their own homes. Cemex got more value out of the product because it recognized the value of brand development in this home market.[21]

After consolidating his hold on Mexico, Zambrano adopted a growth-through-acquisitions strategy. Any cement firm that wishes to grow has to ensure that it has operations near its market. Transportation costs are high in this trade and delivery must be executed swiftly. Therefore, an acquisitions strategy was the main way forward for an aspiring Global Latina in this sector. The only alternative was to run a cement-trading operation, orchestrated by a maritime fleet, which Cemex had also done.

It is important to note that Cemex under Zambrano developed a unique and successful approach to acquisitions that has become a source of admiration in management case studies worldwide (discussed in greater detail in Chapter 4).

The key point here is that Cemex posed itself three questions when choosing an acquisition target: Can it be integrated seamlessly into the overall operations of the company? Will it be compatible with the company's financial targets? Will it offer superior, long-term returns in a growth market? If it met these criteria, Cemex locked its sights on its target. After acquisition, Cemex would implement a sophisticated post-integration process to ensure that the acquisition was welded into the organization and made more profitable.

Cemex's first efforts to break into the US market, before Mexico's accession to NAFTA, were disappointing. First, a joint-venture deal with a US company, Southdown, ended in acrimony, with the latter claiming that Cemex had been reducing the fees of their joint venture and increasing the price of its imported cement. In 1989, Cemex took over the joint venture. But a month later, Southdown and others filed an anti-dumping case against Cemex, claiming that it had been deflating cement prices to gain market share.[22] When the International Trade Commission (ITC), an arm of the US Department of

Commerce, supported the petition in 1989, Zambrano later recalled that at the time he had 'felt furious enough to cry'.[23] Cemex now faced a 58 percent countervailing duty in the United States.

It was at this point, as the company entered a new decade, the 1990s, that Cemex needed to draw on this Latina's famed toughness and resilience to execute its global aspirations in another way. Zambrano rose to the challenge, setting his sights on acquisitions in Europe. This strategy had the virtue of opening up new markets in Europe. It provided a base from which Cemex could improve its credit rating, using its subsidiary in Europe to raise capital, which provided better terms than those that prevailed in Latin America. It also opened a back door through which Cemex could export cement to the United States without having to pay any countervailing duties.

In 1992, Zambrano returned in force, buying two of Spain's biggest cement producers for US$1.8 billion. After the two companies were integrated, Cemex could lay claim to a 25 percent market share. By 1994, after only two years, Cemex had managed to increase its profits from 7 percent to 21 percent. 'They said a Mexican company could never manage in Europe', Zambrano later recalled.[24] After this Spanish acquisition, this myth was dispelled. Mexico is supposed to be a 'natural market' for Spanish companies; Cemex proved the contrary is also true. Spain is often the gateway to Europe for Global Latinas from Spanish-speaking countries, while Portugal plays a similar role for Brazilian companies.

Cemex used its new subsidiary in Spain, which had an investment-grade sovereign rating, to raise money on the financial markets to fuel further acquisitions. Interest rates were also tax-deductible in Spain and Cemex saved about US$100 million per year by consolidating its group-wide debts into its Spanish company.[25]

Cemex's higher-grade financial standing, based on its European subsidiary, proved invaluable worldwide. It was able to make important acquisitions throughout the 1990s, unhindered by the impact of the Mexican Peso Crisis in 1994.

In 1992–1994, Cemex bought two cement firms in the United States, enabling it to circumvent the punitive countervailing duty to some degree. It also gained a position in Venezuela by buying a controlling stake in its largest cement firm, picked up during a local economic downturn. The new Venezuelan position provided a coastal facility for delivering exports to markets in Brazil, Panama and the Caribbean.[26]

In April 2008, however, a new crisis emerged in Venezuela which affected this earlier investment. Its President, Hugo Chávez, announced the immediate nationalization of the country's entire cement industry. Cemex had half the market, with the rest divided between two other multinationals, Swiss Holcim and French Lafarge. The Mexican Finance Minister, Agustín Carstens, is reported to have condemned the measure, saying it showed a lack of respect for property rights.[27]

In the mid-to-late 1990s, Cemex built more market share in Latin America, through acquisitions of, or the purchase of shares in, companies in the Dominican Republic, Colombia, Chile, Costa Rica and Puerto Rico.[28]

From the late 1990s, Cemex had begun to make significant inroads into the emerging markets in Asia. High-growth markets which are investing billions of dollars in the building of infrastructure and other major projects are obviously critical for firms such as Cemex.[29] As already mentioned, China is consuming half of the world's cement to support its fast development plans. There is also a good chance that Cemex can find under-performing local cement firms in the region. It can buy them, integrate them and turn them around, releasing greater value. However, the economies of the region are heavily regulated and controlled by government, making this a difficult terrain to navigate. On the other hand, Global Latinas are used to managing difficult environments.

Cemex has persevered in Asia, despite some early setbacks. For example, the company took advantage of the economic downturn that affected Asia in 1997–1998 and bought a minority stake in the state-owned Indonesian firm, Semen Gresik Group, the country's largest cement producer. Indonesia is important because of its strategic location and its growth potential. However, Cemex's attempts to persuade the Indonesian government to let it buy a majority stake in the company fell on deaf ears. In 2006, Cemex decided to sell its interest.[30]

In 1999, however, Cemex managed to buy APO Cement Corporation in the Philippines, making it the biggest producer in the country. It also used a new investment vehicle – Cemex Asia Holdings (CAH), run in association with US insurance giant AIG – to make further investments in the region. And it was not lacking in funds: Cemex had a war-chest of US$1.2 billion, which it used to purchase Cemex's investments in the Philippines, including APO Cement, and to buy a cement firm in Thailand. In 1999, Cemex also made a move into the Middle East, another growth market, with the purchase of the largest cement company in Egypt.[31]

In the six years from 2000 to 2006, Cemex spent more than US$20 billion purchasing three key acquisitions in the United States, United Kingdom and Australia. It benefited from booming global markets and the willingness of banks to lend money, which were features of this period.

Its first acquisition had an ironic twist. Cemex took over US firm, Southdown, the company that had led the anti-dumping suit of 1989. The US$2.6 billion purchase gave Cemex the access to the US market it had craved for many years. This was in line with its desire to reduce its dependence on more volatile markets in the developing world. It also ensured that a sizeable proportion of its income would be in the more stable US dollar. Post-integration of Southdown, the new US business, accounted for 30 percent of the parent company's revenues by 2001.[32]

The second big acquisition, of UK-based RMC in 2004, provided Cemex with its widest ever range of operations across the world. It cost US$5.8 billion, then the largest acquisition ever undertaken by a Mexican company. RMC was a classic Cemex acquisition, an under-performing company with plenty of growth potential. Cemex also extended the company's position in the United States with an established market in ready-mixed concrete.[33]

The third piece in this mega-acquisition puzzle was the purchase of the Australian-based aggregates company, the Rinker group, for US$15.4 billion in 2006. With about 80 percent of its capacity in the United States, the Rinker acquisition deepened Cemex's grip on the US market, not something that impressed analysts at the time, because of the emerging housing slowdown.[34] The third deal also transformed Cemex overnight into a building material supplier, reducing its dependence on cement. Finally, Rinker also provided Cemex with a small but important strategic position in China, with concrete plants in the northern cities of Tianjin and Qingdao.[35]

When Zambrano began his journey as CEO in 1985, annual company revenue was US$275 million. By 2007, this had soared to US$21.6 billion. He had shown visionary leadership and developed an enviable management machine to undertake acquisitions across the globe, a response to the opening up of the Mexican economy in the 1980s. In addition, Mexico's economic crises of the 1980s and mid-1990s reinforced the need to seek other, more stable markets. Finally, the US anti-dumping petition that caused so much bitterness showed the importance of expanding to other markets in Europe and Asia.

But the company's resilient response to all of these pressures has made its fortune. With strong leadership, a steady nerve and an attention to detail, Cemex was able to take the knocks – and come back fighting. Cemex, like other emerging multinationals, wanted to succeed in the developed world of the United States and Europe, as a way to balance the volatility of its domestic market and its own currency.

However, since the beginning of the so-called 'subprime crisis' in July 2007, the situation has reversed: growth in the United States and Europe has stalled and the dollar has been losing value against most currencies in the world. Succeeding in the United States and Europe has been seen as a 'coming of age' for the emerging multinationals. Cemex came of age long ago and is now a world-class multinational in its own right.

However, in December 2007, while Cemex was finalizing the purchase of Rinker, with most of its assets in the United States, one of Cemex's main competitors, French multinational Lafarge, was buying the Middle East cement company, Orascom.[36] This move increased Lafarge's exposure to emerging markets and secured it a leading position in a region where oil and gas revenues were feeding a construction boom. At the same time, the real estate bubble in countries such as the United States and Spain had burst. To meet the double challenge of this sudden volatility of developed markets and rivals like Lafarge entering pastures new, should Cemex perhaps go back to its natural market in Latin America?

AMÉRICA MÓVIL: AGILE PREDATOR

América Móvil, the Mexican mobile company, has grown sixfold since its spin-off from former state-owned monopoly, Teléfonos de México (Telmex) in 2000. This is a great achievement, even in a fast-growing sector such as wireless telecoms. América Móvil is the fifth largest company in Latin America. In 2006, it earned profits of US$4 billion on revenues of nearly US$22 billion.[37] In 2007, its annual revenues jumped by 34.3 percent, to reach US$28.9 billion.[38] It has built up 153 million mobile phone customers and operates in 17 countries. América Móvil also displays many of the classic characteristics of a successful Global Latina as identified in this book. Under the strong and shrewd leadership of Mexican billionaire Carlos Slim (profiled in Chapter 1), it has crafted a highly successful pre-paid or call-card business model for a market of low-income consumers who lack a good credit rating.

In the years before América Móvil burst onto the scene in 2000, it would have been hard to spot the potential for a company such as this. In the 1980s and 1990s, Mexican monopoly Telmex slowly developed its mobile phone brand, then known as Telcel. A rival brand, Iusacell (its parent company SOS was then owned by the Peralta family) targeted the small high-income market. The pace picked up after 1989, when Telcel won the sole nationwide wireless license from the government, with the proviso that it was always the second player in every Mexican region. A turning point came in 1990, when the Mexican government sold a 20.4 percent controlling stake of Telmex for US$1.76 billion to a consortium run by Carlos Slim; a consortium that included France Télécom and US-based southwestern Bell. Some critics of the bid, dubbed 'Taco Bell', believed that Slim had exploited his political connections with the Mexican President of the time, Carlos Salinas de Gortari to win the bid, something Slim denies.[39]

Since then, Slim has been able to dominate the telecommunications sector in Mexico, in part because of the failure of successive governments to fully liberalize the sector. Critics have claimed that Telmex and Telcel (the local unit of América Móvil) overcharge for their services, something also denied by Slim. In 2007, Eduardo Pérez Motta, president of Mexico's Federal Competition Commission (CFC), was investigating the telecommunications and energy sectors to assess whether they needed to be opened up to more competition. In December 2007, Pérez Motta told the *Financial Times*, 'I've often heard Mr Slim say Telmex has reduced its charges over the years…It undoubtedly has, but it would probably have reduced them more if there had been more competition.'[40] But, until that greater competition is fostered, Slim continues to enjoy a dominant position in his home market.

The new owner's 'pre-paid' model came into its own after the Peso Crisis of 1994. While Iusacell still continued to target the well-off, América Móvil appealed to the much larger group of low-income consumers with its 'Amigo' brand. As was common at the time, Telmex chose to spin off its successful, mobile upstart in 2000, to unlock value for its shareholders and provide a branding vehicle to expand its wireless business.

So much for the domestic market; looking outward, América Móvil had two things going for it that would strengthen its chances of success outside Mexico. First, it was using the most up-to-date roaming technology of the time, GSM, which enabled consumers to use their phones in different countries; second, it had built a strong business around its pre-paid model.

In particular, América Móvil realized that success in the low-income market was all about driving volume sales. It could not count on loyalty. So, América Móvil used teams – often dressed in bright yellow jumpsuits to resemble Formula 1 pit crew members – to sell pre-paid cards to the public. It also flooded the market with mobile handsets, as loss-leader giveaways. At the same time, the company invested heavily in services, to try to hold on to as many customers as possible. In Mexico, where Slim's company had a dominant position, the pre-paid model helped it build 46 million customers by 2007. Its nearest rival, Movistar, owned by Spanish telecoms giant Telefónica, had less than a quarter of this number.[41]

In the 2001–2003 period, Slim seized the moment to buy up a number of key distressed assets in Latin America at bargain prices, strengthening América Móvil's regional position.

In particular, the acquisitions helped to build América Móvil's position in Brazil, where its 'Claro' brand fought for market share against 'Vivo', the joint-venture owned by Telefónica and Portugal Telecom. By 2007, Claro, although still the third player, was catching up with market-leader Vivo and was ahead of Telecom Italia's mobile brand TIM, in terms of numbers of subscribers but behind in revenue.

Everyone needs luck in business. But Slim had an uncanny ability, similar to leaders of other Global Latinas, to seize an opportunity when it emerged. In this period, distressed assets were put on the market, either because foreign companies were worried about economic instability in the region during the so-called 'lost half-decade' in Latin America (1997–2002), or because they were damaged themselves by the global dot.com crash of 2000. In 2002, Slim bought one of Brazil's wireless operators, BCP, from BellSouth, for US$800 million. The US firm needed to free up some money to help finance its joint bid with Cingular Wireless for AT&T Wireless. Compared to a bigger deal, in which Telefónica had paid US$6 billion for some of BellSouth's Latin American assets, it is possible to calculate that on a per-customer basis Slim paid 50 percent less than his Spanish archrival.[42]

In 2003–2004, Telmex, América Movil's sister company – also under Slim's leadership – picked up two key assets at bargain prices. The first, in 2003, was its purchase of AT&T's Latin American assets for US$207 million. Worried by the economic instability that followed the *peso* devaluation in Argentina of 2002, AT&T wanted to leave the region. It was Slim's América Movil that benefited from the fact that AT&T had already invested US$2 billion in building fiber-optic networks in the region. Secondly, US telecoms company, MCI Worldcom, then going through bankruptcy proceedings, needed to sell its assets in Latin America. Therefore, in 2004 Telmex managed to purchase the former state-owned Brazilian long-distance carrier, Embratel, for about a quarter of the original price paid by MCI Worldcom when it bought it from the Brazilian government in 1998.[43]

In 2003–2007, América Móvil continued to build a strong position across the region, using a number of different brands to appeal to different markets. In the two years between 2003 and 2005, it bought assets from foreign companies in Argentina, Chile, Paraguay and Peru, adding several million subscribers to its business. It also had a share of a wider range of other markets, including Colombia and Ecuador, where it is the largest player. More recently, in 2007, it paid US-based Verizon US$3.7 billion for its telecoms assets – fixed and mobile – in Puerto Rico and the Dominican Republic.[44]

In the United States, América Móvil incorporated Telmex's North American business, Topp Telecom, set up in 1996. This had carved out a significant market share in the United States, based on its pre-paid model. Topp is not a provider. Instead, it re-sells pre-paid airtime from other providers. It has become the sixth largest mobile operator in the United States, with 8 million customers.

Carlos Slim is yet to break into the European market. He did make a dramatic bid to buy Telecom Italia, one of the world's biggest firms, in a joint bid with AT&T in 2007. In the end, the Italian government preferred to sell Telecom Italia to a European company, backed by Italian banks.[45] It went to Slim's rival, Telefónica. For both Telefónica and Slim, the main interest in the deal was access to Telecom Italia's assets in Brazil.[46]

As Carlos Slim increasingly hands over the running of his business (he controls both Telmex and América Móvil) to his three sons, Carlos, Marco Antonio and Patrick Slim Domit, the company enters a new era.[47] Slim senior has built a considerable cash-rich telecoms empire in Latin America, based on a deep understanding of local markets, a decisive leadership style and a canny purchasing of assets at bargain prices. Slim has operated on classic Global Latina lines of growth through rapid acquisitions, focusing initially on his 'natural' markets.

Provided the region continues to grow economically and develops an ever-increasing middle class, companies such as América Móvil are set to do even better in the future. The attempted bid for Telecom Italia demonstrates that the company may be poised to seize a major opportunity in Europe. If it does, it will enter a new path as an emerging Global Latina.

BIMBO: THINKING BIG IN THE US

Grupo Bimbo started life as a small bakery founded in Mexico by Juan Servitje, an immigrant from Catalonia in Spain. The same family has retained its dominance over the company as it has moved from its early beginnings to its current status as the biggest food company in Latin America. Servitje's grandson Daniel is the current CEO. Today, roughly 75 percent of the stock is controlled by four families who go back to the company's founding – Servitje, Sendra, Jorba and Mata. The company's executives control another 5 percent and the remaining 20 percent has been floated on the stock market since 1980.

Building on the brand 'Bimbo', inspired by the Disney character Bambi, and the company's manufacturing and distribution capabilities, the company soon became Mexico's best-known producer of packaged bread.

Its success was always based on its use of the latest technology. For example, from early on it used cellophane wrapping to keep the bread fresh for longer periods, at the time a completely new technique.[48] Another key reason for its early success was its decision to vertically integrate backwards into wheat production and flour mills, giving it control over the price of its raw materials. This change occurred when Bimbo purchased in 1986 US-based Wonder Bread's Mexican subsidiary, Continental Baking. It got a flour mill in Mexico City as part of the deal. It took on more mills and by the end of the 1990s had become the second biggest flour producer in the country.[49]

Typical of many family-owned Global Latinas, Bimbo maintains a cautious approach to financing, keeping its debt to a minimal level. This has helped it weather some difficult storms. For example, during the Mexican Peso Crisis of 1994 it did not have large interest payments to make on debt borrowed in dollars when the latter was much stronger against the *peso*.[50]

It has also proved to have the Global Latina's ability to survive against strong competition, brought into Mexico following the opening up of trade barriers. Grupo Bimbo acted quickly to deal with a 1991 threat from PepsiCo to Bimbo's dominance of distribution. Instead of reducing its extensive transport and distribution network to save money, as it had planned, Bimbo changed tactics to meet the threat from PepsiCo. Bimbo increased the number of truck deliveries in order to out-perform its new rival. The tactic worked; Bimbo kept its hold on its local distribution networks.[51]

Bimbo operates in a low-margin business – bakery – where growth is driven by volume sales. That made it want to expand into new markets and not rely solely on its considerable position in Mexico. In 2007, nearly 70 percent of its revenues came from Mexico. It planned to grow fast outside Mexico through acquisitions, with the aim of eventually controlling the entire supply chain and securing major contracts with companies such as McDonald's, as it had done in Mexico.[52] There were attractive 'natural' markets in the United States (the large Hispanic population) which caught Bimbo's eye. In addition, Mexico's entry to NAFTA in 1994 encouraged Bimbo to move northwards.

First, Bimbo expanded into 'natural' markets to the south, in the rest of Latin America. In 1990–1994, it went on an acquisitions spree in Guatemala, Chile, Venezuela and Costa Rica. Its most important purchase in this period was of the bread and snacks manufacturer, Alessa in Chile, which it bought in 1992. It also used joint ventures to gain quick market entry. For example, it joined cracker and biscuit manufacturer, Noel in Colombia.[53] In this way, Bimbo has built strong positions throughout the region.

Following the acquisition of Plus Vita in Brazil in 2001, bought from Bunge, a US-based agribusiness giant, it has built up its market there and now 25 percent of its sales in Latin America come from Brazil. As with Carlos Slim's Telmex, Bimbo was more than ready to pick up a bargain in difficult times. For instance, it acquired a controlling stake in bankrupt Argentinean baked-goods company, Fargo in 2003, during the economic crisis in the country. Along the way, it learnt some important lessons, including the fact that the rest of Latin America does not share the same enthusiasm for packaged bread as the United States and Mexico.[54]

The lure of the United States is strong for Bimbo. It has large Hispanic populations and a considerable general market for Mexican food. It is economical to distribute products there because most of the supply goes to large supermarkets, not small stores, and finally, NAFTA opened up trade between the two nations.

Bimbo's first big move into the United States came in 1994, the same year as the accession to NAFTA. Bimbo formed a joint venture called QFS Foods with Texas-based Mrs Baird's Bakeries. The new company was to distribute tortillas and joined together Bimbo's manufacturing prowess with Mrs Baird's distribution network. Unfortunately, the partnership did not work and it was dissolved in 1996. Bimbo took over Pacific Pride Bakeries, based in San Diego instead. Then two years later, Mrs Baird's was put up for sale and Bimbo bought it for US$200 million.

While its move into the United States was successful, Bimbo had not expanded beyond the 'natural' markets in Texas and California with their large Hispanic populations.

A sea change occurred in 2002, when Bimbo paid US$610 million for the North American assets of Canadian-based food giant, George Weston. This gave it both a market in 23 American states and five production facilities, in Oregon, California, Colorado and Texas. It opened the West to Bimbo and doubled its revenues.[55]

Bimbo had to make some changes to improve the profitability of its US businesses, however. It reorganized to focus on well-performing products and downplayed the Bimbo brand, which had negative, sexist connotations north of the border. Bimbo also encouraged its truckers to leave their trade unions and become 'independent' by providing financial incentives. The unions had opposed some of the company's efficiency plans. Bimbo in the United States became profitable in 2006.

In Europe, Bimbo has so far restricted its expansionary plans to acquiring a candy factory, Park Lane European Candy Distribution in 1998, located in the Czech Republic. It bought the factory to gain access to its know-how – it produces such items as fruit gums, Mexican snacks and tinned candies and peanuts.

Under the direction of CEO Daniel Servitje, Bimbo has started building a position in China, beginning with the acquisition of the Spanish-owned Beijing Panrico Food Processing Center in 2006 for US$11 million. This is part of the company's plans to become the world's largest bread manufacturer by 2010.[56]

From a dominant position at home, Bimbo learnt, as other Global Latinas, about internationalization moving first in 'natural' markets to the south and north. In the United States, Bimbo first entered states with heavy Hispanic populations missing their home products. NAFTA gave it a stable framework to be more aggressive in its US expansion. Its financially conservative approach, perhaps partly due to its being family-controlled, has proved to be helpful in surviving major economic crises in its home market. But will Bimbo be able to remain conservative as it enters the phase to become a major Global Latina?

MEXICAN GLOBAL LATINAS: MOVING FORWARD

The three Mexican multinationals we have looked at in this chapter have grown to world status each in their own way. But what does the future hold for them?

América Móvil was a trail-blazer in its market because Mexico was among the first countries in Latin America to privatize its telecommunications company, Telmex. Clearly, this gave América Móvil a great advantage over its Brazilian competitors, for instance, which did not experience privatization in the telecoms sector until a decade later.

But América Móvil had another great advantage: the stewardship of Carlos Slim. First, Slim preferred to keep a firm grip on the controls. Only once did he try to join in a partnership with other companies, but this reduced his ability to make fast and key decisions over big issues such as financing and technology. This partnership with BCI and SBC, called Telecom Américas, was short-lived (2000–2002). Second, he shrewdly looked for bargain acquisitions during times of economic instability in Latin America and the world economy. As with many Latin American companies, América Móvil grew through its acquisitions. But Slim's skill was to identify potential bargains that would have a huge impact on the business and then ensure that he won them at a good price.

Now, the company's future rests more in the hands of three of Slim's sons, as their father starts spending more of his time on philanthropic work. But its future growth will depend on whether the regional economy continues to prosper and bring forth ever-increasing demand for mobile services. In the future, América Móvil may seek to spread the risk of being over-dependent on its regional market and enter new ones. It might consider new markets in Asia. Slim senior can rest assured that under his watch the company has been transformed from an old-style Mexican telephone company, constrained by engineering and regulatory pressures, to a dynamic multinational, rooted in a strong marketing-based model.

As the protectionist barriers tumbled down in the 1980s, Mexican cement company Cemex faced the toughest battle it had ever experienced in its seven decades of corporate life. Its less than stable domestic position was under attack from two of the biggest companies in the world, Holcim and Lafarge. CEO Lorenzo Zambrano faced up to the challenge, however, and made two key moves: he expanded the company's market at home through some critical acquisitions and recognized that the company needed to expand internationally or risk being swallowed up by one of the giants.

Soon after this, Zambrano faced another character-building moment when a punitive anti-dumping duty was imposed on Cemex's exports to the huge US market. This further convinced Zambrano of the need to diversify Cemex's operations across the globe. As with América

Móvil, Zambrano's growth strategy was built on acquisitions. But he added in some key advantages that would enable the company to break into new markets in M&A deals unheard of before from a Mexican company. His visionary leadership was joined to operational discipline in regard to organizational structure, the use of technology and a rigorous post-merger integration process, all of which became known as the 'Cemex Way'.

In the future, Cemex may find that it needs to loosen its famous centralizing grip in order to let local managers shape the company's subsidiaries to suit the local cultures. That is one challenge presented by becoming global. Cemex's management model has enabled it to grow at an astonishing speed and wrest significant value out of its new acquisitions. Zambrano's insistence on using the latest technology in a supposedly low-tech industry has enabled Cemex to gain superior efficiencies in the way it manages its operations and distribution networks and transform the industry for ever. It also generated greater profitability from its branding strategies, based on its understanding of the consumer market for cement in developing countries such as Mexico, something we explore in Chapter 4. Furthermore, Cemex shrewdly used its acquisitions in Spain to improve its credit rating and debt position, enabling it to continue financing growth regardless of the ups and downs of the Mexican *peso*.

Zambrano had many personal victories: the company's return to the United States when it bought Southdown and the purchase of the Spanish cement companies on the anniversary of Columbus are some examples. But perhaps the greatest overall achievement is the creation of a world-class multinational that won major acquisitions in the developed world and turned them around, as well as spreading risk by expanding into the wider building-material industry.

Last but not least, Bimbo is another interesting case in point. Like other Latinas, driven by the desire to offset the risks of economic and political instability and drawn by the lure of the US market in the aftermath of Mexico's accession to NAFTA, bakery firm Bimbo drove its own remarkable expansion through some key acquisitions. It had developed efficient distribution networks, an innovative approach to operations and product development, a willingness to make acquisitions at critical points and a strong branding strategy in its 'natural' markets in the United States.

Bimbo also gained advantage from its 'backward integration' into wheat production and flour mills, enabling it to hedge against price fluctuations and stabilize its supply of its core ingredients. One possible drawback of the family control at the top of the company, however, may have been an over-cautious financial approach that has perhaps constrained its acquisitions-led growth. Its purchase of Mrs Baird's Bakeries and Canada-based George Weston's Oroweat's operations enabled it to build market share across North America and not just in the Hispanic communities.

Bimbo has become one of the world's leading food companies based on its market position in Latin America and the United States. The company is now in a position to seize new opportunities in other markets, but this will depend on the leaders of the company and their willingness to make major new acquisitions overseas.

As stated earlier, in 2006, Mexico's exports totalled US$214 billion, with an overwhelming 85.7 percent dependence on the United States. In the wake of the economic slowdown in the United States, as a result of the subprime mortgage crisis that started in July 2007, many Mexican firms are looking for ways to reduce this dependence and re-balance their portfolio toward growth markets, such as their Latin American neighbors and China. For example, while the US housing market has been experiencing a downturn since July 2007, China's insatiable demand for building materials continues apace. Currently, China is consuming half of the world's cement, the primary product sold by Cemex.

For the last 15 years, the involvement through NAFTA of Mexico and Mexican Global Latinas in the United States has been a successful model. The knowledge transfer has proven extremely useful. Mexico's geographical proximity to the North at a time when transportation costs from faraway Asia are increasing will remain a competitive advantage for Mexico. However, it may be time for the country to look for a second front to balance the sudden uncertain economic times of its northern neighbor. The second front could very well be closer to their backyard – in Latin America itself.

4

BUSINESS MODEL INNOVATION IN LATIN AMERICA: MAKING THE UNUSUAL USUAL

> Years ago our competitors said: 'How dare those ugly duck-lings from South America try to sell a jet in the Northern Hemisphere?'... Fortunately, they underestimated us.
>
> Satoshi Yokota, Embraer's executive vice-president for
> engineering and development
> *Business Week*, 31 July 2006

Latin American multinationals have not only shown that they are responsive, agile and opportunistic, as seen in the previous two chapters, they have also developed important innovations in their business models, management processes, products and services that have helped to propel them forward.

In this chapter we look at eight Global Latinas, in a wide range of sectors, from the perspective of their innovative business models: Mexican cement manufacturer, Cemex; Brazilian airplane manufacturer, Embraer; Brazilian cosmetics and toiletries company, Natura Cosméticos; Chilean wine-maker, Viña Concha y Toro; Mexican bread manufacturer, Grupo Bimbo; Brazilian IT services firm, Politec; Argentinean pipe and tubing manufacturer, Tenaris; and last but not least, Mexican brewer, Grupo Modelo.

The main competitive advantage of Latin American companies resides in innovation in their business models. Global Latinas have been able to adapt to and change the rules of the game set out by the multinational corporations from developed countries. The wide range of companies covered in this chapter have launched their own business model innovations, inspired by the unique business environment found in Latin America, and have used them to build on a global scale.

We start with Mexican cement manufacturer Cemex, which has already been covered extensively in previous chapters (its leader,

Lorenzo Zambrano, is profiled in Chapter 1, while its history and strategy are covered in Chapter 3). Cemex has developed a unique and powerful globalizing model, based on three pillars: the use of technology; a devastatingly effective approach to acquisitions; and a smart marketing and branding strategy that has particular appeal in low-income markets such as Mexico.

The Brazilian aircraft manufacturer Embraer built a 'reverse out-sourcing' model which has given it great flexibility in production and delivers lower labor costs than its main rival, Canadian-based Bombardier.

Brazilian cosmetics manufacturer Natura Cosméticos and Mexican beer manufacturer Grupo Modelo are both included for their success-ful model of taking a local brand global. Also in the area of strong branding, Chilean wine-maker Viña Concha y Toro has pioneered a completely new industry in Chile and become in the process one of the world's top exporters of high-quality wine.

Mexican bakery firm Grupo Bimbo has built its extraordinary global scale upon its integrated model of production and delivery, which covers everything from the making of the flour to the delivery of its products. This control over a complex supply chain has given the com-pany significant competitive edge over its rivals. Brazilian information technology services company Politec has built its success on its ability to reinvent itself and adapt to new market conditions.

Tenaris, the global Argentinean firm that makes sophisticated high-tech seamless steel pipes for the oil and gas sector, has a unique multicultural model which enables it to span the world and draw on a worldwide talent base to create super-effective multinational teams.

All Global Latinas covered in this chapter represent sectors not rooted in the natural resources industry. They represent the future of Latin America. Latin America needs to develop more of these kinds of companies. The astonishing success of these companies in the past couple of decades (see the Appendix for full details of com-pany performance) can be in large part attributed to the innovative approaches of their business models. We now look at each of these eight Latin-American business model innovators in detail.

'THE CEMEX WAY'

Cemex's business model innovation can be divided into three parts: its utilization of high-tech methods in a supposedly low-tech industry;

its unique approach to mergers and acquisitions; and its approach to branding its cement in Mexico and other emerging markets.

High-tech methods in a low-tech industry

Since taking over as CEO in 1985, Lorenzo Zambrano has tirelessly promoted the use of the latest technology. On his watch, the company has deployed technology and information systems as management and product-delivery tools to keep its cost structure competitive and to leverage organizational knowledge. This approach has gained fame as the 'Cemex Way', which elevates organizational structures to the status of corporate strategy. It is a global business model with standardized processes and systems on a common platform worldwide. As Zambrano puts it: 'Information is your ally. You use it to detect problems quicker and get better faster, or determine who is better, and then you can go and find out why. As we grow, we clearly need more information. I must admit that I want the information for myself.'[1]

A good example of this approach is the Cemexnet satellite-based system, deployed in 1989 to connect and coordinate all Cemex plants and get information to make timely decisions. In the early 1990s, the company created a logistics system called Dynamic Synchronization of Operations, which uses Global Positioning System (GPS) technology to link delivery trucks to a central control center.[2] Since ready-mixed concrete has to be poured within 90 minutes of mixing, a major challenge is the dispatching of trucks so that they can transport concrete from plants to construction sites in a timely manner. This means, for example, that in Mexico today you can get cement from Cemex as fast as a pizza delivery.

Unique approach to mergers and acquisitions

The difficulty of wresting value out of mergers and acquisitions is well known. The so-called synergies are not always realized, or the cultures fail to mesh effectively, or the business fit is not as good as had been previously imagined. Cemex, however, has created a method of identifying acquisitions and integrating them afterwards that seems to be genuinely innovative. Its success in integrating three global giants from advanced economies – Southdown (US), RMC (UK) and Rinker

(Australia) – bears testament to the effectiveness of a management technique honed and refined over several decades.

Cemex generally targets undervalued or underperforming assets, which it believes have the potential for operational efficiency improvements. Cemex focuses on companies that are well-established players and possess a substantial market share. When identifying acquisition opportunities, Cemex also takes the broader view and examines the potential for restructuring the respective market as a whole.[3]

It has three key objectives when targeting an asset. First, the targeted company must be a good 'Cemex Way' candidate – in other words, it must be capable of being streamlined into Cemex's overall operations. Second, the investment must in no way make the company deviate from its financial targets. Third, the investment must offer superior long-term returns and be located in a country that is, or promises to be, a growth market.[4] Accordingly, Cemex's due diligence includes strong emphasis on country-analysis factors, such as population size and GDP forecast.

Like many another Global Latina, Cemex sometimes takes advantage of economic crises to shop for cement assets carrying lower valuations. Shareholders of targeted companies are often more than happy when Cemex starts to look at them as a potential acquisition.

Cemex can integrate acquisitions very quickly due to this unique approach.[5] The post-merger integration has three main goals: detecting cost savings; identifying and retaining talent; and implementing the Cemex business model. This business model is based on a single global identity (acquired companies are almost always renamed 'Cemex'), common organizational structures and operating processes, a common technological platform, centralized back-office functions and a strong emphasis on operational best practices, business process gap analysis, benchmarking and performance measurement. Reporting lines are adjusted, depending on the function: back-office functions such as finance, risk management, procurement and IT must report to global headquarters, while commercial and other activities report to country headquarters. At the end of the day, the Cemex subsidiaries focus on making and selling cement, while centralized functions are tightly controlled by the parent company in Mexico.

The sheer attention to detail of the Cemex Way is captured in a 2001 article in *The Economist*:

In each case, 'post-merger integration teams' – that is, executives armed with laptops – were dispatched to analyze the new acquisition, to cut costs, and to harmonize its technical systems and management methods with Cemex's....(it) specifies everything, down to the make of computers that employees must use. It can seem authoritarian at times, but it does at least ensure that communication across the company is seamless.[6]

Marketing and branding

Cemex's operations in Mexico are among its most profitable, because it has built a consumer brand for its cement, delivered in bags. Mexico is perhaps unusual in the sense that cement is regarded as a consumer good. In a market where many families build their own homes, cement is not seen as a bulk commodity. This knowledge helps Cemex in penetrating other similar markets, largely in emerging markets. The company recognized that branding was critical in this market. Since retail customers of bagged cement regard it as a consumer item, brand management is an important part of the product's commercial success. The Cemex brands are strong throughout Mexico and the prices there are among the highest in the industry.[7]

An excellent illustration of Cemex's understanding of its domestic market was its 1998 launch of 'Patrimonio Hoy' ('Your inheritance, today'), an innovative savings-and-loan program for the low-end housing market.[8] Most of the poor had insufficient savings to purchase building materials, and Cemex at that time estimated this market to be worth US$500–$600 million per annum. Cemex's answer was the 'Patrimonio Hoy' program, which changed the perception of cement from a functional to an emotional one, creating an uncontested market space. Cemex's scheme provided low-income city dwellers with materials through certified distributors. Inspired by the traditional *tanda* credit-rotation system, members got back their investment in the form of construction materials and related services such as assistance in home construction.[9] In some *tanda* schemes, a local NGO gives each person a repayable loan of one and a half times their savings and the state government provides twice their savings in the form of building materials (non-repayable).[10] This innovative marketing scheme, merging business interests with powerful socio-economic needs, was a huge success in Mexico. While the competition sold only bags of cement, Cemex was selling a dream – and demand soared. With 'Patrimonio Hoy', the company achieved differentiation at a low cost.

Mexico is among the world's highest recipients of remittances. Mexican emigrants in the United States send a total of US$25 billion per year to their families back home. Cemex launched 'Construmex' in the United States in 2001, to capture part of the remittance market. It enabled Mexicans working there to send money directly to Mexican-based Cemex distributors, who supplied materials for their families to build houses in Mexico.

Cemex's understanding of its domestic market and its intelligent use of innovative marketing strategies have paid off. In 2007, the company had a dominant market share of 55 percent in Mexico – more than double the share of the number two player, Holcim Apasco.[11]

EMBRAER'S 'REVERSE OUTSOURCING' MODEL

Underpinning Brazilian plane-maker Embraer's great success in recent years has been an efficient manufacturing model that is highly unusual for an emerging market company: it has reversed the expected out-sourcing model prevalent in such economies.

Instead of making components for big firms in the advanced economies of the United States, Europe and Japan, Embraer draws on the best component suppliers in the developed nations to supply its own needs: reverse outsourcing. Owing to the company's earlier obsession with technological prowess over commercial viability, its engineers can design new planes from scratch. As their wages are typically much lower than those in the developed world, this gives Embraer a significant cost advantage. The company also claims that the reverse outsourcing model helps it to respond more flexibly to peaks and troughs in demand. Whereas a firm like Embraer's chief rival, Canadian-based Bombardier, assembles everything, it is slow to ramp up the supply of components for the final assembly. In con-trast, Embraer can exploit its strategic alliance of component suppliers around the world to increase or decrease the flow of components, as and when necessary.

Finally, by getting components from companies that are best in class, Embraer can get the finest components at a competitive price. For example, in its 70-seat Embraer E-170 and E-190, Embraer bought engines from General Electric, avionics from Honeywell, wing stubs and pylons from Kawasaki, titanium plates from VSMPO in Russia, and door and fuselage parts from a number of European companies. Parts of the ERJ-145 were manufactured by Rolls-Royce and flight instruments by Honeywell.

One other key element of the business model that was developed with great success by former Embraer CEO Maurício Botelho was to create a more customer-focused organization. It was clear from the past that the company had been too internally focused and had failed to establish what the market wanted. This flaw in its make-up was painfully evident when the CBA-123 Vector aircraft, produced with Argentina's Fábrica Militar de Aviones, flopped so dramatically in the 1990s. Though technically advanced, it was cancelled without a single aircraft being sold.

Botelho wanted to make sure that the company would not lose sight of its customers' needs again, so, as mentioned in Chapter 2, he created five profit centers to embed a more market-focused approach. An 'entrepreneur' was put in charge of each division to develop and improve customer relations.[12] The mix of customer focus and entrepreneurial spirit was a way to foster innovation at Embraer.

NATURA COSMÉTICOS: BRAZIL'S BODY SHOP

Brazil is the country with the highest cosmetics spending per capita in the world. Natura Cosméticos, the world's seventh largest personal care products company as measured by market capitalization, sells premium cosmetics and related products that have an eco-friendly pedigree, since they are made from the extracts of local Brazilian plants. The biodiversity theme is underscored not only by the company's name, but also by its motto: *bem estar bem* (literally, 'wellbeing well', in other words, 'good for you, good for the world'). Natura's 600-strong product portfolio is divided into eight segments: fragrances, make-up, skin treatment, sun creams, hair care, deodorants, soaps and shaving creams. Among the best-known brands are Ekos, Chronos and Mamãe e Bebê.

Natura's business model has three components: it has an ethical, natural brand which has wide appeal for Brazil, as well as for other markets; it has developed an extremely effective method of selling in its home country, based on an army of female door-to-door saleswomen; and it has found a relatively low-cost way to conduct research and development, a critical component of success in the industry. Well-heeled rivals such as L'Oréal can invest much more money in seeking out innovations; Natura's genius was to discover a lower cost way to support its own product development.

Ethical stance

As with The Body Shop, Natura's ethical stance has been inspired by its leaders. For example, the company's founder, Antonio Luiz da Cunha Seabra, believes that cosmetics can make people more at ease with themselves, and by extension make the world a better place. He recently told French language webzine Afrik.com how at the age of 16 he was struck by a saying of Plato: 'Humanity is part of everything; everything is part of humanity.'

As a result of beliefs such as this, the company has championed good causes connected to its products. For example, it has developed a sustainable approach to the sourcing of the active ingredients in its Ekos range of skincare, launched in 2000. In particular, it has gone further than the Fairtrade NGOs in seeking to support remote Amazonian communities through its procurement policies.[13]

Since the 1990s, Natura has opted to make transparency a key element of its ethical stance as well, building its marketing campaign around it with the motto, 'truth in cosmetics'.[14] This translated into advertising campaigns using real consumers over the age of 30, an approach other brands such as Unilever's Dove would use more than a decade later.

Sales model

Natura has a network of more than 560,000 independent female sales representatives, Brazilian 'Avon ladies' called 'consultoras'. In 2007, the company earned approximately US$287 million in profits on an annual revenue of US$1.9 billion.[15] More than 95 percent of total sales come from the Brazilian market. This sales model has worked so well because the company has won fierce loyalty from its 'consultoras', in part because they agree with its commitment to 'truth in cosmetics' and broader social causes. The model is particularly suited for a country as big as Brazil, because certain areas lack traditional department stores, and women, many of whom lack good job prospects, are attracted to work that can earn them around US$1100 per year, about a quarter of the average annual wage in Brazil's four largest cities.[16]

Natura also provided certain extras that made the sale representatives even more loyal. For example, it developed meeting places (*centros de convivenças*), ostensibly a place where they could use computer terminals. However, these facilities became extremely important to the 'consultoras' as social meeting places, where they could get together and network. The consultora model, though successful in Brazil, has not always worked as well in other cultures.

Low-cost R&D

Innovation is a key requirement for companies wishing to compete in the cosmetics market, driven as it is by the frequent release and marketing of new product lines. Natura found its own way to beat its giant competitors at the innovation game through a joint program called the 'Campus Project'. This program adopted a collaborative approach to research and development through combined projects with universities and research centers in the United States and France. Using this approach to R&D, Natura produced a new product every three days and dozens of patents every year, as well as keeping development spending down. In 2004, for example, its spending was 2.7 percent of net income, compared with 3.5 percent on average for its larger competitors. Natura counted only 150 employees working in research, whereas a giant player like L'Oréal employed 3000 researchers.

In 2000, Natura merged its research and development and marketing units, to bring together technology and sales and, by doing so, accelerated the time in which the company could estimate a new product's commercial acceptance.[17]

VIÑA CONCHA Y TORO: BRANDING MASTERMIND[18]

Some of the Global Latinas have developed an effective branding strategy, which has taken them to the top of their sector worldwide. Chilean winery Viña Concha y Toro is one such example. Founded in 1875 by Melchor Concha y Toro, a lawyer and entrepreneur who bought an estate in the Maipo Valley near Santiago to plant vines imported from Bordeaux, the company grew to become one of Chile's biggest exporters of wine. The company now claims that it is one of the top ten wine companies in the world, with consolidated sales of

US$528 million in 2007.[19] In the company's annual report, Chairman Alfonso Larraín Santamaría has reported that 2007 was one of its best years yet. Business had grown by 37 percent in value and the volume of exports had jumped by 28 percent.[20]

At the heart of the company's success is its branding strategy, based on what is known as the 'silver-bullet' approach. This means that a company commits itself to a dual-pronged branding strategy, developing and promoting volume sales of mass brands along with smaller sales of very high premium elite brands – the 'silver bullet' ones – at the same time. The purpose is to gain an excellent reputation, in this case from the world's elite of wine-tasters. This in turn helps to lift the volume brands to a relatively high price level and maintain in consumers' minds the reality and perception that for the market the wines are of extremely good quality.[21]

In 2007, higher-value premium brands represented 40 percent of Concha y Toro's total exports. The company has shown its continuing commitment to the premium end of the mass market with the launch of a new brand from its recently acquired vineyard in the Limarí Valley in the north of Chile. The company describes the new wines from this vineyard, situated close to the Pacific Ocean, as being 'fresh, mineral, elegant and delicate'. The brand is called Viña Maycas del Limarí and is inspired by Inca culture. The term 'Maycas del Limarí' means 'farmable land' in the ancient Quechua language and the graphic illustration on the packaging alludes to the Inca's sun calendar. Its turquoise color is reminiscent of the Inca's royal stone. In January 2008, the branding on the packaging won an award at the fifth Wines of Chile Awards.[22] Such pride in national history and culture is a repeated feature of the success of many Global Latinas.

Concha y Toro has developed top-end 'master brands' that have continued to enhance its reputation. It created the Almaviva brand in partnership with the Baron Philippe de Rothschild Winery, for example, and has won several prestigious awards for its high-quality wines. For instance, in 2001 its Don Melchor vintage of that year won 95 points out of 100 in *Wine Spectator* magazine. The company has also been extremely good at cultivating wines and its brands for different international markets. For the United States, it produces clean, fruity and fresh wines and for the United Kingdom it produces more complex ones. Its focus on local tastes has paid off hugely. For example, its exports to the United Kingdom, where it has made a particularly focused effort, have risen by 53 percent. The value of this market has risen by 69 percent.[23]

Concha y Toro's successful branding strategy has made the company one of the top world players in a very difficult market. Twice in a row, the United Kingdom's *Decanter* magazine has named the company's CEO, Eduardo Guilisasti, as one of the 50 most influential wine personalities in the world, a fitting testament to the company's successful operating and branding approach.

GRUPO BIMBO: NIMBLE PLAYER

Grupo Bimbo was profiled as a successful Global Latina in Chapter 3. It has built itself up to be the largest food company in Latin America and the world's third largest bakery, behind Japanese-based Yamazaki Baking and US-based Kraft Food's Nabisco.

One of the company's secrets to success is its commitment to handling all of its own distribution through a model of backward integration, in which it controls the whole process, from flour production to baking to delivery. For this reason, it has been able to keep foreign rivals such as Continental Baking at bay in its home market. Globally, it manages a network comprising 980 distribution centers serving 34,600 routes to supply 1,300,000 different points of sale in more than 18 countries.[24]

Bimbo was also prepared to make an investment of US$30 million to build a strong relationship with McDonald's, which eventually made Bimbo its exclusive supplier of hamburger buns in Mexico. Building on this relationship as it expanded into other Latin American countries where it also controlled the whole logistics chain, Bimbo gained a significant advantage over rivals who depended on third-party logistics companies. A recent case study noted, 'Bimbo then set up new plants in foreign markets along with McDonald's: every sandwich McDonald's sells in Peru, Colombia, and Venezuela comes on a locally baked Bimbo roll.'[25] It even had a distribution tussle with PepsiCo, which Bimbo won.

Bimbo's successful international expansion has been based on its triple commitment to people, processes and technology. As the first Mexican company to launch an employee stock-purchase program, Bimbo has shown through its actions that it is committed to treating its people with respect. It likes to promote people from within and upholds a positive approach toward its employees, based on the notion of the dignity of labor. It has also shown an ability to use the latest technology to improve operational capability and thereby gain a competitive edge. For example, in the 1990s, the company introduced computers to establish speedy response delivery or 'just in time', as it is known. The result has been an extremely effective fast delivery system, which has been translated into other markets. From an organizational point of view, in 2003 the company cleverly divided the organization into two groups to optimize efficiency. It set up Bimbo to manage all domestic bakery operations, and Barcel to manufacture salted snacks, candies and chocolate products.[26]

POLITEC: GLOBAL DELIVERY MODEL[27]

Looking at medium-size companies in Brazilian information technology services firms we find Politec, which has always been a master of reinvention (see Chapter 5 for more information). It started life in 1970 as a mainframe processor working on bank accounts, accounting systems and payroll data. With advances in technology, global corporations started managing these services internally, taking advantage of the arrival of the microcomputer. Fast-footed, Politec was ready for the change and searched for new opportunities. It found them in Brazil's banking sector, then experiencing a period of downsizing which meant banks wanted to outsource some of their data entry, digitalization work and document scanning.

At around that time, the three principal shareholders of Politec – Carlos Alberto Barros (the chairman), Hélio Oliveira (the CEO) and Newton Alarcão, the company's maestro of delivery models and technology – redefined their business model. They established new processes and facilities to cope with the challenges of the industry. For example, along with several other companies, they took on work scanning 400 million forms for Brazil's compulsory saving scheme, FGTS (Fundo de Garantia do Tempo de Serviço). Employing 600 people dedicated to the task in a building in Rio de Janeiro, Politec did the work in 90 days, much faster than the other companies that had won part of the contract. In 2000, the company was awarded work automating Brazil's census.

Further technology advances brought in new changes and Politec had to reinvent itself again. The kind of digitalization work it had done was no longer required and the company developed another niche, providing short-term information technology services for global corporations in their human resources management. By this time, Politec had fine-tuned what became known as its Global Delivery Model, the ability to link together hand-picked talent across 16 technical centers, so as to be able to create the perfect team for a particular job immediately. The company managed a complex web of partnerships with technology providers and global IT companies and encouraged the spread of knowledge within the system through its portal website. For example, Politec joined Oracle US in a pilot project to create a system of electronic invoicing for the central-western Brazilian state of Goiás. It also developed a partnership with a high-tech Israeli firm, which specialized in image-recognition systems to be used by banks.

Being able to reinvent itself continuously, to develop a web of partnerships and manage talent across vast distances to conjure up effective, fast teams when needed form the essence of Politec's business model innovation.[28]

TENARIS: INNOVATIVE GLOBAL OPERATOR

Seventeen new companies entered BCG's '2008 BCG 100 New Global Challengers'. The list identified '100 dynamic companies based in Rapidly Developing Economies (RDEs) around the globe'. Five of the 17 come from Latin America: two from Brazil, one each from Mexico, Argentina and Chile. Their stories demonstrate how Global Latinas with strong business models are taking the world by storm.[29]

Argentinean tubular technology company Tenaris, one of the 2008 newcomers, displayed at least three of the attributes, as highlighted by BCG, of a fast-moving global company from an emerging market. Tenaris was able to develop a business model that went beyond competing on cost; it was successfully attracting and developing top talent; and it had developed operations on a truly global scale.[30] By 2007, it had become the world's leader in seamless steel pipes and tubing for the oil and gas market, with roughly a 20 percent share of the world market.[31]

As the BCG report noted, Tenaris spanned the world, with a network of five research and development centers, located in Argentina, Italy, Japan, Mexico and the United States. This has enabled Tenaris to use innovation to go beyond cost improvement: 'Each centre specializes in one type of technology or product, and, collectively, the centers employ more than 200 researchers, half of whom have doctoral or master's degrees. This effort has enabled the company to add more high-end products to its portfolio.'[32]

Many of the BCG 100 Challengers had adopted 'sophisticated internal systems to foster training and continuing education'.[33] Tenaris definitely passed that test, as it had created its own corporate university, claiming that its average white-collar employee spent more than 65 working hours each year in class or taking online courses. An article by consultants Pablo R. Haberer and Adrian F. Kohan in the *McKinsey Quarterly* in 2007 noted that many Latin American firms struggled to develop international talent for their global operations, especially in the area of leadership development with cross-cultural capabilities. Tenaris was one of the few exceptions to this rule, according to Haberer and Kohan: 'The recently-created Tenaris University trains the company's employees around the world and introduces new hires to Tenaris.'[34] Tenaris University has four different schools, offering training in industry, commerce, finance and administration and management. It has, for example, an advanced management program for mid-level managers who come from across the world and meet in Tenaris's mill in Campana, province of Buenos Aires, Argentina.[35]

Finally, BCG noted that Tenaris succeeded on a truly global scale. Its operations 'span the globe', with subsidiaries in four Latin American countries as well as in Canada, Italy, Japan and Romania. In addition, Tenaris had acquired welded-products plants in the United States.[36]

Tenaris' roots go back to 1945 when Italian steel engineer Agostino Rocca, who had founded his own seamless pipe company in Milan called Techint, went on to create a subsidiary known as Siderca in Argentina to produce seamless steel pipes for the local energy industry. Just after the World War II, Argentina was flourishing, in stark contrast to Italy, then just emerging from the war, and Siderca benefited from a closed market, protected by import-substitution policies, as was usual at the time.

Siderca also benefited from a succession of strong leaders, from the founder Agostino Rocca to his son Roberto and grandson Paolo. Roberto ensured that the company made the proper investment in technology and operations in the 1980s. Following a long period of protectionism through import substitution, Siderca had not developed products that were competitive in the world market. It was able to depend on the fact that import-substitution policies meant locally based companies were obliged to use its products. During the 1980s, when the Argentinean economy was hit by runaway inflation, Roberto, then in charge of the company, realized that it could not depend on the domestic market forever and decided to build a strong export capacity for the far more demanding world market.[37]

Similarly, at another turning point in the company's history, it was the founder's grandson Paolo Rocca who transformed the enterprise into a multinational that spanned the world through a major top-to-bottom reorganization. In December 2002, in the middle of the Argentine crisis, he brought together three subsidiaries, all of which were listed companies from different countries (Siderca in Argentina, Tamsa in Mexico and Dalmine in Italy) into one company under the brand name Tenaris (which was then listed on the New York Stock Exchange).

This move helped the company leverage one of the most unique elements of its business model: its multicultural character. By working across borders in a seamless way, the company has made the best use of its diverse engineering talent from different countries, capitalizing on the best elements from each one.

One example of this was what became known as the Tenaris 'Blue' research team, comprising engineers from Japan, Italy and Argentina, which came up with a breakthrough in pipe technology. As author Antoine van Agtmael explains,

> Besides passing the most exacting tests with flying colors, the Tenaris Blue team came up with a breakthrough in 'dope less' technology, a seamless joint that permits oil service companies to dispense with the often costly and toxic lubricants typically required to make a seal tight and seamless at high pressures and temperatures.[38]

The company's director of technology, Carlos San Martín, described the advantages of being able to work across different cultures, as demonstrated by the Blue team: 'The Italians are great designers, the Mexicans experts at welding technology, but nobody surpasses the Japanese in product testing, and one of the Argentinians, with a PhD from MIT, invented some of the complex models that are part of the Finite Element Analysis computer modeling we used.'[39]

Tenaris was also a pioneer of a unique service model in its industry. It introduced an integrated service in which it installed all of the tubes in customers' oil wells and only charged for non-defective ones. This policy was so popular that Tenaris introduced an additional service later in which it could manage customers' tube inventory for them.[40]

The company also developed a unique 'just-in-time' service in Mexico during the 1990s, which it later rolled out to other markets. This example demonstrates yet again how Global Latinas can navigate through turbulent waters and pluck advantages out of difficult conditions. Tenaris purchased the Mexican seamless pipe manufacturer Tamsa just before the 'Peso Crisis' of 1994, when the Mexican currency was suddenly devalued. As a consequence of the economic crisis in Mexico, the state-owned oil firm Pemex stopped all of its drilling and cancelled its orders for seamless pipes from Tamsa. Also, an anti-dumping suit in the United States closed down some of the market to the north. In response, Tenaris came up with a just-in-time service, supplying Pemex with seamless pipes quickly when it made an order. The practice was then expanded to other markets in the world, making Tenaris not only one of the biggest players in its sector worldwide but also a nimble logistics supplier too.[41]

Techint also took advantage of the state privatizations in Argentina in the 1990s to build a diversified business, intended to offset the risk of dependency on one market and to leverage the company's networking and project-execution capabilities across different sectors. In the 1990s, for example, it bought the Italian state-owned glassmaker SIV jointly with the United Kingdom's Pilkington.[42] Techint was an 'early bird' in internationalization. It began investing abroad in Brazil and Mexico in the late 1940s and early 1950s. But by 1997, just half of its assets and staff were overseas. In 2007, Tenaris' annual revenue reached US$10 billion, up from US$7.7 billion the previous year.[43]

GRUPO MODELO: TAKING LOCAL BRANDS GLOBAL

During the Peso Crisis of 1994, Carlos Fernandez, CEO of the Mexican beer manufacturing company, Grupo Modelo, faced plunging sales in his home market. He knew then that he had to bet the company's future on its capacity to build a strong export market. Today, the company is known for its strong branding strategy, in which it has taken local brands global. Grupo Modelo, another one of BCG's 100 Global Challengers of 2008,[44] notched up annual revenue of US$7.7 billion in 2007, up from US$5.8 billion in 2006. Gross profit in 2007 was US$4 billion.[45]

Much of Grupo Modelo's success in the past few decades has come from its extraordinary success in selling its beer brands abroad, especially in the United States. Three of its brands are among the top imported brands into the United States, with Corona Extra in the number one slot, above Heineken. Modelo Especial is in the number three position, above Guinness, at number five, and Corona Light comes in at number six.[46] Corona, an amazing success story in its own right, emerged as the world's fifth most popular beer brand in 2005 and 2006, with a market share of 1.9 percent.[47]

Some five decades after the company had been founded by Pablo Díez Fernández in Mexico City in 1922, CEO Carlos Fernández in the 1970s discovered that Corona was attracting a cult following among young consumers in the United States. It began when Americans returned from beach and surfing holidays in Mexico, with the unusual long-necked empty Corona bottles as souvenirs. Sales of the beer in San Diego, California, near Mexico, proved that a significant number of Americans identified the beer brand with surfing, beaches, sun and carefree holidays. This was a stroke of luck. But winners in business take advantage of such moments and build their future success upon it. This is what Grupo Modelo did when it began to build a global branding strategy around Corona and its other beer brands.[48]

The company developed the brand image around the universal themes of sun and carefree holidays and by the mid-1980s exported a million cases of Corona to the US market every month.[49] One US bartender's decision to add a slice of lime to the drink completed the brand image that Corona enjoys today. The idea to sell it at a higher price than the rest helped Corona move away from cheap to 'premium'. A momentary crisis in 1986 temporarily halted the company's progress, after a US rival spread the rumor that there were traces of human urine in the bottles of Corona. The company's sales were affected but eventually recovered after it successfully campaigned in the United States to demonstrate that quality had always been paramount. By 1997, Corona had knocked Heineken into second place as the United States' most popular imported beer.[50]

Grupo Modelo's successful branding strategy was built around four components: dominating the home market; building a distinct, international brand; going global; and joining top global brands. In Mexico, it has built a strong brand presence by arranging exclusive deals with bars and retailers and it also owned a sporting arena, a soccer team and two baseball teams, all good promotional tools. It has also built strong partnerships with major global firms, which helps to protect the company's fortunes in a world in which more beverages firms are consolidating and dominating world markets. For example, Grupo Modelo has cemented a strategic alliance with Nestlé Waters to produce and distribute bottled water brands Santa María and Nestlé Pureza Vital in Mexico.

It also imports Budweiser, Bud Light and O'Doul's premium non-alcoholic beer, through an arrangement with Anheuser-Busch. It has just started to import China's leading beer, Tsingtao, as well as Denmark's Carlsberg.[51]

MODEL BEHAVIOR

The Global Latinas covered in this chapter have developed innovative and effective business models, which have driven their success first in home markets and then elsewhere. The ability of these companies to build success on such innovation makes them formidable players on the world scene. Judged by their past performance, they are unlikely to rest on their laurels and will continue to drive new efficiencies and advantages through fresh thinking in the future.

Companies reared in emerging markets such as Mexico and Brazil have often been forced to develop innovative business models and be flexible in their turbulent local markets. This equipped them with a definite competitive edge when they moved into foreign markets. As they become more international, they are also realizing that they may have to change further to innovate in their new global markets.

Cemex, for instance, has proved adept at growth through rapid integration of acquisitions. As it copes with its new global organization, Cemex may find that it needs to relax its centralized controls. It may find that greater local autonomy is needed when it develops its business in new growth markets.

Natura Cosméticos has also seen that its business model does not always translate across borders. In the 1980s, Natura found that its salesforce 'consultora' model did not work as well in Chile, because people there tended to shop for their cosmetics in retail stores.[52] Nonetheless, it managed to build a force of just under 10,000 'consultoras' in Argentina, Chile, Peru and Bolivia by 1996, achieving an annual turnover of US$100 million by 2000. In 2003, Natura's Argentinean business had grown by 100 percent.[53] In 2005, the company opened a shop in Paris, experimenting with a different approach to selling its products, more suited to the French market.

Global Latinas have often outsmarted slower-moving corporate super-tankers of the developed world through the agility and survival skills that they honed in their home markets. However, they need to watch out for new developments on the horizon – the appearance of global Asian firms. Asian companies are also appearing on the global stage and they carry much of the same survival-orientated DNA of Global Latinas. Global Latinas will have to innovate in their business models to both cooperate and compete with them. More on this in Chapter 6.

5

LATIN AMERICA AS A BRAND: HARD SELL AND SOFT SELL

> In an industry constantly facing new challenges and increasing competition in markets everywhere, a strong brand is more valuable than ever and indispensable for future growth.
>
> Interview with Eduardo Guilisasti,
> CEO, Viña Concha y Toro, 2007

Creating the right brand can have incalculable benefits for a country, or even a continent. The United Kingdom is known worldwide for the financial resourcefulness of the City of London and for its innovative service industries, such as media and advertising. The United States produces some of the world's most innovative technology firms, such as Apple, Google and Microsoft. And emerging economies have their own branding strengths. China has been known for quality manufacturing for a couple of decades and India has recently gained recognition as a high-tech star, with an increasing number of IT services firms, such as Wipro, Infosys, TCS and others, adding to the country's renown.

Such reputations can help drive national economies, providing a virtuous circle in which rising companies can enter new markets, boosted by their association with national expertise. This in turn reinforces the country's reputation.

The brand of Latin America is in the making. The world has yet to catch up with the continent's economic realities. It still associates Latin America with soccer, salsa music or a fun-loving culture epitomized by Brazil's annual Carnival. On the economic front, Latin America is best associated with its immense natural resources such as coffee, copper, gold, soy, iron ore, oil and gas and, last but not least, water and rain forests.

This association is not without solid foundations. About 14 percent of the world's daily oil output comes from Latin America, which has the largest proven oil resources in the world. Mexico and Venezuela are major oil exporters and Brazil may become one in the near future. The region is home to 28 percent of worldwide mining spending, with 40 percent of the world's copper mines in Chile and Peru, while Brazil produces a third of the world's steel. There is silver and sulfur in Mexico, nitrate in Chile, nickel in Cuba and emeralds in Colombia, to name but a few. In terms of biodiversity, 40 percent of the world's plants and animals and 20 percent of the planet's water resources are to be found in the region. Brazil has become an agricultural powerhouse and is now the world's biggest exporter of soy and orange juice.

However, Latin America is more than a supplier of commodities to the world. Its commodity companies are moving up the value chain into more knowledge-intensive or specialized areas. Brazilian mining and logistics company Vale, for example, provides a range of non-ferrous products for the steel industry, and is not just an extractor of iron ore. Brazilian energy company Petrobras is committed to developing a capability in ethanol production, drawing on several decades of experience in the Brazilian sugarcane-based ethanol industry.

Some companies are developing high-value global positions in new industries. For example, Viña Concha y Toro, the Chilean winery, has elite brands of wine that have won awards across the world, based on a sophisticated branding strategy. It has been able to wrest greater value for its products by lifting everything to a higher level, even its mass products. Other companies covered in this book are competing in non-commodity sectors, such as food and restaurants, beverages, manufacturing, cosmetics and telecommunications. This sort of diversification is essential if Latin America is to make itself less dependent on the volatile commodities market.

In the future, what will Latin America become known for? Will a distinctive brand emerge? And will it generate greater value for the region beyond commodities with cyclical prices? Can the region take advantage of high commodity prices to move up the value chain, both in commodities and in other sectors? We explore in the following sections examples of areas where Latin American companies and countries can build on their successes on the global stage and help transform the brand of the region. The companies covered below are flag-bearers for a dynamic and positive image of Latin America, and one devoid of past associations with military dictators and economic crises. Beyond the usual images of soccer and samba, they also offer a deeper dimension to the underlying knowledge and competencies that will drive the region forward in a positive way.

BRAZIL, A GREEN CHAMPION?

In light of the climate-change debate, there has been increased interest in ethanol production in Brazil. In 2007, investors were planning to spend some US$12.2 billion on 77 new ethanol plants over the following five years and US$2.4 billion on existing plants, which by 2012 would be producing 9.5 billion gallons of ethanol.[1]

Brazil is one of the largest producers of sugarcane-based ethanol in the world, manufacturing 37 percent of the world's total output. Brazil pioneered ethanol production in the 1970s, after the oil crisis[2] and long before any concerns about climate change, and today all cars manufactured there must run on a blend of ethanol and petrol. The government aimed to become self-sufficient in oil and by 2007 Brazil reached its goal of self-sufficiency, producing 16 billion liters of ethanol per year.

Might Latin America become known for its contribution to the global environment? Should the region – and Brazil in particular – focus on sustainable-development initiatives? Green is after all a predominant color of the Brazilian flag, and Petrobras is committed to becoming a global producer of 'green fuel' ethanol. It is possible, therefore, to imagine a time when Brazil leverages its long experience in green matters and intensifies its capabilities to become one of the biggest contributors to this more environmentally friendly fuel. Not only could this provide Brazil, and perhaps other countries in the region, with a boost to its exports but it could also help to save the planet from the unsustainable consumption of fossil fuels. 'Green branding' is something that both Brazil and Latin America could make their own.

In March 2007, the United States and Brazil signed an agreement making ethanol an internationally traded commodity and committing themselves to promoting ethanol production in Central America and the Caribbean. Both countries also agreed to pool their expertise and technical knowledge.[3]

This agreement was a significant gesture on the US side, as President Bush had staked his reputation on a hugely ambitious goal to increase ethanol-based fuel for cars in the United States. In his 2006 State of the Union address, Bush had called for the nation to use 35 billion gallons of biofuels, including ethanol, by 2017. In 2006, the United States used 5.4 billion gallons.[4]

While the target is going to be hard to reach, the United States has another major concern with the policy. It produces its ethanol from corn, which is much less efficient than the sugarcane base used for ethanol in Brazil. One hectare of sugarcane produces 7080 liters of ethanol. The same amount of corn produces about half the amount. Sugarcane also needs less energy to produce it and emits less carbon, making it a greener form of ethanol.[5]

Brazil already has the capacity to meet its stated commitment to increase ethanol production from 17 billion liters per year now to 40 billion in the next five years. The other important advantage of Brazil's ethanol industry is that sugarcane-based ethanol production does not use up arable land, as does corn-based ethanol in the United States. The use of corn for fuel rather than food is also helping to drive up food prices, leading to environmental concerns that the demand for greener fuel will increase the problem of starvation in countries where people spend a larger proportion of their income on the basic foods.[6]

So, in many ways, Brazil is in a unique position to become the world's green supplier of fuel. It has developed significant expertise in the area, based on 30 years of research and development.

Today, Brazil has the best technology for alternative-fuel vehicles. In 2006, 70 percent of the 2.2 million vehicles built in Brazil used 'flex-fuel' engines, which can run on a mixture of gasoline and ethanol. Brazil also developed biodiesel, a mixture of diesel and vegetable oil made from soy or castor beans. A 2007 Latin American market report summed up the opportunity: 'The Brazilian government and the Brazilian ethanol industry aim to export the country's techno-logical know-how, acquired on the back of over 30 years of ethanol research and development. This would, once and for all, do away with the country's stigma of being mainly an exporter of commodities.'[7]

There is even more potential in a new area of ethanol production called cellulosic ethanol, based on sugarcane bagasse (the biomass remaining after sugarcane stalks are crushed to extract their juice).[8] It can also be distilled from timber. The bagasse does not require extra land to grow crops and is therefore potentially even more environmen-tally friendly than the sugarcane-based ethanol. However, the tech-nology is expensive and untested. But estimates suggest that it could one day be more energy-efficient than any other ethanol; the energy produced from corn-based ethanol is only 30 percent greater than the energy needed to create it, while it is predicted that cellulosic ethanol could produce between twice the amount of energy and as much as 16 times the amount.[9] Nilson Boeta, director of the Sugar Cane Tech-nology Center (Centro de Tecnologia Canavieira or CTC), a leading research center in São Paulo state, has said that Brazil could have a large-scale facility producing cellulosic ethanol from sugarcane bagasse at competitive prices by 2013.[10] CTC is running a small-scale unit to produce cellulosic ethanol and Petrobras has set up a pilot plant.

As the world seeks to reduce its dependence on fossil fuels, it could turn to Brazil for its ethanol needs. The more energy-efficient and cost-effective sugarcane variety of ethanol will be particularly attractive to consumers concerned about the price of fuel at the pump. Environmentalists will also prefer a source of ethanol that does not cause the price of food to go up, hurting the poorest people in the world. Brazil is putting pressure on the United States to lower its tariff against Brazil's ethanol exports, currently set at 54 cents per gallon. In the March 2007 meeting between George W. Bush and Brazilian President Luiz Inácio Lula da Silva, the US President said that the tariff would remain in place until 2009.[11] But if it does come down, Brazil could become a major exporter of green fuel to the United States. The Chinese market also beckons. Currently, it is the third biggest, with sales of seven million cars in 2006.[12]

However, there are a number of short- and long-term challenges facing the ethanol industry in Brazil. In the short term, ethanol producers are struggling to make a profit because of the doubling of production costs over 2007–2008 caused by global factors such as a rise in the price of fertilizer and diesel. Brazil's producers also suffered recently because of the appreciation of the Brazilian *real* against the US dollar. There has also been a fall in the price in the market for ethanol. Carlos Murilo Barros de Mello, commercial director at Cosan, Brazil's largest sugar and ethanol producer group, told Reuters in July 2008 that, 'Prices have to reach 17 cents (per lb) for Brazil to resume planting cane. At 15 cents, no mill will be built.'[13]

In the long term, investors and industrialists in the field believe there will be an increasingly attractive market for ethanol, but the industry lacks leadership. However, there is a trend toward consolidation among Brazil's 350 or so ethanol producers and Maria Borges, director at sugar and ethanol consultants Job Economia, predicted to Reuters, 'In ten years, we'll certainly see Brazil harvesting one billion tons of cane with only 20 industrial groups'.[14]

Another trend is that ethanol producers are seeking to vertically integrate so that they can control the whole process, from the planting of sugar cane to its distribution. At the moment, they are dependent on oil companies for distribution. As a signpost to a more integrated future, in April 2008 Cosan purchased Exxon's fuel-distribution assets in Brazil in a US$826 million deal. This will make Cosan the first ethanol group to operate all stages of production, from cane planting to fuel distribution.[15]

Meanwhile, Petrobras is continuing to deliver on its promise to develop a strong capability in ethanol production. In June 2008, it inaugurated its first ethanol factory and announced that it would complete the first of two ethanol-only pipelines. The new plant is to be 80 percent owned by the Itaruma Group from Goiás state, while both Petrobras and Japanese trading house Mitsui will own 10 percent each. US$200 million is being invested in the plant, which is expected to produce 200 million liters of ethanol per year.[16]

Through partnerships such as these, Petrobras aims to create a number of 'CBios' – bioenergy complexes which consist of an industrial unit for the production of fuel ethanol, powered by electricity generated by the company itself using its sugarcane waste. Ultimately, these complexes would include a biodiesel production unit to supply tractors, trucks and sugarcane harvesters.[17]

Petrobras's first ethanol pipeline, due to be completed in 2009, will run between the center-west state of Goiás and Paulina in São Paulo state. The second will be built between the center-west state of Mato Grosso do Sul and Paranaguá Port, in the southern state of Paraná. The pipelines will help improve efficiency and reduce production costs.

Petrobras has announced plans to export 4.7 billion liters of ethanol per year from 2012, and intends to sign around 20 contracts with local ethanol groups to build similar partnerships. To show its long-term commitment, Petrobras created a new biofuels subsidiary, Petrobras Biocombustível.

Building a brand is never easy and Latin America cannot rely on there being no competition for the green crown. The long-term challenges come from the biotech research labs of California and elsewhere, which are promising to produce a significant revolution in biodiesel and ethanol production. Innovative methods, some derived from genetic engineering, are being applied to fuel production from the C4 grasses (switchgrass, miscanthus, sugarcane and sorghum), as well as from sea-based algae.

Biotech firm Amyris, for instance, based near San Francisco, California, is working on a method that uses micro-organisms (both bacteria and yeast) to turn sugar into isoprenoids, a more cost-competitive fuel than ethanol. And Synthetic Genomics of La Jolla, California, a company set up by Craig Venter (who founded the privately funded Human Genome Project), is working on a method whereby algae are genetically modified to make it easier to extract their oil.[18]

BP Chief Scientist Steven Koonin believes that this area of research might produce the next great unexpected breakthrough and has persuaded BP to plough US$500 million into an academic project on biofuels, the Energy Business Institute (EBI), in partnership with the University of California, the Lawrence Berkeley National Laboratory and the University of Illinois. Steven Chu, the head of the Lawrence Berkeley Laboratory, talks of a 'glucose economy' replacing the oil economy.[19]

If successful, such technology might enable the United States to provide for 65 percent of its current petrol needs with plant matter collected from American soil. A special June 2008 report in *The Economist* noted,

A study by America's Departments of Energy and Agriculture suggests that even with only small changes to existing practice, 1.3 billion tonnes of plant material could be collected from American soil without affecting food production. If this were converted into ethanol using the best technology available today, it would add up to the equivalent of 350 billion liters of petrol, or 65% of the country's current petrol consumption.[20]

Petrobras and other ethanol producers in Brazil will have to ensure that their technology is equal to the potential breakthroughs in the labs of the United States and Europe and elsewhere, if they are to stay ahead of the curve. They might also consider constructing their own partnerships with small biotech firms in high-tech clusters such as California. Equally, they will need to ensure that their production efficiencies help them make the fuel as cost-competitive as possible.

Clearly, Brazilian producers have to hope that the United States will bring down the tariff wall currently set against Brazilian exports of ethanol fuel. But they will also need to be mindful of the possibility that cutting-edge biotech firms will provide North America with viable alternatives, drawn from its own soil.

For now, Petrobras appears to be maintaining an impressive technological lead in biofuels. Petrobras CEO José Gabrielli has set a country target to become 'the Saudi-Arabia of biofuels', with the goal of exporting 4.75 billion liters annually by 2011.[21] The company has reiterated in a recent edition of *Petrobras Magazine* that it intends to become the 'world benchmark in biofuels'. In its strategic plan, which goes up to 2020, Petrobras has set aside US$1.5 billion for biofuels out of a total investment of US$112.4 billion. It plans to become dominant globally in the production, commercialization and logistics of the biofuels industry. But it is cleverly maintaining a focus on supplying the home market of Brazil with ethanol.

Petrobras also has an eye to the future. In terms of its global strategy for exporting ethanol, it has a two-tiered approach. On the one hand, it is focusing on a selection of 'long-term and differentiated' markets with great potential, such as Japan, Korea, Taiwan, Venezuela and Nigeria. An article on the future of ethanol in *Petrobras Magazine* said that,

> Japan, for example, still doesn't use ethanol for fuel, but, as it has the second largest fleet of cars in the world, it will begin to use this fuel, probably to comply with the greenhouse gas emission-reduction targets it accepted as signatory to the Kyoto Treaty. Then it may become the world's largest ethanol importer.[22]

Historic ties between Brazil and Japan could turn this into a fantastic opportunity for Petrobras and other players in the ethanol industry.

The company also plans a second-tier strategy, operating in Europe and the United States. It is studying the formulation and commercialization of two fuels, E85 (85 percent ethanol and 15 percent gasoline) and E10 (10 percent ethanol and 90 percent gasoline), to develop a stronger and more integrated approach to these advanced markets.[23]

Brazil's natural resources, combined with science and innovation in areas from biofuels to stem-cell research, create a unique opportunity for the economy to develop. A recent report from UK think-tank Demos refers to Brazil's economy as the 'natural knowledge economy'.[24] It talks of Brazil's prescient and impressive record in R&D in such areas as biofuels. It notes that innovation continues to the present day, with the world's first aeroplane fuelled by ethanol. This is a small crop-duster plane known as the Ipanema, which has been manufactured by Indústria Aeronáutica Neiva (IAN) – one of Embraer's subsidiaries – since the 1970s. In the last few years, IAN has sold some 50 of the new ethanol-powered models.[25]

The Demos report says that the numbers of Brazil's PhDs in science have grown by roughly 12 percent per year for the past decade and that the country is 'making waves' in areas from software to stem-cell technology. Demos singles out the impressive commitment to R&D from private companies such as Petrobras. But Demos also highlights the research carried out by a state-owned company affiliated to the Brazilian Ministry of Agriculture, Embrapa, the Brazilian Agricultural

Research Corporation, whose network of 37 research centers and over 2000 scientists has helped to make Brazil one of the most productive agricultural nations in the world. The high-tech nature of its business was described by one of Embrapa's professors: 'Here tractors have dashboards like the control centre of a jumbo jet – linked to satellites that give information about soil humidity.'[26]

Counter-intuitively, the Demos report argues that Brazil does not need to develop away from its current bias toward natural resources to become a more advanced economy. It offers an 'alternative trajectory' in which Brazilian science and innovation will enhance and support an economy heavily geared toward the development of natural resources. 'From oil and hydropower to biofuels and agriculture, from biodiversity development to the climate-change properties of the Amazon rainforest, Brazilian innovation is at its best when applying the ingenuity of its people to its natural assets', said Demos.[27] Green innovation – now there is a brand.

EXPORTING EMOTIONS: MEXICAN 'SOAP OPERAS'

The origins of the *telenovela*, the 'Latin American soap opera', are pre-television, and can be traced to Cuban radio in the 1930s and 1940s. It is believed that the owners of tobacco factories used the *radionovelas* to keep their workers content. The workers did not have enough money to own a radio so the five-days-a-week format of the *radionovela* helped to ensure attendance at work.

After the Cuban Revolution in 1959, several *radionovela* writers, typically middle-class women, left Cuba and started writing for television in Mexico and other countries. This was the case with Caridad Bravo and Delia Fiallo, two of the main *telenovela* writers of Mexico's Televisa, the largest media company in the Spanish-speaking world, founded in 1950.

Televisa aired its first *telenovela* in 1957. *Senda Prohibida* ('Forbidden Path'), written by Fernanda Villeli, was a drama involving a love triangle that would revolutionize Mexican TV and set a trend for future *telenovelas*. Its creation responded to a dual need. On the one hand, by the late 1950s, most of the Mexican upper class had a TV set, so it was the moment to encourage the middle class to acquire a TV by offering more popular programming. On the other hand, advertising agencies realized that serials were effective in promoting home articles. *Senda Prohibida* was sponsored by Colgate Palmolive, on exactly the same model as the original US radio 'soap operas' of the 1930s. In fact, initially the production of Mexican *telenovelas* was financed mainly by Colgate Palmolive, Procter & Gamble and advertising agencies.

The *telenovela*'s target audience is housewives and families. A typical storyline features a beautiful young girl from a lower social class and a handsome 'prince' from a higher social class; they fall in love but must face endless obstacles before they can finally live happily ever after. In most cases, it also includes *'la villana'* ('the wicked woman'), the rival of the heroine who uses her sexuality and malice to try to steal the prince, but who ultimately pays for her evil acts. In a *telenovela*, rich and poor co-exist in a friendly way – but only the heroine manages to climb the social ladder, and does so conventionally, through marriage. Since the classic *telenovela* storyline promotes social stability rather than social development, critics argue that it is used by the powerful to suppress the working classes and 'keep them in their place'.

A *telenovela* consists of 60–100 one-hour episodes, aired daily from Monday to Friday. The storyline is easy to follow, with a beginning, a happy ending, and references to the main developments so far to update those who have missed an episode. The *telenovela* defends traditional values, such as family and fidelity, and generally contains moral or educational messages. Each episode finishes with the traditional 'cliffhanger', a key revelation to keep the viewer intrigued until the next episode – this will be particularly important on a Friday.

The *telenovela* differs from the *sitcom* in several main aspects. (i) Duration: one hour vs 30–40 minutes. (ii) Storyline: the *telenovela* has a clear storyline from the first to the last episode, while the *sitcom* is more fluid. (iii) Frequency: daily vs weekly. (iv) Values: the *telenovela* defends and promotes traditional values and sends a clear moral or educational message, not generally the case in a *sitcom*.

Nonetheless, the recent worldwide success of *Betty la Fea* (*Ugly Betty*), a *telenovela* produced by Colombian network RCN, might suggest that it is time to start changing the Cinderella-like fairy tale. *Betty la Fea*, unlike other *telenovela* heroines, is no poor beautiful girl, but a seemingly plain-looking professional woman able to support herself financially. However, it is still a love story with a happy ending. Betty works in the finance department of a fashion company and falls in love with her boss, who is not at all attracted to her. She has to put up with the constant humiliations of her co-workers, the *'villanas'* who make fun of her looks and clumsiness. Finally, Betty metamorphoses into a beauty (good-bye the thick glasses, dental braces, unflattering hairstyle and old-fashioned clothes) and wins the heart of her boss.

One of Televisa's main objectives is to focus on producing quality content and expand the reach of its library. Televisa licenses more than 60,000 hours of programming to other countries (excluding US/Univision). Latin American TV chains such as Brazil's Globo TV, Venezuela's Venevisión and Colombia's RCN and Caracol are also exporting *telenovelas* all over the world, mainly to Russia, Middle East and so on.

In terms of branding, the *telenovela*, like it or not, is a key part of the Latin American – and the Mexican, in particular – construct. Despite the *Ugly Betty* challenge, an exception that proves the rule, soaps in Latin America are innately conservative, supportive of the status quo. It would be crass to try to make direct links between a cultural phenomenon such as the *telenovela* and the continent's need to transform itself economically, but the nexus is a fascinating one. Roll on the first Global Latina *telenovela, El mas grande*: 'Armando, you look after the niño, I am going online for an ethanol teleconference I have to attend...'.

TWO LATIN FOOD MISSIONARIES

It might seem strange to suggest that a chef would have a mission to improve the brand of his country. But this is exactly what the passionate Peruvian cook and entrepreneur Gastón Acurio wishes to do (see Chapter 1 for a profile) with his burgeoning empire of up-market restaurants. Beyond building his business, his wider mission is to put Peru's cuisine on the map, and enable people around the world to see the country in a more positive light than before. At the other end of the chain, in the fast-food sector, Guatemalan entrepreneur Juan José Gutiérrez is also raising his own banner of Guatemalan cooking, in the shape of his Pollo Campero company's home-reared chicken meals, launched around the world in direct competition to the mighty Kentucky Fried Chicken. Pollo Campero's uniqueness is rooted in Guatemalan cooking culture and, in its own way, is taking that Latin American culture into the world. For both Acurio and Gutiérrez, business excellence is tied to the promotion of a country.

A: Peru's Exporter of High-Quality Cuisine

Since at least the Incas, Peru has experienced a rich and varied influx, with people coming from all over the world in successive generations, eventually forming the unusual mix that exists today.

This cultural melting pot has contributed to an unusual and unique mix of styles in Peruvian cooking.[28] In the early period, traditional Incan cuisine was mixed with new ingredients introduced, first by the Spanish conquistadors, who arrived in the early 1500s, and then by the African slaves who were brought to the country from the 18th century on. After independence from Spain in 1821, immigrants from France, Germany and Italy added further elements to the Peruvian melting pot. In the mid-19th century, Chinese immigrants brought with them new frying techniques, along with soy and ginger. Finally, Japanese immigrants added new knowledge about fresh raw fish and seafood.[29] In addition, with 80 of the world's 120 microclimates, Peru offers a rich variety of ingredients, including a wide variety of potatoes (which originated in southern Peru, just north of Lake Titicaca).[30]

Acurio began his business after he and his German wife Astrid graduated from Le Cordon Bleu hospitality college in Paris, opening their first Astrid y Gastón restaurant in Lima in 1994. The *haute cuisine* restaurant targeted premium customers, serving cocktails with tropical fruit and *pisco*, a grape brandy from Peru and Chile.

Acurio has acknowledged that it was a mistake to open a French-style restaurant and ever since the business has developed around various themes and business models, but all rooted in Peru's culture and cooking. For example, in 2003, Acurio launched T'anta, which means 'bread' in the ancient Quechua language. This was designed as a bistro-style restaurant aimed at the mass market, and it earned about one-fifth of the company's revenue in 2007.[31] Another successful addition, which has translated well across the world, is the fish and seafood chain, La Mar. Offering such dishes as traditional lime-marinated raw shellfish, the chain attracted a fashionable following.[32]

Heading off in yet another direction, Acurio developed a traditional Peruvian sandwich chain called Hermanos Pasquale, offering people the chance to try food cooked on the traditional Andean barbecue.

Acurio, as the entrepreneur-chef, ensures that the ingredients are rooted in Peru's long and varied culinary heritage. He regularly visits the street markets of Lima, trying out new tastes and ingredients. Discoveries are written up on the whiteboards in his office, ready for use in his business around the world.[33]

So far, Acurio's globalizing mission has taken his restaurants into Chile, Colombia, Venezuela, Ecuador and Mexico. He has also launched an Astrid & Gastón outlet in Madrid, following other Global Latinas in using Spain, its 'natural market' in Europe, as a springboard for countries on the other side of the Atlantic. There is also a plan for an opening in Hong Kong in 2009 and for further launches across Latin America. One of the most exciting ventures is the planned opening of a La Mar outlet in the Ferry Building in San Franscisco. This US$6 million venture will be located in the heart of the renovated San Francisco harbor district. A further 20 La Mar outlets are planned in the United States, from Las Vegas to New York.[34]

Running a hugely successful and widely differentiated business, Acurio is driven by his belief that a love of Peruvian food worldwide will both help to boost the country's tourist trade and promote Peruvian products abroad, boosting 'brand Peru' in a virtuous circle that also helps his own business. He often refers to the way in which Mexican food has taken off in markets such as Europe and the United States. If something similar happened to Peru's cooking, then its ingredients would be in great demand around the world, he believes. If it does not happen, it will not be for want of trying on Acurio's part.[35]

B: Guatemala's Answer to Kentucky Fried Chicken

When Juan Bautista Gutiérrez emigrated from Spain to Guatemala in the early 20th century, he could not have known that his grandson, Juan José Gutiérrez, would be in charge of an empire of several hundred fast-food chicken outlets in the world's major cities, such as Shanghai, New York and Madrid, as well as across Latin America.

Originally, Juan Bautista plied his trade buying and selling wheat to local mills. Then one day a baker could not pay for the flour in cash and offered a chicken farm instead. The rest, as they say, is history. First, Juan Bautista branched out into selling processed chickens to supermarkets[36] and then, in the 1970s, he and his son Dionisio (father of current CEO, Juan José Gutiérrez) launched the first 'Pollo Campero' ('country-style chicken') restaurant. Pollo Campero opened a string of restaurants in Guatemala and El Salvador, successfully competing with the likes of Kentucky Fried Chicken.

The owners of the company showed their commitment to the local community in Guatemala and beyond by supporting humanitarian missions. Tragically, it was on just such a mission – this time to take food to hurricane victims in Honduras in 1974 – that the plane carrying Dionisio and his sister's husband crashed, killing them both. Without Dionisio, the business' development slowed down for a period.[37] In 1982, aged just 24, Juan José Gutiérrez took over the family company, bringing with him fresh drive and focus to take the business worldwide.

The Pollo Campero brand offers Guatamelan-style marinated, breaded and fried chicken, sold in family restaurants. It increased the number of restaurants in Guatemala from a handful to the current 112.[38]

In developing the brand, the company has taken care to ensure that it is rooted in Guatemala, as expressed by its slogan, 'As Guatemalan as you' ('Tan guatemalteco como tú'). It also continues to act on a commitment to social and humanitarian causes, enhancing its appeal to local people. For example, Pollo Campero founded the Universidad Campero to offer continuous education in business skills and the Instituto Campero to provide basic education for employees. It also sponsors two foundations: the Ayuvi Foundation for children with cancer and the Juan Bautista Gutiérrez Foundation to promote the ideals of community service.[39] As with Acurio's Astrid y Gastón business, Pollo Campero has identified its brand with the country's standing, creating another virtuous circle.

Pollo Campero has made a significant impression already on the United States. Its first franchise operation in Los Angeles, the city with the highest Hispanic population in the United States, opened in 2002. It set a record in reaching revenues of US$1 million in three weeks, compared with the fast-food average of between US$650,000 and US$2.5 million per year.[40] This was followed by further successes in New York and Washington.

Pollo Campero's success was based on the use of the tried-and-tested franchise model used throughout the food industry, ensuring that people with local knowledge were running the operations. It also rooted its outlets in areas with large Hispanic populations. By 2007, it had 41 restaurants across the United States.

It has also moved to Europe, beginning with a partnership with Spain's Tele Pizza, in which each company shares restaurant space in its respective territories. Spain, as usual, for Latin American multinationals was the first stop in Europe and a symbol of coming back home for the descendants of the founder. Pollo Campero plans to have 50 outlets in Spain by 2010.[41] In 2007, it was also the first Latin American restaurant chain to move into Asia, initially with outlets in Jakarta and Shanghai.[42]

POLITEC: PLAYING THE HIGH-TECHNOLOGY GAME

The last company in this chapter, Politec, operates in a very different space – the Brazilian IT industry. But it is also emerging as an important global brand in the IT services sector, drawing on the experience and knowledge that exist in Brazil and revealing to the world a perhaps less-known strength rooted in Latin American soil. Most people immediately think of India as an emerging market that has built a strong IT services industry. But Brazil has been highly advanced in IT for some time, in part driven by a very sophisticated banking sector, which has demanded the most up-to-date technology services. With the image of India before it, Brazil too is looking to information technology to add luster to its branding worldwide.

In 2006, Politec ranked second on Gartner's list of the top 15 emerging outsourcing players in the world published by *Business Week*. The company has become known for its services in developing, maintaining and operating high-tech systems for large-scale clients in the banking and financial industries and the public sector. With a strong base in Brazil, including 16 technology offices, it has developed offices in the United States and Japan.

Many may not realize that Brazil's IT industry generates almost as much revenue domestically as India's.[43] Global players such as IBM and Accenture have bases in Brazil, making the country a part of their international network of resource centers.

Ironically, it was the old problem of soaring inflation in the 1970s and 1980s that drove early development in the Brazilian IT industry. In particular, the banks had to learn to process information quickly, to cope with the problem of runaway inflation.[44] Brazil's banks are efficient and among the most technologically savvy in the world. In fact, they are able to clear bank checks electronically on the same day, in contrast to the United States, where it can take a week.

Today, political stability, a strong telecommunications sector and a diverse mix of cultures make Brazil a popular country for international firms wishing to outsource their IT. However, in comparison with outward-looking India, Brazil's IT industry is more inward, servicing clients in the domestic market, and there are fewer English-speaking technicians than in India. Some of the processes are not as up-to-date as in India, and Brazilian IT lacks the same government backing that has helped to drive success in India. For instance, Brazilian IT firms do not yet get the export tax credits that their Indian counterparts enjoy.[45]

Currently, there are efforts spearheaded by the Brazilian Association of Software & Service Export Companies (Brasscom) to increase IT exports from US$800 million in 2007 to US$5 billion by 2011. In May 2008, the Brazilian government announced a Production Development Policy which finally included a tax relief encouragement to exporters, cutting in half their social security taxes. The President of Brasscom, Antonio Carlos Rego Gil, was optimistic about the change and said at the time that, 'With this new policy the government is telling the world that Brazil is getting into the game. The world needs an alternative to India. This is a niche that will be filled by Russia, China or Brazil, and we have great advantages over the competition.'[46]

One of the Brazilian IT success stories is Politec, which for nearly four decades has stayed ahead of the curve. Since its creation in 1970, Politec has had to reinvent itself a number of times to survive. In one recent incarnation, Politec leveraged its knowledge of security systems – developed in its work for its banking clients in Brazil – to offer services to the United States. It strengthened its offering by acquiring Washington-based Sinergy in 2000, a pioneer in iris-recognition technologies. Following this, Politec won US government contracts, including the provision of iris-recognition systems to hospitals. The business increased following the September 11 terrorist attack on the Twin Towers, an event that intensified the demand for security support.

Since 2004, the company has stepped up its efforts to penetrate global markets through a program called 'Global Reach'. Politec chose four target markets where it felt it could offer cost reductions and where there was an affinity between the market and the company's know-how: the United States, Japan, China and Europe. In the United States, it offered 'near-shore' services and in Japan it built on cultural connections with the Japanese community in Brazil. After a long period of negotiating and selling, Politec won some small but significant contracts in Japan. In China, the company spotted opportunities as the major banks needed to upgrade their systems.

The image of Brazil as a commodities exporter and not as an IT powerhouse has certainly not made it easy for companies such as Politec to win major contracts abroad. Also, the appreciation of the Brazilian *real* vis-a-vis the US dollar since 2005 has made Politec less cost-competitive. Drawing on this experience, the company has begun building a capability in low-cost countries such as China, following a joint venture agreement with Chinese-based Neusoft, announced in 2006. Politec is hoping it can win a contract to help the Chinese government conduct its 2010 census. This is not normally offered to foreign companies. But Politec has impressed China's National Bureau of Statistics with its experience in this area, having engaged in census data-processing in Brazil. Politec will lobby the Chinese to change this rule forbidding outsides involvement, and it hopes the Brazilian government will use its influence as well.[47]

Politec is looking for ways to finance its growth, such as through an Initial Public Offering listing, to take it to the next level. Already, it has made significant inroads into building new contracts outside its home market, where it is currently strongest.

Sustained work by companies like Politec – and there are many of them in Brazil – will help diversify its brand from that of cheap commodity supplier to the world to perhaps the India of Latin American IT.

CREATING A LATIN BRAND

Latin America was the 'emerging market of choice' from the 1950s until the early 1980s. Before the fall of the Berlin Wall in 1989, half the world (including Russia, China and India) did not take part in the market economy. All this changed after the fall of the Wall, when emerging economies in Asia and Eastern Europe started competing fiercely in the global market economy. It soon became clear that it was impossible for Latin America to compete on labor prices with China and other countries in Southeast Asia, such as Vietnam and Cambodia. Commodities themselves, for so long Latin America's trump card, became a vulnerable area with the increased competition.

Coffee provides a stunning example of the shifts in global competitiveness. After oil, coffee is the world's second most widely traded commodity. Latin American countries including Brazil and Colombia have traditionally been the world's biggest producers and exporters of coffee. Although Vietnam has cultivated coffee since the middle of the 19th century, it was not until the end of the 1990s that the country entered on the world stage as a serious coffee producer. Taking advantage of a World Bank loan, Vietnam's coffee production tripled from 1995 to 1999, causing coffee prices to plummet.

Colombia and Brazil could not compete with Vietnam's cheap labor and many coffee growers in Latin America went bankrupt, while Vietnam grew rapidly to become the world's second largest exporter of coffee after Brazil. Coffee prices, along with those of other commodities, soared in 2007 and 2008, but it was the shock of the 1990s, triggered by the sudden appearance of a competitor from Southeast Asia, that is still remembered in the region and that urges Global Latinas to think of a bigger picture beyond commodities when building their brand.

Carnival, music and soccer, among other things, make up the popularly recognized Brazilian brand. But emerging companies such as Politec and other Brazilian technological companies are challenging the conventional wisdom.

In the restaurant business, both Pollo Campero and Astrid & Gastón have made significant gains in spreading their brands, rooted in Guatemala and Peru respectively, around the world. Firmly linked to the profit motive – certainly in Acurio Gastón's case – is the view that their global expansion will increase people's awareness of and liking for their countries, boosting tourism and trade, country and company mutually reinforcing each other's brand.

Another Latin American branding opportunity is green energy. Brazil's Petrobras is set to become one of the world's leading suppliers of biofuels, based on its unique knowledge. It is making a bet on the rise in demand for such fuels, as the quest for reducing carbon emissions intensifies. In July 2008, at their summit on the Japanese island of Hokkaido, the G8 industrialized nations (Britain, Canada, France, Germany, Italy, Japan, Russia and the United States – Latin America is not yet at the table) vowed to cut carbon emissions by at least half by 2050, to tackle global warming.[48] So Petrobras seems to be making the right bet. It is also cleverly focusing both on its home market and on high-potential markets abroad such as Japan, while attempting to make inroads into richer markets such as the United States and Europe. In the future, Petrobras will have two strong businesses supplying oil and gas, on the one hand, and future greener fuels on the other. As nations such as China come under greater pressure to develop their economies using cleaner fuels, they will become huge markets for companies such as Petrobras. This may put Brazil on the map as one of the world's most advanced suppliers of green energy.

The examples covered in this chapter and in the rest of the book show that it is possible to create a new brand for Latin America that leads to success on the global stage. Sun, sand, soccer and *telenovelas* will continue to be associated with and create a positive image for Latin America across the world. However, the global economy is changing rapidly and Latin America must not look back. It needs to create its brand for the future.

6

ASIA'S CHALLENGE TO LATIN AMERICA: COOPERATION AND COMPETITION

> We pray every day that China will keep growing and investing so that we can keep surfing this wave that China is sending around the world.
>
> Roger Agnelli, Chief Executive, Vale, *Financial Times*, 11 January 2007

China and India's rapid growth in the last couple of decades is unparalleled in terms of scope and impact in recent history. If one includes Japan, Indonesia, Vietnam and other Asian countries, it is not a surprise that many call the 21st century the Asian century. The prominence of Asia will continue to grow, in both absolute and relative terms in the global economy; so Latin America can ill afford to ignore Asia. Global Latinas will have to both cooperate and compete with Asian firms to succeed on the global stage.

Trade between Latin America and Asia is not a new phenomenon. It started in the 16th century with trade routes between the coastal regions of China and Acapulco in Mexico, via Manila, and lasted till 1815 – the time of the Independence wars in the region which coincided with Napoleon's invasion of Spain and Portugal (1808–1814). There were other factors influencing trade between Asia and Latin America at the time. British exports to Latin America were replacing the demand for Chinese goods, China was controlling its exports and Spain and Europe in general were finding other maritime routes. In Manila, the Spaniards bought pearls from India and Persia, ivory and silk from Cambodia, in exchange for silver from Mexico, Peru and Bolivia. Other products exchanged for silver included spices, porcelain, cotton clothes, artwork, jewellery, gunpowder and agricultural products, from China, the Philippines, Japan and Southeast Asia.

The first diplomatic relations between the two continents came in the second half of the 19th century, when China established relations with Peru, Brazil, Chile, Mexico, Cuba and Panama. During this period, Latin America needed labor for agriculture, fisheries and the construction of its railways – and half a million Chinese laborers arrived to work in Latin America. For a while, the Mexican *peso* was also used as legal currency in the coastal areas of China.

Coming to the present, Japan started investing in Mexico in the late 1970s and early 1980s, as a consequence of the increase in manufacturing wages in Japan. In an attempt to maintain price competitiveness in the US market, Japanese companies took advantage of the free-trade zones by establishing *maquilas* (assembly factories) in Mexico through their US subsidiaries. By the early 1980s, eight of the largest Japanese manufacturers had footholds in Mexico. Latin America itself, however, benefited from Japanese investments only to a limited extent. In 1996, for instance,[1] 46 percent of Japanese FDI was directed to the United States, and 24 percent to Asia, whereas Latin America was the destination of only 9 percent of Japanese overseas investments.

China has provided interesting challenges and opportunities for Latin America in recent decades. For starters, the Middle Kingdom supplanted Germany as the world's third-biggest economy in 2007 in purchasing power parity terms. China's global trade moved from US$20 billion in 1978, the year its economy started opening up, to US$2.17 trillion in 2007, making it the third-biggest trading power in the world. China has emerged as a major player in the global economy of the 21st century.

China provides an attractive market for Latin America's commodities and in return supplies the region with exports of high-quality manufactured goods. In 2007, China consumed 25 percent of the world's steel and zinc and 40 percent of its cement. In 2006, China overtook Japan as the world's second-largest importer of oil after the United States. These are all sectors that Latin America is strong in. China's currency reserves of US$1700 billion exceed those of Japan. China is expected to become the world's biggest exporter in 2008, with US$1 trillion of exports.[2]

At the same time, China threatens to challenge the flow of investments into Latin America and the future success of some of its own industries. China is still a recipient of one of the highest totals of FDI, amounting to as much as 6 percent of the world's total, according to a recent investment report.[3] The same report predicts that China will continue to attract yet more investment, reaching an expected figure of US$90 billion by 2011.[4] In the competition for FDI, there are fears that China will divert funds from Latin America.

The success of Chinese manufacturing exports has also raised worries about the sustainability of manufacturing in Latin America. Across Latin America, both industry associations and government ministers have voiced concern about China adversely affecting the competitiveness of the home industry.

India is at a preliminary stage as compared to China in economic relationships with Latin America, with a bilateral trade of US$5.5 billion in 2005, representing 1.8 percent of total Indian trade. Over the past two years, India's exports to the continent have tripled and imports have doubled. Indian exports to Latin America include spare parts for cars, pharmaceuticals, textiles and machinery.

The most spectacular Indian investment in Latin America was announced in June 2006, with the victory of Jindal Steel and Power, India's third-largest steelmaker, in the auction for a concession of 40 years for developing the deposits of iron ore in Motún in Bolivia. Jindal is committed to investing US$2.3 billion in this project.

The concerns around China and India can be attributed both to the rapid growth in the importance of these two countries in recent years and to the decreased relative economic importance of Latin America in the global economy. In 2006, China and India's share of world exports was 5 percent larger than Latin America's; the reverse was true as recently as 1990. In 1980, Latin America's GDP was twice as large as that of China and India. Today China's economy is larger than that of Brazil and Mexico combined. Even though Latin America has been enjoying robust growth as a region over the last decade, China and India have been progressing at faster rates.

Taken together, Japan, China and India (and indeed Asia as a whole) are places Latin America can ill afford to ignore as it builds toward global success. Traditionally, Latin America has focused on its links with North America and Europe. However, the global landscape is changing fast. Over 50 years ago, the member countries of the OECD represented more than 75 percent of the world's wealth, while today they only represent 55 percent. Since 2005, trade within emerging markets themselves has amounted to more than their trade with OECD countries. The East beckons, and Global Latinas will have to both cooperate and compete with Asian companies to achieve their global ambitions. This chapter examines the complex economic links between Latin America and the Asian giants of Japan and China.

BENEFITING FROM JAPAN

Japanese investment in Latin America has been relatively modest, compared to that from Europe and the United States, accountable for 3.9 percent of FDI to the region from 1990 to 1994, and only 2.9 percent or US$5.147 billion from 1995 to 1999, when it was the seventh largest source of FDI to the region.

Some of the largest Japanese investments in Latin America have been in Mexico. However, the raw numbers there can be deceptive. Of the US$91 billion that was invested in Mexico between 1994 and 2001, just over US$3 billion was directly attributable to Japanese companies. However, it is estimated that only 22 percent of Japanese investment in Mexico comes directly from the Japanese parent company. A large part of the capital of *maquilas* (assembly factories) is held by the United States subsidiaries of Japanese firms, and hence appears in most official statistics as part of US FDI into Mexico. While there was no free-trade agreement between Mexico and Japan till 2004, NAFTA allowed Japanese manufacturers investing in Mexico through their US subsidiary to take advantage of cheaper raw materials in Mexico, while also avoiding the increasing tariffs and protectionism that characterized the US economy of the 1980s.

Japanese manufacturers have become an essential part of the Mexican *maquila* economy, with over 100 Japanese-owned *maquilas* employing over 100,000 workers in 2008.[5] Indeed, the third and fourth largest *maquila* employers in Mexico are Yazaki North America and Alcoa Fujikura respectively, both Japanese automotive-parts manufacturers. While the largest *maquilas* by numbers of employees are both from the United States (Delphi Automotive Systems and Lear Corporation), Yazaki has 41 *maquila* plants and employs 33,400 employees while Alcoa Fujikura employs almost 24,000 people in 26 *maquila* plants throughout Mexico. Due to the importance of these plants for the local economy, they enjoy lower employee turnover, at around 3 percent.[6] Yazaki has excelled in training Mexican staff and setting up operations in remote locations.[7]

Japanese investments in Latin America have helped to upgrade the technological sophistication and the skills base of the region. For example, Sony's facilities in Mexico are fully-fledged manufacturing sites with sophisticated technology and highly trained workforces, unlike the general impression of labor-intensive, semi-skilled, low-cost production typically associated with the *maquila*. Sony opened its first production plant in the city of Nuevo Laredo, on the Texas border, in

1979. The Sony Nuevo Laredo (SNL) plant started out as a complement to the recording-media production facility at Sony Magnetics Products of Dotham, Alabama in the United States. As time passed, SNL proved to be both cost-effective and of high-quality and eventually replaced the Alabama facility in its entirety.

With its first experience proving a successful one, and with further cost pressures coming from new southeast Asian competitors, Sony expanded its Mexican manufacturing base by opening a facility in the city of Tijuana, on the US border, in 1985. Within the first ten years of its operations, Sony Tijuana Este (STE) had produced 6.7 million television sets, and had around 5000 employees. In 1995, Sony expanded its operations in Baja California, in the state capital of Mexicali. Sony de Mexicali (SML) began to manufacture TV components for Sony manufacturing sites in San Diego and Pittsburgh. In March 1995, STE manufactured the first locally designed television set for the Latin American market, and, in 1997, in order to localize the design activity, STE established the state-of-the-art Azteca R&D center. One of Sony's few R&D centers outside Japan, Azteca has helped STE design more than 80 percent of North and Latin American TVs.

Another major Japanese investor is the Toyota Motor Corporation. Toyota first entered Latin America in 1953, when Distribuidora de Automóviles SA began operations in El Salvador. It rapidly expanded its Latin American presence with successive entries into Honduras, Costa Rica, Panama, Venezuela and Brazil.

In May 1959, Toyota opened its first production facility in Latin America, with the commissioning of its Toyota do Brasil manufacturing operations in Brazil. Today, Toyota has become the world's biggest car manufacturer and has several Latin American manufacturing facilities, in Brazil, Peru, Ecuador, Venezuela, Colombia, Argentina and Mexico, with distribution offices in numerous other countries in the region. Toyota's sales in Latin America increased from 135,000 vehicles in 2000 to 211,200 vehicles in 2007.

Japan and China represent growing sources of finance for Latin America, being the top two creditor countries in the world. Both Japan and China have made extensive investments in the *maquilas* in Mexico, given its unique competitive advantages such as quick access to the United States because of its geographical proximity and the free-trade agreement (NAFTA). Mexico is capable of ensuring that access can be certified as 'safe' and this is important given the growing concern in the United States on security matters. Similarly Mexico can integrate the value chain between the two countries and facilitate the implementation of manufacturing best practices such as 'just-in-time'.

The main Japanese trading houses are also active in Latin America, the most important being Itoh, Marubeni, Mitsui, Mitsubishi and Sumitomo. These trading houses conduct a wide spectrum of activities, including the sale of Japanese goods, the arrangement of the finance for transactions and serving as a channel for export of Latin American goods to Japan. For example, Nissan Marubeni,[8] representing Nissan in Chile, and owned by the Marubeni Corporation of Japan, started operations in Chile in 1979, under the name of Nissan Datsun NDC.

Japan is very dependent on the import of energy and minerals, given their scarcity in Japan. In a policy of development imports (called *kaihatsu yunyū*, 'develop and import'), Japanese companies provide capital and technical assistance to develop and process natural resources overseas, for eventual export to Japan or a third country.[9]

Japanese economic-security priorities demand diversified sourcing, and Latin America is of great importance within that perspective. The Los Pelambres Copper Mine Project in Chile is one such venture, financed by the Japanese with the aim of supplying 10 percent of Japan's demand for refined copper. The mine is scheduled to produce copper ore concentrate for at least 30 years and deliver half of this production to Japanese refiners. It is owned by a consortium composed of Antofagasta, Nippon Mining & Metals, Mitsubishi Materials, Marubeni, Mitsubishi and Mitsui.

Japanese firms have also actively invested in the steel sector in Brazil. Nippon of Japan has an 18.4 percent shareholding in Usiminas,[10] the leading Brazilian steel producer. Japanese shareholders account for 20.51 percent[11] of common shares, amounting to 7.91 percent of Companhia Siderúrgica de Tubarão, now part of Arcelor Mittal, one of Brazil's leading steel producers, with a 2001 revenue of US$881 million. They also have an important stake in Cosipa, part of Usiminas.

Latin America is a vital supplier to Japan in areas such as iron ore, aluminium, cotton, lead and zinc, in addition to being a source of oil (from Mexico and Venezuela).

These Japanese investments have strategic importance for Japan in terms of supply of commodities. But Japanese FDI is important for Latin American firms too, helping them to absorb the latest technologies and to move up the value chain and become more competitive in the global economy. Japanese investments in Latin America have not only provided valuable employment in the region, but have also facilitated the absorption of new technologies and the upgrade of skills in the region. Firms such as Sony and Toyota have brought new R&D capabilities into the region.

There are strong cultural links between Japan and Latin America, given the large Japanese immigrant community in the region. Known as *dekasegi* ('working away from home' in Japanese) in Japan, the Japanese immigrant community in Brazil traces its origins to the end of feudalism in Japan in the 19th century: it generated great poverty in the rural population, so many Japanese began to emigrate in search of better living conditions. In 1907, the Brazilian and the Japanese governments signed a treaty permitting Japanese migration to Brazil.

Today the Japanese immigrant community in Brazil numbers around 1.5 million individuals, and while celebrating in 2008 the hundredth anniversary of the arrival of the first 217 families in 1908, it has achieved enormous economic clout. The community has made significant contributions to Brazil, and has set up prosperous farming settlements from the south to deep into the Amazon. The Japanese Brazilian community, the largest outside Japan, has also been used strategically to buffer the cultural shock of Japanese firms entering into Brazil. São Paulo, the business center, has one of the largest concentrations of Japanese Brazilians. Hundreds of employees of Japanese origins are employed by giants such as Sony, Mitsubishi and Honda.[12]

The presence of these Japanese immigrants has resulted in Brazil coming closer to being a 'natural' market for Japan, and a suitable entry point into the continent. The *dekasegi* in turn have also made Japan a natural point of entry for many Latin firms as they sought new technologies and access to developed markets. For example, Brazilian software services firm Politec found it easier to build alliances in Japan, as compared to India and China. It was easier for Politec to use its Brazilian colleagues of Japanese origin for the management of links with Japan than to negotiate with other firms in China and India. As a result of this, in April 2008, Mitsubishi of Japan bought a 10 percent share in Politec, giving this Global Latina access to capital and know-how from a Japanese multinational.

LEARNING TO WIN WITH CHINA

China has been playing an increasingly active role in the Latin American arena, quickly catching up with Japanese trading volumes in the region. The Chinese are eager to ensure a continuous supply of raw materials, minerals and energy essential for the progression of the

Chinese economy and industrial infrastructure. In the fashion of oil diplomacy, they have been active negotiating and building operations in the petroleum sector in Latin America.

In Venezuela, for instance, a country with some of the largest oil and natural gas reserves in the world, China National Petroleum Corporation (CNPC) has successively taken stakes in exploration, drilling and processing operations, in search of natural resources. Latin American countries, on the other hand, look toward China for Chinese goods such as machinery and textiles, and for technical expertise.

Latin America as a region will continue to benefit from strong Chinese demand for oil and non-oil commodities. But China's domestic industrial strength creates problems for Latin America. It will pose a growing threat to Mexico's *maquila* economy, for instance, as a cheaper destination for investors wishing to establish manufacturing operations overseas to gain economies of scale and lower production costs. Simultaneously, Chinese companies have opened about 30 *maquilas* in Mexico, mainly in the technology sector, to take advantage of NAFTA.[13]

Despite recent increased commerce between China and Latin America, trade between the two regions still represents only 5 percent of the total trade of Latin America. There are also points of friction, stemming in part from the cultural differences and geographical distance between these two blocs. China is already a formidable competitor to Latin American manufacturers in low value-added sectors such as footwear (China manufactures 40 percent of the sector), toys (70 percent) and textiles (60 percent).

As China expands its manufacturing strength in high-technology domains such as aircraft and steel plants, it will compete more directly with successful Global Latinas such as Embraer. Thus it is not a surprise that many Latin countries consider China as a threat. Mexico, for example, has faced direct competition from China since 2003. Also, Mexico has a trade deficit with China of US$2.8 billion dollars and China is the main destination of US manufacturing investment. It is no accident that Mexico was the last country to sign China's accession to the World Trade Organization in 2001.

Bilateral trade between China and Latin America grew from US$200 million per year in 1975 to US$100 billion per year in 2007, according to the Chinese Ministry of Commerce.[14] Latin America now represents a fifth of the US$100 billion of outward Chinese investment.

Countries such as Brazil, Chile, Peru and Venezuela have benefited most from trade with China. They have exported their commodities there, taking advantage of a period of high world prices (in large part driven by demand in China). Latin America supplies much of China's increasing need for soybeans, copper, crude oil, coffee, cocoa and tea. The rise in demand has been staggering. For example, China's imports of soybeans from Brazil and Argentina increased tenfold in the five years, 1999–2004, from US$360 million to US$3.6 billion. Chile and Peru accounted for half of China's copper imports and, overall, Latin America's share of the Chinese commodity boom has doubled in recent years, to a value of US$50 billion. While the region is benefiting from Chinese demand and the boom in commodity prices, it is of concern to policymakers that the region does not become dependent on a volatile market subject to price fluctuations.[15]

At the same time, Latin America has a relatively small manufacturing sector and one which is vulnerable to Chinese competition. Mexico, as mentioned, and some Central American countries, for example, have fared less well from trade with China. Their manufacturing base in sectors such as automotive components and textiles has struggled to compete with Chinese imports.[16] On average, light manufactured goods from China, such as textiles and footwear, are three times cheaper than those produced in Latin America, and these cheaper Chinese goods have taken away a significant share of the US market from Latin America. *Latin Business Chronicle* noted that,

> Within seven months of the 2005 expiration of the Multi-Fiber Agreement that governed quotas in the textile industry, the share of the US market held by Latin American manufacturers fell from 25 per cent to 8 per cent, while the People's Republic of China's share jumped from 26 per cent to 56 per cent. Similarly, in Mexico and Central America, a significant number of *maquiladora* (assembly) jobs have been lost or moved to China.[17]

Clearly, not everyone in Latin America has benefited from the increase of Chinese–Latin American trade. This has given rise to a debate between what can be classified as the pessimists and the optimists. The former believe that the impact of China on Latin America will, on balance, be negative, that China's sheer economic firepower will produce an imbalance. One recent report noted that all the commodities happily exported to China, such as iron, soybeans, crude oil, wood pulp and refined copper, return to the region in the form of cheaper, manufactured goods, such as cars, white goods, computers and textiles – that then undercut local manufacturers.[18] Even Brazil, the strongest economy in the region, ended up importing more from China than it exported. China's trade surplus with Brazil increased from US$62 million in 2005 to US$524 million during the first quarter of 2007.[19]

Furthermore, say the pessimists, China is using its considerable financial resources to build sales networks for its new multinationals in hitherto neglected parts of the region, challenging local firms in areas where they had felt secure from competition. Chinese auto company First Autoworks has been selling its pickups and small vehicles in Ecuador and Guatemala, while the Hong Kong-listed privately owned auto company Great Wall Motors has been selling cheap cars in Venezuela. *Latin America-Asia Review* wrote, 'What is worrying for Latin American policymakers is that China has the financial firepower to build up the distribution networks it needs to dominate Latin America.'[20]

According to a China–Latin America Taskforce, trade with China was preventing the region from developing into other higher-value industries, encouraging a continued focus on lower-value-added, low-tech sectors such as commodities.[21] Officials in countries such as Brazil and Argentina felt 'deceived' in that the promised investment for opening up their economies had not been as beneficial as they had been led to expect and, when it did come in, was often tied to Chinese workers or companies.[22]

The *Latin Business Chronicle* described the split between optimists and pessimists:

> Although certain elements within Latin American society may look to China with unrealistic hopes that the nation will serve as an engine of development that will enable the region to escape its problems, China is also regarded in Latin America with an element of fear that is arguably distinct from attitudes toward a previous generation of Japanese and European investors. Both the 'fear of China', as well as the 'dream of China', are probably rooted in the degree of cultural differences that exist between China and Latin America and will likely continue to influence the dynamics of engagement.[23]

However, the more optimistic commentators suggest that trade with India and China has created a great opportunity for Latin America. Indeed, a 2006 report from the World Bank suggested that Latin America had not taken full advantage of the opportunity to trade with China. During 1990–2004, the estimated growth in China's demand for goods and services from Latin America and the Caribbean was 28 percent higher than the observed increase in exports in that period.[24]

The same report also claimed that there were 'complementarities' between Chinese exports to third markets and Latin American goods. An increase in China's exports to third markets in 2004 resulted in a substantial increase in exports to the same markets from Latin America. The report also stated that many imports from China had a positive effect on regional trade, as they provided 'intermediate goods', such as partly finished goods or raw materials, that local manufacturers used to produce the goods they exported.[25]

The World Bank report called for a number of changes in the region to develop the economy in a different direction. Overall, it wanted to see a shift to higher-tech natural-resources industries and greater investment in scientific and technology-intensive activities.

> Partly under pressure from China and India, the LAC [Latin America and the Caribbean] specialization patterns have been shifting toward higher natural resource-based and S&T [scientific & technology]-intensive activities and products. To facilitate this shift and increase the potential benefits from it, LAC countries should improve their natural-resource management and rural-development policies, while at the same time strengthening policies and institutions for the promotion of skills and innovation (patentable or not).[26]

Another report, from the World Economic Forum, stressed that China's growth was a fact that had to be accepted and that the region needed to sharpen its competitive edge to take advantage of the New World that was emerging. First, it said, China's success in manufacturing has not been based on cheap labor alone. The cost of labor would continue to rise, the report said, and eventually the disparity between wages in China and Latin America would narrow or even disappear. But China would continue to have a competitive advantage, based on the wide availability of capital and its high levels of productivity.

Second, the report claimed, it was too simplistic to say that China had a negative impact on foreign investment flows into Latin America. China did attract flows of money that might have gone into Latin America during 1995–2001, the report agreed. But the two areas attracted different kinds of investment. Investments in China tended to be related to technology transfer while investors in Latin America were looking for high returns. Also, China had huge reserves of money and would become a major exporter of money, creating a new opportunity for Latin America.[27]

Rather than see trade with China as a threat, the report argued, Latin America should see it as an opportunity to improve its global competitiveness. For instance, Latin American businesses have a number of advantages over China in relation to the US market. They have proximity; they can maximize their cultural ties; and they can exploit strong existing networks.

The report suggested a number of strategies that Latin American companies could adopt to raise the value of their products and services. For example, Brazilian IT firm Bematech used closer integration with China to achieve lower production costs, while keeping the valuable segments of its business under its own control, using its base in Argentina and beyond as its 'hub in innovation'.[28]

Mexican auto parts manufacturer Nemak has carved out a very successful niche market for itself in aluminium cylinder heads, engine blocks and other aluminium components for the auto industry. It has expanded across the world, gaining economy-of-scale advantages, and has strengthened its technological edge. Its production facilities in China were not a large part of the company's operation but, according to the report, the presence in China was 'important to keep the development of other potential, more sophisticated players at bay'.[29]

The report recommends a number of policies to help improve the region's competitive edge. These include maximizing the geographical advantage of its closeness to the United States by improving infrastructure. The region contributes about 2 percent of GDP per year to infrastructure, but this would need to be increased to 4–6 percent if it intended to catch up with Asia, the report recommended.[30]

A second recommendation was to encourage the release of more intra-regional trade through a deeper free-trade agreement that integrated the region's economies more closely.

The third recommendation was to encourage innovation.

The Latin American business sector has traditionally been uncommitted to innovation strategies in the region, with a low propensity for funding innovation in most industries. This to a large extent is the result of a Latin American culture that lacks in innovation: innovation-oriented human capital and funding have been scarce and poorly integrated, unlike in other hubs (such as Boston and Bangalore).[31]

Brazil leads the region in its investment in R&D, with just over 1 percent of GDP spent on it, but this lags far behind countries with high-tech industries such as Israel (4.5 percent) and Switzerland (3.7 percent).[32] Brazil passed an Innovation Act in 2004, demonstrating its commitment to improving matters.

But the region's innovativeness, as measured by the number of patents issued, is poor. There were four patents per million people in Argentina during the period 2000–2005, the highest in the region. In the same period, Norway registered 103 patents per year per million people, Japan had 857 and the United States had 244.[33]

There are some significant exceptions to the rule that innovation is low in Latin America. For example, Brazilian aircraft manufacturer Embraer is now a world leader in mid-sized aircraft production, based on its hugely innovative design and processes (for more details, see Chapters 2 and 4).

Most firms in the region, however, have tended to adapt technologies rather than create or improve existing ones. Some industries have blazed a trail, and may be Global Latinas in waiting. For example, a cluster of companies in the salmon industry in Chile have proved a great success, drawing on their own R&D. Equally impressive has been the growth of a thriving wine industry in Chile, of which the company Viña Concha y Toro is a big part (see Chapter 4).

Too many Latin American countries, the World Economic Forum (WEF) report continued, base their research on universities (although this has proved a success for Brazilian cosmetics company, Natura Cosméticos) and fail to finance a healthy research environment. 'Overall research infrastructure in Latin America is weak: centers are underfunded, researchers and academics receive meager compensation and postgraduate enrolment is scarce', said the WEF.[34]

The report calls for an urgent rethink on innovation policy, with the encouragement of interaction between business and research communities, and greater collaboration between technological institutes and universities and other research institutions.

Finally, the report called for Latin American governments to encourage as much economic diversification as possible, to avoid over-reliance on commodity-based industries. It concludes that China's economic rise is a reality that must be accepted, that one day the Middle Kingdom will be as significant as the United States.

The answer is not to go on the defensive against what the region may regard as unfair competition. The challenge for Latin America is to build a new competitiveness that will take the region forward.

'The new world brings threats and risks, but also many opportunities. As the examples of successful companies show, business strategies and public policies must be bold, ambitious, mutually reinforcing and forward-looking,' the WEF report continued.[35]

China and India in particular, and Asia as a whole represent enormous markets and opportunities for growth for Latin America. The growth in demand in Asian markets has helped raise prices and demand for commodities and natural resources from Latin America. This has proven to be a boon for firms such as Vale and Embraer, which have benefited from this to improve their global reach.

China and Brazil have entered into an agreement for the joint production of remote sensing satellites for space imaging. Other bilateral agreements have been formed between both of these countries for advances in the domains of mining, geosciences and forestry. All of this has helped Latin American firms to build new competencies for succeeding in global competition.

Latin American governments and businesses are learning to win with China and India. But there is still a long way to go to encourage local industry to move up the value chain, diversify and avoid an over-dependence on the temporary good fortune of a price boom in commodities.

LATIN AMERICA AND ASIA: COMPETITION AND 'CO-PETITION'

Countries on both sides of the Pacific can exchange knowledge – 'co-petition', the theory of 'collaborative competition' – to realize their economic potential in the new century. Latin America must seize this favorable economic environment born of high commodity prices to learn from similar Asian experiences, in the same way as India and China are drawing lessons from the processes of privatization during the 1990s in Latin America to avoid making the same mistakes in their own processes of privatization.

At the level of monetary policy, these Asian countries are studying the Argentinean decision to leave the 'currency board' very closely. China wants to avoid at all costs the same fate as Argentina in its crisis years of 2001–2002. At the corporate level, the emerging multinational companies on both sides of the Pacific have similar global ambitions and can share the successes and mistakes of their respective expansions.

Brazil and China share common interests in sectors such as high technology. In 2005, China announced the purchase of Brazilian Embraer aircraft to a value of US$200 million, with a projected of sales in the coming years of US$2 billion. In 2002, Embraer set up a joint venture with Chinese consortium Aviation Industry Corporation II to produce the ERJ145 in China. China and Brazil have developed joint science and technology strategic projects of high added value. The two countries have formed the company INSCOM, International Satellite Communication, an alliance between China Great Wall Industrial Corporation and the Brazilian Avibras Indústria Aeroespacial. The Committee on Science, Technology and Industry for National Defence of China is working closely with space exploration company Brasilsat on the China-Brazil Earth Resources (CBERS) satellite program, developed by the two countries and aimed at collecting environmental and geological data necessary to monitor environmental changes. In 1999 Brazil and China manufactured and launched into space the CBERS-1 satellite, which was replaced by Ziyuan 2/CBERS-2 in 2004.

With regards to oil exploration and production, there is a sense of specialization and skill transfer between Brazil and China. Petrobras has been tasked with deep-sea activities in the China Sea, while the Chinese company Sinopec is assisting Brazil with the recovery of mature oil fields. Both companies also want to cooperate in their activities in third countries.

Renewable energy is another sector of possible co-petition. The sector is highly developed in Brazil, and Asian countries are very interested, particularly India, Japan and China, which all need to import most of the oil they consume. This also applies to green energy: for instance, ethanol produced from sugarcane in Brazil is profitable when the price of a barrel of oil exceeds US$30. China introduced a new law in 2006 on renewable energy, whose goal was that 15 percent of energy should come from renewable sources. Brazil's sugarcane ethanol technology is of great interest on the other side of the Pacific.

The Panama Canal plays a very important logistic role for maritime trade. Singapore, with the world's busiest port by shipping tonnage, is interested in Panama and Brazil. International Enterprise Singapore opened an office in São Paulo in September 2005. Singaporean firms APL and Pacific International Lines (a subsidiary of Singapore-based global transportation firm Neptune Orient Lines (NOL)) are investing in Panama and connecting the ports of Brazil and Singapore. Singapore companies such as commodities trading company Noble Group and agricultural products and food ingredients multinational Olam are already in Brazil to buy coffee, soybeans and spices such as nutmeg. In return, Brazilian companies such as Embraer, Petrobras and frozen food king Sadia have their Asia regional operations, marketing and distribution based in Singapore, given its role as regional hub.

Asia should be a source of inspiration for Latin America. The previous chapters described the case of Vietnam, which, in the space of a few years, became the second-largest coffee producer in the word after Brazil, displacing Colombia.

Another example is India, which in a few years has managed to be the country of reference in information technology outsourcing. Companies such as TCS, Wipro or Infosys are synonymous with quality and technology in the domain of software. The Brazilian technology industry is made up of 3265 companies and more than 100,000 employees. Yet the Indian technology industry is double the size of Brazil's, with a turnover of US$30 billion and a diametrically opposed profile: India exported 80 percent of its technological products, while Brazil only managed to export 3 percent.

In response to this situation, in 2004, Brazilian technology companies set up Brasscom (Brazilian Association of Information Technology and Communication Companies), similar to the Indian organization Nasscom (National Association of Software and Services Companies). Brasscom is a public–private partnership to promote technology industries in Brazil. The country has everything it takes to succeed: scale, with a large domestic market and thousands of excellent engineers who graduate every year; quality, with advanced technological solutions for the financial sector online, electronic payments (among the most advanced in the world) and electronic government (all Brazilians pay their taxes and vote in elections electronically). Brasscom is aware of the need to ensure that Brazil sells its technological success. To achieve that, the government, private sector and civil society must work together to achieve a country brand similar to India's.

So Asia, be it China, Japan, India or Vietnam, has become an intriguing symbol for Latin America: a mentor to learn from and a pupil to teach, a competitor to beat, a driver up of commodity prices and a driver down of local industry, a source of FDI and high technology, an inspiration and an annoyance, the friendly rival, the enemy within. For Global Latinas, Asia, more than the Old World, represents the future they must aim at.

7

FROM GLOBAL LATINA TO A CORPORATE CITIZEN: ARE POVERTY AND INEQUALITY BUSINESS ISSUES?

> My vision is to globalize Peruvian cuisine and contribute to the reduction of poverty in Peru.
>
> Gastón Acurio, founder of Astrid & Gastón,
> Interview with author, October 2007

The rise of Global Latinas has been driven by their resilience and agility as well as the economic boom and soaring commodity prices. But Latin American multinationals are unique in the sense that they have emerged within societies which are among the most unequal in the world. These regional factors offer local companies distinctive business opportunities as well as business obligations, but does it mean that they have stronger social responsibilities beyond making a profit?

Today, most Latin American multinationals feel obliged to take part in the development of a subcontinent still plagued with extreme poverty and huge inequality. For most of them, corporate social responsibility (CSR) translates as a business commitment to contribute to sustainable economic development, by working with employees, the local community and society at large to improve their quality of life. CSR is high on their agenda for a variety of reasons, but it is unclear if, beyond that, they should consider that they also have a duty to contribute to the alleviation of poverty.

Since the 1960s, there have been increased efforts to regulate corporate activity and numerous attempts, including within the United Nations, to establish international codes of conduct for multinationals. Those codes have been seen as supporting the efforts of the governments of developing countries to maintain the balance between growing corporate power (often multinationals from North America) and the increasingly vulnerable state. The current wave of interest in CSR dates from the early 1990s and focuses on the longstanding debate over the relationship between business and society.

In the mid-1990s, some leading brands from the textile industry and the energy sector, for instance, were discovered to be running sweatshops, using child labor, and indulging in corruption. This added fuel to the fire of protest from civil society, environmental groups and human rights organizations which subsequently demanded greater acts of corporate social responsibility from international business.

By the end of the 1990s, it became obvious to many that trade liberalization in Latin America was sometimes making the problem of poverty worse for many of those still trapped at the bottom of society. There was a growing awareness that the market alone was not sufficient to bring about development. In particular, critics of free-market policies stressed that if firms were driven by short-term financial profitability, they would not make long-term investments to promote human development or benefit the poor.

Today, companies are largely concerned with the potential damage to their reputation that could result from exposure as guilty of corporate malpractice. This partly explains why CSR is seen in negative terms, with an emphasis on things that companies should not do, rather than on seeking positive developments, such as helping to eradicate poverty.

It is also noteworthy that the impact of big business on poverty has not been included as one of the criteria upon which corporate performance is measured. This is in spite of the growth of ethical investment funds. Even the 'Global Compact', created by the UN in 2000, does not refer to key concerns such as poverty reduction or equity; a missed opportunity as this commitment was signed by 4700 companies in about 120 countries, along with worker representatives, Non-Governmental Organizations (NGOs) and governments.

So far, labor conditions, human rights and sustainable development have been at the heart of CSR policies, while poverty alleviation has not been a high priority, even though it has remained the principal social problem in regions such as Latin America.

Furthermore, the tools and methodology of CSR are not geared to solve this particular problem. As some specialists explain, CSR has been shaped by the North and therefore reflects its specific characteristics and needs. The success of CSR in Latin America, as well as other developing regions, will not only be about the number of local companies signing up to the concept. It will also be about whether business and others can drive forward their own home-grown version of CSR, which addresses local issues and improves society, while also strengthening the capacity of governments to solve those problems.

A number of factors have changed society's views of CSR, raising its importance as a means to drive development. First, international agencies began to regard it as an important method for positive change. Second, beginning in the 1990s, Latin America saw the implementation of the so-called 'Washington Consensus' policies, which placed an emphasis on deregulation and the liberalization of economies. Milton Friedman, the high priest of free-market economics, used to argue that business has one overriding responsibility, which is to use its resources and engage in activities designed to increase its profits. The new CSR policies, on the other hand, were often accompanied by what is called 'triple bottom line reporting', which includes not only financial results but also the social and environmental impact of the business.

CORPORATE SOCIAL RESPONSIBILITY: THE LATIN AMERICAN WAY

CSR is about the way a company manages its business so that it can become 'co-responsible' for social and sustainable development, according to Marcello Linguitte from the Ethos Institute, a non-profit organization that advises Brazilian companies on social responsibility issues.[1] In this view, a socially responsible company is one that has the will and the ability to listen carefully to the various claims of its many stakeholders, including shareholders, employees, contractors, suppliers, consumers, communities, government, labor unions, NGOs and so on.

There are four main elements that need to be integrated for the development of a successful and permanent CSR process: a strong ethical basis; a perception that the company is part of society and has the moral obligation to help society and the environment; projects with a clear stakeholder orientation; and finally, a process that supports the sustainable development both of the business and of society as a whole.

Since 2002, and thanks to economic growth, there has been a significant reduction of poverty in Latin America. Between 1990 and 2007, the poverty rate (those living with less than US$1.25 per day) reduced by close to 12 percent and cases of extreme poverty (those living with less than US$1.00 per day) decreased by 9.1 points. Nevertheless, in 2007, the region was still home to 190 million poor people,

35.1 percent of the total population, including over 69 million, about 12.7 percent of the total population, living in extreme poverty.

The problem is that despite the sub-continent's booming economy, the figures for the poor and indigent are still higher in absolute numbers than the figures for 1980[2] (136 million poor and 62 million indigent in 1980 vs 190 million and 69 million in 2007). There are large differences across Latin American countries but the region as a whole is on track to meet the Millennium Development Goals, to halve the 1990 rate of extreme poverty by 2015.

As regards inequality, ethnical and regional variations are making things worse and cause Latin America to be the most unequal in the world. The data shows that the top 20 percent of income earners receive about 15 times more than those in the bottom 20 percent. In the most unequal countries, such as Brazil and Guatemala, the disparity is as high as 30 to 1. We can compare these figures with those of more equal countries, such as Sweden and Taiwan, where the ratios are 5 to 1; or the United States, the most unequal country among the developed world, where the ratio is 9 to 1. From 2005 to 2008, according to the 2008 Wealth Report by Capgemini and Merril Lynch, the wealthiest Latin Americans have increased their assets by 20.4 percent amassing US$6.2 trillion in financial assets, excluding homes and art collections. The same report in 2007 mentioned that Latin America's rich are the world's least generous – only 3 percent of their assets go to charity compared to Asians or Americans who give 12 percent.

The endemic poverty of the sub-continent seems all the more shocking when set against the fact that Global Latinas have benefited from surging economic growth over the last few years, driven by high commodity prices.

Unlike most proponents of CSR who appreciate its wealth-creating capacity for all stakeholders, certain NGOs, such as Oxfam and Christian Aid, remain critical. They consider current policy to be completely inadequate faced with the devastating impact that multinational companies can have on development. For the critics of CSR, growth has led to improvement in the overall standard of living in Latin America; but its supporters say poverty remains the fault-line threatening the future.

Ironically, the problem with CSR in regions such as Latin America may be the fact that the poor do not have a stake in multinational businesses. CSR, as currently practiced, is geared to taking account of its stakeholders, not those who are outside of this group.

How can businesses launch market-based initiatives in poor communities to achieve meaningful progress in the alleviation of poverty?

Recent thinking has identified three channels for raising people out of poverty: enterprise, distribution and government revenue.

One immediate and direct way that enterprises can alleviate poverty (the 'enterprise channel') is when a foreign firm employs people locally. In addition, companies can have an indirect effect on wealth creation when they raise demand for products and services from local suppliers. But FDI in the 1990s was directed mainly at the service sector. Foreign multinationals bought privatized assets mainly in telecoms, banking and energy. This investment represented a change of ownership, which rationalized and made those formerly state-owned companies more efficient and in some cases actually reduced employment instead of creating it. The enterprise channel's positive impact seems to be limited to the relatively small number of people who are offered employment.

The 'distribution channel' involves the poor as consumers. This approach was made popular by CK Prahalad's theory concerning the fortune at the bottom of the pyramid.[3] He was the first to emphasize the huge untapped market represented by the poor population. Successful attempts to eradicate poverty through this channel have taken place, but two main challenges remain. To be effective, all firms need to contribute to a reduction in poverty to 'create' those new markets. The other difficulty lies in the fact that most products produced in the South by companies with CSR policies are meant for export under well-known brand names. Most of these branded goods and services are not bought by the poor, excluding them as customers altogether.

América Móvil, however, is a good example of what can be achieved for the lower-income population through the 'distribution channel'. One of the keys to América Móvil's success is the fact that its 'prepaid' calling cards and services appealed to low-income customers with no established credit rating and a very limited budget for telecom services. This market model has since proved tremendously successful in Latin America and all over the world, where mobile phones are a popular alternative to high-cost fixed phone lines. Carlos Slim's strategy to extend the use of portable phones to tap into the lower-income consumer market revolutionized not only the Mexican but also Latin American and global markets. It showed that you can improve your bottom line while allowing a relatively poor population to have access to services that, until then, it had found to be unaffordable.

Another similar initiative comes from Venezuela, where a start-up company called Diemo is launching mobile banking with GSM network provider Digitel. The service will give remote and generally poor residents the ability to transfer money wirelessly via a cell phone to a store where a third party can receive the cash. This service is 'virtuous' for two reasons. It is ideal in areas where there is neither a wired infrastructure nor easy access to banks for the poorest residents, but the advantage of the system is mainly financial for a low-income population. Western Union, a US-based global leader in money transfers, charges up to 15 percent or US$30 to send US$200 in cash to another party, while Diemo's fee would be about 1.5 percent – or US$3 – on US$200. The fee reductions have a direct impact in improving the lives of the poor who receive those transfers directly. The IDB estimates that Latin America and the Caribbean received US$66.5 billion in remittances in 2007. Most of the money sent by migrants goes to pay for basic expenses such as food, shelter, clothing and medicines. The largest recipient is Mexico with almost US$24 billion. And about three-quarters of the remittance flows to the region come from the United States. Spain and Japan are other major sources.

The last channel is the 'government revenue channel' which operates through tax contribution. The efficiency of this channel depends on the extent of taxes levied by the state as well as the use that is made of tax revenues. But some factors limit the state's revenue gains, including that of FDI in Latin America: competition to attract foreign investments means that governments often offer tax rebates to investors to minimize their tax burden; and overall, globalization has made it difficult for governments to secure tax revenues from internationally mobile capital.

In this regard, it is surprising that the debate about CSR, which has touched on virtually every area of corporate engagement with broader society, has scarcely begun to question companies in the area where their corporate citizenship is the most tangible and most important – the payment of tax. With the exception of Brazil, which has a high tax rate of 35 percent, the other Latin American countries have very low tax rates of about 10–12 percent. Mexico, for instance, collects 12 percent of its GDP from taxes while most of the government revenues (40 percent) still come from oil.

The idea is beginning to take root though, that extreme inequality in the distribution of the fruits of progress constitutes a social and economic problem and that there is a link between fiscal policy, democratic governance and economic development. But so far, no Latin American country can pretend that it has a successful fiscal policy. As a matter of fact, only 25 percent of the region's population believes that their taxes are being well spent.[4]

OVERCOMING OBSTACLES

CSR is taking root in the larger businesses located within Latin America, but the growth of better business practices is neither comprehensive nor uniform. One major issue is that large multinationals are paving the way, but small and medium enterprises (SMEs), which provide 80 percent of the region's employment, are lagging behind. The biggest challenge is to convince SMEs to incorporate CSR in their business plans. More vulnerable than large corporations, they focus on ensuring their survival rather than spending money and energy to improve their business brand and reputation.

Nonetheless, Latin America is moving toward more ethical standards in business. Brazil is leading the way, due to a combination of factors. It has a fairly healthy economy, while a huge divide still exists between rich and poor. Brazilian companies want to be seen as part of the solution rather than as part of the problem.

Fifty-nine percent of Brazilian businesses participate in social initiatives, according to a study produced by Brazilian research organization IPEA (Instituto de Pesquisa Econômica Aplicada),[5] and Brazil is one of the first countries to have adopted tough legislation in this area. Under the 1995 Environmental Crime Laws, the executives, officers and directors of a company can be sued in a criminal or civil court for failing to ensure that the company meets the necessary health, environmental and safety standards. As a result, CSR has grown dramatically in recent years, with companies of all sizes and sectors developing innovative strategies. Growing demand has also sparked the proliferation of a number of CSR instruments, like codes of conduct, good practice and so on.

FROM CORPORATE PHILANTHROPY TO SOCIAL RESPONSIBILITY AND GLOBAL CITIZENSHIP

Corporate philanthropy has existed since the 19th century as a by-product of industrial capitalism. CSR seems to offer a progression that goes beyond corporate philanthropy. The motivations are different in each case. Companies engage in philanthropic activities because they are convinced that in doing so they will be able to gain a significant advantage in terms of reputation, social capital or business development. On the other hand, the ultimate purpose of implementing a CSR policy is the enhancement of social welfare and economic performance as a necessary condition to achieving this goal. In this second case, economic profit is a means to an end – the betterment of society – rather than an end in itself.

Looking into the figures, it seems that most business managers in Latin America do not understand the nuances between corporate philanthropy and CSR. According to a *Latin Trade* survey of 'the best Corporate Citizens 2004', 20 percent of the Latin American companies that took part in the poll considered that the practice of social responsibility meant providing corporate donations to charities. For 17 percent of them, it represented corporate grants, for 16 percent, it was an action taken in the field of community services. Yet 9 percent of the companies involved in CSR in Latin America have set up a company foundation and 15 percent of CSR actions are based on partnerships with organizations or charities.[6] Such partnerships, however, might become the focal point where corporate philanthropy meets CSR, as setting up a partnership with public and private organizations enables corporations to extend social projects to new areas. Corporations supply the financial means while other organizations provide the network and the projects. One business leader explains why this type of partnership works so well. Arturo Elias Ayub, head of the Telmex Foundation, created by Carlos Slim, says that there are other people who know better how to manage and implement social projects while companies have the economic capacity to help fund them.[7] The Telmex Foundation, established in 1995, focuses on nutrition, justice and environmental conservation issues.

According to Professor Michael Porter of Harvard Business School, CSR brings a competitive advantage that lies in integrating societal demands with strategy and operations.[8] This opinion is backed by the 2007 edition of the sustainability guide published by the Brazilian business periodical *Exame*.[9] It explains that out of the 140 companies that recently answered a questionnaire sent out by the magazine, 72 percent publish an annual sustainability report and 31 percent adopt a system whereby executive pay is tied to the social and environmental results achieved. In Brazil alone, the 32 companies that appear on Bovespa's Sustainability Index (ISE) on the São Paulo Bovespa stock market are worth US$400 billion.

Support for Brazil's Ethos Institute of Business and Social Responsibility is yet another indication of the increasing regard for CSR in the country. Founded in 1998, Ethos has already attracted over 1000 companies and its membership is growing by 15 percent every year.

Latin American companies that venture into developed markets tend to develop an even greater commitment to CSR, as they perceive it as a way to protect shareholder value through the awareness of social, environmental and corporate issues.

Mexico pioneered the development of philanthropic organizations with the creation of The Mexican Centre of Philanthropy (Cemefi, El Centro Mexicano para la Filantropía) in 1988, with 59 companies, 92 foundations and organizations and 45 individuals. Its aim is to promote philanthropic culture, civic engagement and sustainable development. The organization started a CSR program in 1997, with the idea of helping companies to implement CSR initiatives. Manuel Arango, Cemefi's founder and one of the most important Mexican businesspeople, organized one of the first CSR conferences in Latin America in 1997.

The next step for companies is to embrace global corporate citizenship, which means that businesses must not only be engaged with stakeholders, but be stakeholders themselves, alongside government and civil society. This new concept was publicized by Klaus Schwab, executive chair of the World Economic Forum, in an article that appeared in *Foreign Affairs* in 2008, called 'Global corporate citizenship: working with governments and civil society'.[10]

This concept draws on the fact that since companies depend on global development, which in turn relies on stability and prosperity, it is in their interest to contribute to improvements in the state of the world. It integrates both the rights and the responsibilities that companies have as global citizens.

The intensified pace of globalization due to technological advances is the most significant fact in the weakening influence of the state. Therefore global corporate citizenship is a logical extension of corporations' search for a sustainable framework of engagement.

THE MORAL CASE FOR CSR

Global Latinas often feel morally compelled to help society and the environment. As a consequence, they have approached CSR as an obligation rather than as a way to add value to their businesses. There are various reasons that explain why Latin American multinational companies feel obliged to embrace CSR policies. Their own history is one, as most Latin American multinationals have started as public companies, or at least have benefited enormously from government subsidies.

Is it fair that a state-owned 'national champion', relying for years on orders from the domestic market, public procurement, protection against market forces and import duties as well as financial, fiscal, marketing, regulatory and international responsibilities, once privatized, creates a fully owned financial structure in the Cayman Islands tax haven as part of a global financial-engineering process?

Most Latin American former state-owned industrial giants owe part of their success to these ties to the state. Arturo Elias Ayub of the Telmex Foundation says that at the end of the day people realize that Mexican companies have a social responsibility to their country and its people, in return for everything that Mexico and the Mexicans have given to the company.[11]

Another reason for Latin American companies having a sense of obligation to their country and community is that they have been created sometimes 'for' the people, with a particular ethics and sense of service to them.

Grupo Bimbo, for example, the family-controlled Mexican bakery, has always had respect for the human being as a core corporate value. Promoting managers from within, rewarding loyalty, Bimbo was one of the first Mexican companies to introduce an employee stock-purchase program. Attentive to the well-being and dignity of its staff, the company naturally became involved in various CSR programs.

The same goes for the Brazilian cosmetics company Natura Cosméticos. The whole company is based on an environmental concept, in which its products are created through the sustainable use of natural products sourced from the Amazon rainforest from poor indigenous communities. However, Natura not only promotes products with a therapeutic idea originating from Brazilian biodiversity, but its business model has improved the life of about 400,000 Brazilian women working in direct sales, the 'consultoras' described in Chapter 4. The company, which has fully integrated the concept of CSR, considers that responsible practices are not a separate activity but rather form a part of the company's everyday operations, from production to its business relationships. There is an understanding within its ranks that CSR generates a positive impact throughout the company's chain of productivity.

Astrid & Gastón (A&G) constitutes yet another example of CSR from a moral standpoint. A&G's specialized Peruvian restaurant concept is an example of a socially responsible enterprise that uses its home country's natural ingredients as a national resource to leverage. Co-founder

Gastón Acurio is also reviving the tradition of small vendors of grilled food in the streets, banned earlier because of a lack of health standards. The Peruvian chef is training those street vendors, who are mainly women from a poor background, so that they are able to meet the regulations and get back into business.

The moral ground for CSR is spreading beyond the companies themselves to their wider networks. Increasingly, managers recognize that they are responsible not only for their own CSR performance, but also for 'upstream' and 'downstream' activities connected to them. Their goal is then to extend their corporate practices into the supply chain and ensure that their partners follow in their footsteps. In that regard, Chile's Viña Concha y Toro, Latin America's main wine exporter and one of the most recognized wine brands worldwide, has decided to get involved in research projects on water-management technologies to improve current irrigation practices and to develop an advanced, efficient and sustainable management of agriculture.

THE BUSINESS CASE FOR CSR

Beyond moral grounds, it seems that most companies, including those located in Latin America, hope to draw a competitive advantage from their CSR programs. And they are right to do so. CSR can offer both short-term and long-term advantages to business. Interestingly, the number-one reason why companies in Latin America undertake social programs is to motivate their own workers; slightly ahead of public-image concerns.[12]

The partnership between bakery giant Grupo Bimbo and community bank FinComún, a pioneer in urban lending in Mexico and a true microfinance intermediary, also had an immediate impact. The partnership takes advantage of FinComún's expertise in providing micro-loans, while the community-based financial institution is tapping into Bimbo's comprehensive distribution network and product delivery. To understand the virtue of the system one has only to look into Bimbo's business model. In Mexico, the bakery derives 80 percent of its income from small stores, of whom 20 percent regularly ask for credit. Previously, Bimbo had an informal program to provide credit services to these stores. But thanks to the partnership with FinComún, Bimbo expects to reduce its bad debt and achieve its goal of providing credit to about a quarter of its clients.

INVESTING FOR THE LONG TERM

Latin America at 81 percent (compared with an average of 63 per-cent in the developing world) has one of the highest enrolment ratios at all levels of the educational system. However, the emphasis is on higher education, producing a situation where middle-class children coming out of private schools enjoy world-class universities, while lower middle-class students coming from public secondary education are unable to go to university because the quality of public educa-tion is poor. Results of mathematic tests are among the lowest in the world. Companies that help to improve the level of education of their employees, as well as their employability, provide long-term benefits to those who set up specific programs. Bimbo, for exam-ple, was able to resist the arrival on the Mexican market of the global food giant PepsiCo, thanks to its people-orientated approach. Bimbo is well known for its policy of avoiding lay-offs even in times of crisis.

Working for Bimbo means a lifelong employment. This policy helps Bimbo to retain talent in the face of aggressive recruiting policies from US companies such as PepsiCo. Bimbo has not only adopted agile strategies when faced with competition but has also introduced pay rises and various other incentives to strengthen loyalty and build the notion of common interest among its staff.

Researchers have studied the impact of '*Raizes e Asas* (Roots and Wings)', the educational program launched by the Brazilian Banco Itaú, the only Latin American bank listed on the Dow Jones Sustain-ability index since its inception in 1999.[13] They concluded that the long-term benefits of investing in education were significant. Using statistical analysis, the study looks at the future salaries of students in the program, compared to their estimated earnings without the schooling. The bank found that an investment of US$12,000 in each student would yield a lifelong salary 14.3 percent higher than that if the student had not participated in the program.

Brazilian oil producer Petrobras's commitment to a wide variety of development schemes shows that long-term involvement in CSR can also lead to long-term benefit. Involved in a wide array of social and environmental projects, including the 'Zero Hunger' program (mentioned later in the chapter), the Brazilian 'national champion' was recently ranked as the world's most sustainable oil/gas company, by the rating firm Management and Excellence (M&E Madrid and São Paulo).[14]

Vale, the Brazilian mining corporation, is also involved in various pioneering projects. Vale Florestar, a reforestation program, is one of them. It seeks to recover 300,000 hectares in the Amazon region to restore the Atlantic Forest to its original state by planting 165 million trees in the next few years.

In April 2008 Vale announced the establishment of the Vale-Columbia (University) Center on Sustainable International Investment. The first of its kind, the center will promote learning, teaching, policy-oriented research and practical work within the FDI area, paying special attention to the sustainable development.

The business case for CSR also has to do with the fact that best practice in a variety of fields has become a crucial issue for Global Latinas interested in extending their market abroad. They are required either to invest in policies that are perceived as 'ethical' or to risk being penalized by consumer protection groups in those markets.

The growing impact of ethical investment funds has also contributed to increased pressure on multinationals to adopt CSR procedures, as it influences stock value, consumers and market leaders. Bad publicity can translate into lower stock prices and, on the other hand, there is often a business opportunity behind a CSR strategy – whether it means increasing profit, reducing risks or being less exposed to liabilities of various kinds.

Chile-based GrupoNueva is a private holding company that implements the 'triple bottom line' (economic, environmental and social) management system. It is heavily involved in forestry activities with operations in 15 countries, a good illustration of the growing impact of ethical management practices. Making an early commitment to social responsibility provided GrupoNueva with an exclusive access to premium markets. To sell to customers such as Home Depot in the United States or Canada, for example, the group had to prove that it was socially and environmentally responsible, something its forestry work amply demonstrated. This ultimately brought GrupoNueva a significant competitive advantage over its rivals from northern markets. And research by the company has shown that customers were willing to pay a few cents more for a product, knowing this investment would be returned to the community. The company changed its approach to forecast long-term (15 years) revenue growth taking into account how to provide profitable goods and services for a larger base of customers at the bottom of the pyramid. One of its companies Masisa works all over the Americas to provide basic furniture for the lower-income clients and carries out training courses for micro-entrepreneurs in furniture-making.

CSR offers a variety of avenues for poverty reduction, including job creation, investment in infrastructure and a deliberate effort to make a company's products available to the poor. But current reports offer different verdicts on the effectiveness of CSR practices in terms of the bottom line and competitiveness. But whatever those conclusions might be, experts stress that the future of the planet – as well as the shifting balance between rising economies and the developed world – cannot be left to the business sector alone.

Petrobras' commitment to 'green fuel' ethanol perfectly illustrates this assessment.

REDUCING INEQUALITY WHILE IMPROVING RETURNS

In the world's most unequal region, it is interesting to note that some companies, local and multinational, manage to bridge the gap between rich and poor, create hope, bring a sense of entrepreneurship to low-income populations – and turn a profit. For them, the idea is to try to balance the moral and business cases for CSR.

In 1998, Cemex launched 'Patrimonio Hoy', already described in Chapter 2 and as such the company is one of the pioneers of social innovation in Latin America. This initiative has a strong CSR component. It is a micro-credit system, through which low-income families can improve or fix their houses by receiving free designs and advice through the company as well as offering fixed-priced materials. Cemex managers volunteer their free time to do that. In Nicaragua, for instance, one of the Latin American countries with lowest GDP per capita, more than 1000 families have been benefiting from this program, while in Latin America as a whole, more than 180,000 families have received more than US$67 millions in loans, with a loan repayment rate of 99 percent which has made the program profitable.

This has changed the perception of cement from a functional product to an emotional one, creating an uncontested market space for the company. Cemex's scheme provides low-income urban inhabitants with materials through certified distributors. Inspired by the traditional *tanda* credit-rotation system, members get back their investment in the form of construction materials and related services, such as assistance in home construction. The operation has been a huge success and has allowed the multinational to achieve differentiation at a low cost.

In 2001, Cemex launched a related scheme called 'Construmex', to capture part of the remittance market,[15] Mexico's second-largest source of foreign revenue. This program enables Mexicans working in the United States to send money directly to Cemex distributors in Mexico, who supply materials to their families to build houses in their homeland. Collaboration with different social actors proved fundamental, as Construmex partnered with Mexican immigrant associations and Mexican Consulates; the whole success of the operation was based on building trust. The idea was to channel part of the 'remittances' from the United States to Mexico in a win-win way for both the immigrant workers and their families at home.

The impact of both initiatives has been strong and these innovative strategies have not only improved the global company's corporate image in Mexico, but also constituted a significant barrier to entry for potential competitors by allowing Cemex to secure a dominant position in the bagged cement local market.

Desarrolladora Homex, a Mexican builder of low-cost housing founded in Culiacán, Mexico in 1989 and expanding in India and Egypt, serves communities in highly populated and underserved areas. Meeting the needs of lower-middle and middle classes who had never owned a house before has helped the company to develop an innovative business model and special pricing very appealing in other emerging markets such as India and Egypt.

These cases, like others, demonstrate that the private sector can and will respond to Latin America's low-income majority, given the right incentives. However, some critics argue that private intervention in what should be regarded as a public service undermines the state's fundamental role. In fact, governments that encourage these types of enterprises acknowledge that public spending will never be sufficient to eliminate poverty and that in the absence of private intervention, the poor themselves will be prepared to pay for services.

One way or another, poverty alleviation through business action is happening throughout Latin America. Organizations engaged in service to low-income consumers have actually set in motion powerful forces that promote social change and bridge the gap between rich and poor. But whether that business model can work on a large scale remains to be seen.

COMPANIES VERSUS GOVERNMENTS

In most parts of Latin America, the role of the state has been shrinking and has been gradually replaced by that of the private company. The business sector plays a central role in the expectations of civil society, as people sense that government paternalism or nannying has failed. The fluctuating roles of business versus the state are particularly interesting in the mining industry, which plays such a central role in Latin American economies.[16]

The general perception is that mining, as a source of fiscal revenue and foreign exchange, brings important macroeconomic benefits to Latin America. At the same time, there is a view that environmental and social costs are caused by businesses at the local level that have a direct impact on local communities, but without a meaningful response from the state. For instance, environmental damage done locally by a profitable mining enterprise is tackled neither by the businesses nor by the government agencies.

In a paper[17] on the sustainable development of the Latin American mining industry, a group of experts explains how the low administrative and technical capacity of government regulators means that the financial resources to promote and implement sustainable mining strategies are not available. They also emphasize that many governments have not set clear rules that could make social responsibility and governance in the sector financially viable and economically sound.

Although the distribution of economic benefits through taxes and royalties is a central issue, mechanisms to transfer economic benefits from the mining activity to local communities often remain inadequate. Consequently, and because financial transparency is still not universal in Latin America, both mining companies and communities tend to focus on short-term advantages, disregarding long-term projects.

The other issue is that local communities rarely benefit from centralized taxes. As for gaining from local projects initiated by mining companies, such as new schools and clinics, the local populations often sense that the companies are making a fortune out of locally extracted minerals in exchange for relatively little benefit to their immediate environment. People also suspect that the environmental and social costs for the local population exceed the benefits granted by the mines.

This debate shows the limits of CSR policies on the ground. There is a perception that corporations should complement social investment from the state, rather than replace it. It also casts a light on the use of FDI stemming from those corporate investments.

Many people believe that foreign investment helps to reduce poverty in the region because it contributes to overall economic growth. But to prove that it does have a lasting and positive impact on widespread wealth creation, there needs to be a link between foreign investment and greater income equality.

Meanwhile, the one area in which foreign investment does have a significant impact on the poor today is in investments in infrastructure, such as water, sewage and transport. But those projects also involve both the state and official development assistance (ODA) – the subsidies injected by northern economies into emerging countries. Considering that FDI is now running at three times the level of ODA (known to increase significantly the well-being of the poorest and to have an impact on reducing inequality), one can see how social expenditure is subject to strong budgetary constraints.

The problem of shrinking taxes in Latin America is made worse by the Free Trade Zones that have been set up all over the continent (and all over the world), from Manaus in Brazil to Costa Rica in Central America to Monterrey in Mexico with the *maquila*[18] assembly factories. Multinationals from Asia, Europe or the United States have set up assembly plants in those areas to take advantage of cheap labor costs as well as fiscal incentives.

Tax evasion by companies and individuals is a social problem in the region, but many Latin American companies professing allegiance to CSR would be shocked if the reduction of tax evasion became a key CSR issue. The problem is a critical one though, especially when one considers that the rise of social tension is closely associated with the failure of fiscal policies. And as far as Latin America's fiscal policy is concerned, it is considered ineffectual in term of redistribution. The numbers speak for themselves: the combined effect of taxes and transfers in Europe reduces inequality by as much as 15 percentage points, whereas in Latin America the reduction is only 2 percentage points.[19]

A 'NEW DEAL' AGAINST INEQUALITY?

Some countries manage to launch public programs to tackle extreme poverty. Chile has a record in that respect, and poverty has fallen further and faster in that country than anywhere else in Latin America. In recent years, public policies such as the 'Chile Solidario' scheme have contributed to that relative success. It aims to help the poorest support themselves by ensuring that they keep their children at school. It also offers them training or grants to set up small businesses. Within four years, 250,000 poor Chilean families have benefited from the scheme.

The Mexican government started in 2002 a program called 'Oportunidades' which now benefits 5 million households (about 25 million Mexicans with annual cost of US$4.5 billion, about a quarter of the total population) and the idea is to give mothers of families about US$100 on the condition they meet certain education, health and nutrition goals.

'Fome Zero' ('Zero Hunger'), President Lula Da Silva's high-profile program to stamp out hunger in Brazil, has received far more media attention and is also considered to be an overall success. The program was important for various reasons. First, because 40 million Brazilians – a quarter of the population – lived in poverty and had difficulty feeding themselves when Lula came to power. And this in a country which is the world's top exporter of beef, poultry, soybeans, sugar, coffee and orange juice and poised to overtake some time soon the United States as the world's leading exporter of food products. But it was also unique in the way it brought together many social actors, being built on partnerships of all kinds, within Brazil and beyond its borders. Fome Zero was funded by a combination of over 1400 companies, actors from the private sector and civil society, international support and government contribution. It stands as a model of global corporate citizenship.

The Fome Zero program, launched in 2003, has already improved the living conditions of over 11 million poor people in Brazil. Its initiatives include giving direct financial aid to the poorest families, creating cisterns in Brazil's most arid zones, supporting family farming or offering micro-credit. Zero Hunger includes the Bolsa Familia ('family grant') scheme – a program which gives cash payments of between US$23 and US$44 a month direct to mothers, according to the number of children they have in school. The decision to grant the money to the female head of household, as in the case of Mexico mentioned before, is the result of research that showed that they were 'more zealous in controlling family resources'.[20]

Between 2002 and 2005, Brazil's social spending has tripled to reach US$8 billion, but international institutions, generally conservative about social spending, have not criticized Brazil's strategy this time. Supporters of the program, including the World Bank, even consider that the operation 'Zero Hunger' provides a model that can transcend national boundaries, showing countries how to streamline bureaucracy and give people skills to lift themselves out of poverty.

Of course the program has also been criticized for its uneven distribution, the risks of corruption and its potential for breeding dependency, but although controversial, the model has eventually won such support that half a dozen African states are contemplating the idea of importing the concept to alleviate the continent's endemic poverty.

'Zero Hunger' benefits from having specific goals. It combines emergency measures with structural changes – such as family agricultural programs, agrarian reforms, literacy training and even initiatives to educate families about nutrition. The fact that President Lula has rallied private and public interests, and that the program has been coordinated between federal, state and local government is rare enough to be noteworthy. Last but not least, multinationals that had so far argued that they preferred to donate money directly to social projects or foundations rather than to Latin American governments suspected of widespread corruption are heartily contributing to such a project, on the grounds that it is closely monitored and built on partnerships and consensus.

REACHING A CONSENSUS TO MOVE FORWARD

Governments of Latin America must establish fair business environments, enforce the law, encourage access to credit and create reasonable infrastructures so that business can truly play its role. With that state support in the background, CSR is vital for businesses in emerging economies because it can be a useful tool to tackle issues such as poverty, inequality, violence, environmental problems, corruption, or child labor. Solving those problems is of paramount importance and will require a great deal of integrated action and the forging of new partnership arrangements between companies, government and civil society.

Various countries have widely benefited from consensus-based reform initiatives. In Europe, the 1978 Moncloa Pact was one such, a turning-point in the history of post-Franco Spain. It was prompted by the country's economic turmoil after the 1974 oil crisis. The government, unions, political parties, businesses and civil society came to a consensus on the way forward for the country. They agreed to sign a pact which included political and economic commitments that paved the way to Spain's transition toward democracy and prosperity.

Today, Global Latinas have been transformed into healthy businesses. Their strength is proven by the vast amount of outward flows of FDI from Latin America that they have helped to generate. But does this mean that those companies, which managed to emerge in a difficult economic and political context, are responsible for all the woes of Latin America? Surely not; that is why there needs to be a Moncloa-style broad consensus on the future of social responsibility in the continent. If business could do more, it is also clear that most Latin American states have not done enough, so far, to reduce inequality. Both sides should endeavor to make growth more equitable. It probably means that the tax issue should be revisited, as it is the basis for a fair re-distribution of wealth creation. But this only applies if Latin American states demonstrate that they can avoid any future corruption and inefficiency that would squander tax-generated income.

There is also the question of the very concept of CSR, rooted as it is in developed countries, in the Latin American context. For example, should CSR be tailored to meet different countries' needs, to include poverty reduction and ensure that sustained growth spills over to the poorest parts of the population? Or should it remain a global concept, designed to secure sustainability and a peaceful co-existence between inter-dependant world economies? The debate needs to continue, but not for too long: action is necessary.

ACKNOWLEDGMENT

The contribution of Anne Dumas, Research Associate at INSEAD, as co-author of this chapter is gratefully acknowledged.

CONCLUSION: GLOBAL LATINAS AND GLOBALIZATION 3.0

A new breed of multilatinas is emerging...What they share is excellent, tight management, good cost controls and the flexibility that comes from thriving in high-risk markets.

J. Rumsey, *The Banker*, 4 March 2008

A NEW OPTIMISM

In summer 2008, as I was finishing the writing of this book, there was optimism in the streets of Latin America, despite there being concerns about the impact of the North American financial crisis on the region.

Just over a decade after the Peso Crisis of 1994, economics there had become 'boring', according to a banker based in Mexico City.[1] But, he continued, was this a good thing? A question well worth asking more generally, as we come to the end of this book on Global Latinas. Is it just business as usual, or are there surprises in store?

In Mexico, the budget was balanced and inflation was being kept under control. A middle class was growing. The number of families earning between US$686 and US$1500 (Mex$9000 and Mex$20,000 (Mexican *pesos*)) a month had increased from 5 million to more than 12 million. The finance minister also announced plans to increase spending on infrastructure from about 3.2 percent of GDP in 2007 to 5 percent in 2008.[2] However, two dark clouds hovered over Mexico, according to the *Financial Times*: the potential impact of the economic slowdown in the United States on Mexico's export industry (more than 80 percent of its exports go to the United States) and the failure of successive governments to open up big sectors, such as energy, to more competition.

In Brazil, a very optimistic story emerged in 2008. Social assistance programs, combined with policies which made credit more widely available, had helped to lift six million Brazilians out of poverty. A more vibrant consumer economy was on the rise, with 1.6 million new jobs created in 2007. Liberalizing reforms, the *Financial Times* enthused in July 2008, had created a booming and stable economy.

At a time of rising global demand for food and energy, Brazil is uniquely placed. Already the world's biggest producer of almost any farm product you can think of, including ethanol made from sugarcane, Brazil is the fourth biggest manufacturer of cars and will soon become an important oil exporter.[3]

Big challenges remain: there is too much red tape and enterprise is crushed by a complex and burdensome tax system that is in much need of reform.[4]

Overall, however, years of economic stability have brought increased rates of growth from which more and more Brazilians are benefiting. Average growth rates have doubled to 4 percent a year.[5] An annual global CEO survey from PricewaterhouseCoopers reported that 63 percent of respondents from Brazil said they felt confident about future business prospects, almost double that of the respondents from the United States.[6]

The new prosperity of these two countries and of the continent in general is attributable in part to the strong multinationals they have nurtured, the Global Latinas. It is all very different from the environment of economic and political instability out of which the Global Latinas have sprung. They are resilient survivors who have developed an impressive armory of skills and capabilities, which have enabled them to navigate safely through turbulent waters. While they can enjoy a more stable environment at home, the Latinas paradoxically now face more instability in the world economy. Their history of overcoming great odds at home means that they are well prepared to cope on the global stage.

FROM NATIONAL CHAMPIONS TO GLOBAL LEADERS

Latin American firms that have emerged as global leaders in recent years are those able to survive a period of intense change

157

and competitive pressure in their home country. In particular, from the 1990s on, they have had to contend with tough foreign competitors on their doorstep, as local economies in the region were liberalized. On top of this change they also had to survive several major economic shocks, from the debt defaults of the 1980s to the major economic crises in Brazil in 1999 and Argentina in 2001. To paraphrase President Harry Truman, the Latin American 'kitchen' had become very hot, and yet the companies that later emerged on the world stage did not seek to get out of it for calmer and cooler places: they stood the heat.

Instead of giving up the struggle, the Latinas retooled, readjusted to the new environment and managed to navigate their way through difficult times with skill. In this way, they developed the ability to manage risk and seize new opportunities when foreign multinationals preferred to withdraw. Some of the companies, such as Mexican building-materials leader Cemex and Brazilian mining giant Vale, maintained a sharp focus on their core business and shed their conglomerate baggage. Most made sure that they had a dominant position in their home markets, as the ballast to the global vessel they were about to launch. One of Lorenzo Zambrano's first decisions on becoming CEO of Cemex in 1985 was to buy up two major companies in Mexico in order to create a stronghold in his home market. Vale bought assets in the mining sector in Brazil for similar reasons.

The present Global Latinas emerged from an era in which many foreign multinationals invested and then, following economic instability, chose to sell their assets. This presented a perfect opportunity for many of the Latin American firms to purchase important businesses at rock-bottom prices. Carlos Slim's phone companies Telmex/América Móvil were a notable example of this ability to acquire distressed assets, gaining such prizes as AT&T Latin America, the Brazilian telecoms firm Embratel from MCI Worldcom and BellSouth's Brazilian assets. Similarly, Petrobras bought up retail gas stations in South America from Shell and Exxon. Where multinationals from the developed world saw risk, Global Latinas perceived an opportunity they could profit from during unstable economic conditions.

Operating in a period of instability at home, many Latin American businesses realized that they needed to internationalize their operations as a natural hedge against domestic economic and political uncertainties and reduce the risks associated with the habitual currency devaluations common to the region at that time. The exemplar is again Cemex, which needed stable cash flow and access to cheaper financing to drive its acquisition-based growth strategy. After 1992, Cemex used its Spanish subsidiary to borrow money at a more favorable rate and to reduce its debt repayment burden. As with others, it also found that generating revenue in dollars (and later in euros) protected it from holding cash in local currencies (such as the Mexican *peso*) subject to great volatility.

There were other factors driving Latin American companies to internationalize. Mexico's accession to the NAFTA with the United States and Canada in 1994 helped to encourage firms such as bakery firm Grupo Bimbo and Cemex to expand into the United States. Large-scale firms in the extractive industries such as Petrobras often needed to expand with global partnerships to reduce risk and leverage expertise while exploring for more oil, gas and minerals. Industrial sectors like cement required firms to be close to their markets, since it is expensive to export heavy materials across long distances.

DIFFERENT GLOBALIZATION STRATEGIES

The firms covered in this book have displayed many types of strategic approaches. Cemex focused on its core business, Brazilian airplane builder Embraer gambled successfully on the medium body plane business and Petrobras used its knowledge of deep water drilling and exploration to put together a string of lucrative partnerships across the world. Others, such as Chilean winemaker Viña Concha y Toro, focused on a single line of business. They found their competitive advantage by achieving high levels of quality and efficiency. Most of them expanded organically in their domestic markets through 'greenfield' activity, while their international growth was fuelled by acquisitions mainly.

Global Latinas saw world markets as an extension of an expansionary process begun in their home country. Acquisitions provided a good way for these companies to increase their size quickly and access new knowledge and technologies. Being able to effectively manage the post-merger acquisition was a skill that many of these companies excelled in.

Global Latinas followed a similar and successful pattern of internationalization, focusing first on their 'natural market', that is, countries geographically close and/or sharing the same language and history. When entering the United States, Global Latinas chose first those states with a large Hispanic population and in Europe, Spain (for most of Latin America) or Portugal (for Brazilian companies) as the gateway.

Thus Global Latinas mirrored what Spanish multinationals had successfully done in the 1990s. Most Spanish companies started their international expansion in their 'natural market' – Latin America. Although geographically very far, the region was culturally 'close' – sharing the same language and history.

Latin American firms tended to gain a much greater understanding of the market dynamics in developing countries than their foreign rivals, and could use this knowledge to gain a competitive edge in Latin America and other developing regions. A classic example is América Móvil, which developed a unique prepaid business model for its mobile business in Mexico, a model it was able to roll out with great success to other countries in Latin America. It is natural that such firms would start their expansion program in markets where they have the greatest understanding of the consumers.

Other firms such as Embraer, Vale, Politec and Petrobras, rather than focusing on the end consumers, needed to obtain more resources or assets, such as unique knowledge. Therefore, they scouted the world in order to find the best opportunities for their growth strategies. Politec found a company in the United States, for example, to advance its capability in optical-recognition security software.

Some of the firms covered in this book have been constrained by their own conservative attitude towards financing, often due to family control or a history of being state-contolled. Therefore, there is a contrast between firms such as Vale and Cemex, which each engineered audacious acquisitions of major global companies to further their growth and firms such as Grupo Bimbo and Natura Cosméticos, which pursued a more cautious approach. As a consequence, Bimbo, for instance, is largely limited to Latin America and the United States, with only a minor presence in China. If they are to expand more fully across the world, these Latinas will have to be more willing to deploy cash and buy major assets.

There are some differences between Brazilian and Mexican firms, shaped by historical and geographical factors. For instance, it is no surprise that Mexico does so much trade with the United States, given the fact that it shares a 3000-kilometer border with its northern neighbor. NAFTA fostered even closer ties, but basically built on a connection that already existed. Brazil, which makes up half of South America's territory, is a melting pot of different cultures, with more of a connection with the rest of Latin America than the United States. It is perhaps not surprising, therefore, to find that while Natura Cosméticos has focused on Brazil and other South American markets it has not built a strong presence in the United States – home of its greatest rival, Avon. While around three-quarters of Mexico's exports go the United States, only one-fifth of Brazil's go in the same direction.

A NEW JAGUAR

The leaders of the Global Latinas have acquired some unique capabilities of resilience, drive, focus and flexibility. They have also been more than willing to import best practices in management from developed nations and to invest in their people. Cemex CEO Lorenzo Zambrano, for example, gained an MBA from Stanford and Cemex encourages its managers to be open to similar training in the best business schools and to experience other cultures. Zambrano's obsessive focus on the best use of technology demonstrates very well his adherence to the best international standards of management. And of course, the Cemex Way of the careful integration of acquisitions has become a shining example of good management for companies all over the world. Other Latinas, from Vale to Tenaris to Pollo Campero, have their own corporate universities or training centers, displaying their commitment to operational and management excellence.

A personal mission has driven figures such as Carlos Slim and Lorenzo Zambrano to international expansion. In the food business, Pollo Campero's Gutiérrez family and Astrid & Gastón's CEO Gastón Acurio want to promote their national cuisine across the world. Opening outlets in Madrid represented a great moment for both of them, a return to their ancestral home. These leaders of the Global Latinas have now become role models for the young and are spawning a whole new generation of young entrepreneurs and leaders across Latin America.

Many of the firms that have emerged have also been controlled at the top by the founder or their descendants. Pollo Campero, Grupo Modelo, América Móvil, Tenaris and Cemex, for instance, all benefited from the advantages that this can bring: long-term vision, strong leadership and the ability to make fast and flexible decisions. At Tenaris, the founder's grandson Paolo Rocca engineered a major organizational transformation that turned the company into the global giant it is today. And at América Móvil, Slim's detailed, flexible and fast responses to the opportunities that unfolded during times of economic tumult enabled the company to purchase some key assets at bargain prices. Like other family businesses around the world, many Global Latinas have felt the continuing influence of the founding families, even after listing on various stock exchanges.

Global Latinas have also responded to challenges in an extraordinarily innovative manner; particularly in the way they have shaped their business models. Not previously known for such innovation, Global Latinas have perhaps attempted to reverse stereotypes about Latin American firms and the region. Grupo Bimbo developed a unique logistics model while Cemex developed its world-class approach to pre-and-post-merger management of new acquisitions. Tenaris leveraged its multicultural character to create highly effective global teams. Others have exploited the unique strengths and traditions of their home markets for global success. Natura Cosméticos has created its cosmetics from ingredients taken from the Amazon while Gastón Acurio continues to scour local markets in Peru for the latest flavors and ingredients.

WINNING IN GLOBALIZATION 3.0

If Globalization 1.0 was the Old World discovering the New, Globalization 2.0 meant multinationals from the North, the developed world, going global in the North and in the South. Those two phases were largely in the hands of European and US firms. Now we are in the era of Globalization 3.0, which is taking place in a connected world with virtual and real global access in real time to knowledge; Globalization 3.0 will be in the hands of companies from the South moving North and into neighboring southern countries – unbounded opportunity for Asia and Latin America.

If the performance of Global Latinas over the last decades has proven they have the skills to survive and thrive on a global stage, the parallel rise of Asia has shown that the field is not Latin America's alone. China, Japan and many other countries of Asia – witness Vietnam's supplanting of Colombia in coffee production – are seen by many as a significant challenge to Global Latinas. If the pessimists are right, Asia spells trouble for Latin America. Optimists see Asia as both competition and opportunity.

Despite recent decreases in prices, Latin American businesses are likely to benefit from high commodity prices and large inflows of FDI. Unusually, the region looks set to enjoy favorable times, while the United States is entering a sluggish economic period caused by the credit crunch and the housing slowdown. This provides a good stimulus for local firms to rediscover their natural markets in Latin America. Resource-based giants such as Petrobras and Vale are likely to continue to build on a global scale, while consumer firms such as América Móvil, Bimbo and Natura will face different challenges. To maintain their international position, some Latinas will need to integrate, manage and expand their global operations, subject to economic and political ups and downs. Others will need to secure further acquisitions or alliances to survive, lest they become takeover targets.

Future business growth would be greatly enhanced if the region agrees on a new trade agreement for Latin America that provides a stable legal framework as well as a structural forum to resolve disputes and promote economic integration. There have been regional meetings like the Ibero-American Summit, the biennial Latin America, Caribbean and European Union Summit (LAC-EU). And there are multilateral trade agreements such as NAFTA, Mercosur and UNASUR, bilateral trade agreements and established regional funding agencies. But the region still lacks a solid, all-embracing institution or agreement to foster increased levels of trade. If conditions of economic stability and growth continue, the relatively small markets in the region will nonetheless become richer ones, with plenty of new potential for local businesses to exploit. A common currency should follow.

Companies and nations will need to reconcile economic performance with social inclusion to solve what has been called the 'social debt' of Latin America. This is perhaps a historic opportunity, for business leaders and politicians alike, to foster closer economic cooperation in the region. As employers, tax-payers and generators of wealth, corporations have a major role to play. In this climate, international financing agencies such as the World Bank's International Finance Corporation (IFC) and the Inter American Development Bank might consider financing more businesses, as they have done in the past with Bimbo, Embraer and Vale. Such investments may promote desired social and economic goals and they are equally important in providing money for state-managed infrastructure projects.

As the region is approaching the bicentennial celebrations of independence – starting with Bolivia in 2009 and finishing with Brazil in 2022 – Latin America wants to move away from an era of mutual suspicion between countries and blaming others for their own crisis. The region is searching for a sustainable second wind of prosperity to integrate all its citizens to the developed world. Latin Americans definitely want to be on that prosperous path.

The Global Latina model is beginning to be recognized both in Latin America and on the wider world stage. Coming up behind the Global Latinas of today is a plethora of emerging multinationals from Latin America. They are from all parts of the continent and in all sectors of business. They have a tough act to follow. The game is on.

This book celebrates the success of the Global Latinas and their leaders who are role models for others to follow and, at the same time, need to find a compromise with governments and civil societies to collectively achieve sustainable and equitable economic growth. Globalization 3.0 beckons.

APPENDIX: GLOBAL LATINAS, FINANCIAL DATA AND SELECTED RANKINGS

TABLE A.1 **Globalization Index of Latin American Companies,** *América Economía* **2008**

Rank	Company	Home country	Globalization Index	Sales US$ million	% Sales outside home country	% Investments outside home country	Employees outside home country
1	Cemex	Mexico	77.3	21,673	82.3	70.8	29,200
2	Techint	Argentina	75.8	39,770	62.5	63.0	33,400
3	Odebrecht	Brazil	71.0	4,950	76.7	15.0	26,900
4	Vale	Brazil	60.6	33,115	84.0	46.0	12,000
5	Sud Americana de Vapores	Chile	59.6	4,131	90.0	58.2	5,800
6	Tenaris	Argentina	55.7	9,496	81.0	88.2	16,900
7	Grupo Alfa	Mexico	53.2	9,750	53.1	69.9	19,300
8	Embraer	Brazil	48.0	4,896	96.4	45.0	3,100
9	Gerdau	Brazil	47.3	17,283	54.0	39.0	14,500
10	Grupo Bimbo	Mexico	46.8	6,758	31.2	59.8	42,800
11	PDVSA	Venezuela	44.4	110,000	97.8	N/A	5,600
12	Brightstar[1]	United States	44.1	4,300	13.0	N/A	2,800
13	Cencosud	Chile	40.8	7,623	37.0	63.0	48,200
14	Grupo Maseca	Mexico	40.6	3,347	65.6	15.0	1,400
15	Petrobras	Brazil	39.2	87,476	21.0	12.0	6,800
16	Femsa	Mexico	39.0	16,453	16.7	44.4	24,300
17	Lan	Chile	38.3	3,525	85.0	72.5	6,200
18	Sadia	Brazil	37.9	4,874	46.1	2.1	900
19	Grupo JBS-Friboi	Brazil	36.7	2,012	45.8	10.0	5,000
20	Arcor	Argentina	36.0	1,850	16.8	26.0	5,400
21	Andrade Gutierrez	Brazil	35.7	5,096	7.0	4.0	5,400
22	WEG	Brazil	35.5	2,117	31.3	24.0	1,780
23	Camargo Corrêa	Brazil	35.1	7,175	19.0	28.0	2,500
24	América Móvil	Mexico	32.5	28,924	50.3	31.8	N/A
25	Impsa	Argentina	31.7	600	65.0	N/A	3,000
26	Laboratorios Bagó	Argentina	31.8	409	10.0	60.0	600

Continued on next page

TABLE A.1 (Continued)

Rank	Company	Home country	Globalization Index	Sales US$ million	% Sales outside home country	% Investments outside home country	Employees outside home country
27	Perdigão	Brazil	30.7	3,745	41.1	N/A	N/A
28	CMPC	Chile	30.4	2,976	70.0	5.7	8,900
29	Grupo Nacional de Chocolates	Colombia	30.2	1,660	25.2	25.9	7,500
30	Pollo Campero	Guatemala	29.4	N/A	N/A	12.8	N/A
31	Grupo Vatorantim	Brazil	29.2	13,589	15.5	5.0	2,000
32	Grupo Vitro	Mexico	29.1	2,560	57.9	N/A	4,000
33	Natura Cosméticos	Brazil	28.6	1,735	4.0	22.0	500
34	Madeco	Chile	22.2	1,278	49.0	54.4	400
35	Tam	Brazil	28.0	4,248	10.0	N/A	1,700
36	Falabella	Chile	27.8	5,560	29.0	26.7	21,700
37	Telmex	Mexico	27.4	12,142	51.9	52.0	N/A
38	Grupo Elektra	Mexico	27.1	3,647	54.9	12.0	5,400
39	Viña Concha y Toro	Chile	26.6	536	68.7	6.9	242
40	Aje Group	Peru	26.5	300	10.0	N/A	N/A
41	Pl Mabe	Mexico	26.4	400	47.5	48.6	800
42	Grupo Modelo	Mexico	25.6	17,291	36.7	N/A	N/A
43	Sabó	Brazil	25.3	347	43.0	16.0	1,300
44	Gol	Brazil	25.2	2,804	5.0	N/A	400
45	Grupo Gloria	Peru	25.0	537	33.3	N/A	N/A
46	Banco Itaú	Brazil	24.4	31,185	12.7	22.8	N/A
47	Sonda	Chile	24.3	540	42.4	74.6	N/A
48	Mexichem	Mexico	24.0	2,117	500.0	31.2	N/A
49	Braskem	Brazil	24.7	9,981	20.1	5.6	N/A
50	Marcopolo	Brazil	23.8	2,129	42.2	30.0	2,700

Source: Lourdes Casanova, Henning Hoeber and Samantha Rullán based on *América Economía*, 1 April 2008.
Note: N/A – Figure not available.
[1] Brightstar is a Bolivian company which recently moved its headquarters to the US.

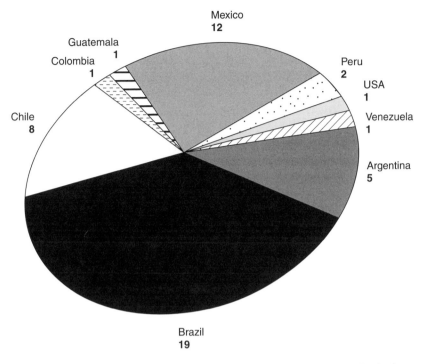

Figure A.1 **Country Distribution of the top 50 Latin American companies in the Globalization Index of** *América Economía* **2008.**
(Source: Lourdes Casanova, Henning Hoeber and Samantha Rullán based on *América Economía* Multilatinas Ranking, 1 April 2008.)

TABLE A.2 Latin America, Internationalization Phases

Phase 1 Emerging Foreign Direct Investment (1970–1982)		Phase 2 'The Lost Decade' (1982–1990)	
Selected Company milestones	Market characteristics	Selected Company milestones	Market characteristics
• Exports to AirLittoral, France (Embraer, 1977) • US subsidiary, Embraer Aircraft Corporation (Embraer, 1979)	• State protection facilitating the emergence of large-scale, family-owned conglomerates • Family-owned local companies expanding in domestic markets • Structural obstacles to international expansion • Latin American companies start international expansion	• Consortium acquisition of California Steel Industries, US (Vale, 1984) • Joint venture with Southdown, US (Cemex, 1986) • Acquisition of Mrs Baird's, US (Bimbo, 1988) • Acquisition of Sunbelt (Joint Venture, Southdown and Cemex, 1989)	• Mexico defaults on debt payments in August 1982 • Beginning privatization, deregulation • Internationalization slows down
• Acquisition of Valencia and Sanson, Spain (Cemex, 1992) • Acquisition of Southdown, US (Cemex, 2000)	• Liberalization of Latin American economies, privatization of telecom, utilities, gas and steel, deregulation and the adoption of pro-market strategies • Upswing of inward foreign direct investment	• Acquisition of George Weston, US (Bimbo, 2002) • Joint venture with Avic II (Assembly line), China (Embraer, 2002) • Acquisition of Pérez Companc (Pecom), Argentina (Petrobras, 2002)	• Growing role of Global Latinas in region's merger and acquisition (M&A) activities • Commodity boom strengthens resource firms • Shift in investment patterns toward China • Rising levels of outward FDI • Higher growth rates

Phase 3 The Washington Consensus (1990–2002)		Phase 4 Going Global (2002–Present)	
Selected Company milestones	Market characteristics	Selected Company milestones	Market characteristics
	• Halving of the number of state-owned firms • Purchase of local banks, oil companies and telecom players by MNCs (mainly Spanish) • Ratified the NAFTA between the United States, Canada and Mexico (1994) • Stock market collapse triggered by the 1997–1998 Asian and Russian crises • Multinational companies (MNC) start leaving Latin America, after 2000 • Latin American firms consolidated their positions in local and regional markets at the end of the decade	• Acquisition of Ogma, Portugal (Embraer, 2004) • Acquisition of RMC Group, UK (Cemex, 2005) • Acquisition of Verizon Dominicana (Dominican Republic), US subsidiary (América Móvil, 2006) • Acquisition of Panrico (China), Spain (Bimbo, 2006) • Acquisition of Inco, Canada (Vale, 2006) • Acquisition of Rinker, Australia (Cemex, 2007)	• Bold takeovers, conquering of markets in the US and Europe • Diversification of export basket, away from commodities

Source: Lourdes Casanova, Henning Hoeber and Samantha Rullán based on ECLAC (Economic Commission for Latin America and the Caribbean's) *ECLAC 2007 Statistical Yearbook for Latin America and the Caribbean* and own research.

TABLE A.3 External and Internal Internationalization Drivers, Strategic Approach and Uniqueness of Selected Global Latinas

	External drivers *(macro level)*	Internal drivers *(company level)*	Strategic approach	Uniqueness
AMÉRICA MÓVIL *(Telecommunications, Mexico)*	• Saturated domestic market • Economic crises in the region • Mobile growth	• Economies of scale • Market-seeking • Risk reduction • Asset seeking and exploitation	• Acquisition of controlling stakes in target companies • High coverage in and focus on natural markets • Leverage of market know-how in emerging markets • Bypassing customer default risks to expand customer base	• Pioneering with prepaid cards • Unique adjustment of serving a low-income customer base • Client outreach (people in yellow selling phone cards in strategic points) • Marketing • Leadership
ASTRID Y GASTÓN *(Restaurants, Peru)*	• Rising demand for innovative restaurant concepts • Shift to more exotic tastes	• CEO with a mission to position Peruvian cuisine among the best in the world • Market-seeking	• Greenfield operations in the high end market • Franchise model for the mass-market • Establishment of flagships in the high-end markets of foreign countries • Natural market	• Local resources from Peru • Innovative combinations of different Peruvian cooking styles • Country-rooted branding and marketing of *Novo Andino* cuisine concepts • Visionary leadership

Company				
BIMBO (*Consumer Goods, Mexico*)	• Highly-fragmented industry structure in consumer goods sector • Offset economic risks and political volatility in its domestic market • Trade agreements (NAFTA)	• Expertise in complex local logistics • New markets needed for its branded products • Market-seeking	• Natural market • Acquisitions and joint ventures • Marketing know-how in emerging markets	• Pioneering packaging and 'just-in-time' delivery • Foco Bimbo (intranet)
CEMEX (*Building Materials, Mexico*)	• Saturated home market • US market tariffs forced expansion south of border • Global cement industry consolidation trend • Trade agreements • Building booms	• Growth as defense against possible takeover • Expanded markets enable economies of scale in a commodity industry • International exposure in order to lower cost of capital	• Focus on emerging markets with higher profit margins • Pre-entry cement trading • Fast acquisitions and integration of major local players with turnaround potential • Natural market	• Integrated exposure to all elements of the value chain • Business model innovation as global building materials solution provider • Easy adjustment to serve both low-income customers (branding) and industrialized markets • Visionary leadership
CONCHA Y TORO (*Wines, Chile*)	• Demand shift from Old World to New World wines	• Export diversification • Increase export revenues • Low per capita consumption in domestic market • Market-seeking	• Implementation of an ambitious investment plan • Development of a wine portfolio • Joint ventures • Marketing	• Innovative branding • Product innovation • Geographical location

TABLE A.3 (Continued)

	External drivers (macro level)	Internal drivers (company level)	Strategic approach	Uniqueness
EMBRAER (Aviation, Brazil)	• Benefiting from state sponsorship • Geographical location	• Achievement of economies of scale • Offsetting development costs • Risk reduction • Asset- and knowledge-seeking • Competitive advantage	• Direct sales contracts • Risk sharing: manufacturing partnerships and alliances • Leveraging operational expertise	• Niche player in the production of low-cost medium body business jets • 'National champion' • Lowest labor cost in the world to develop prototypes
NATURA (Body Care, Brazil)	• High per-capita spending on cosmetics • Growing demand for natural/green products	• Risk reduction • Market-seeking • Learn about global market dynamics • Looking for knowledge and competitive advantages	• Natural market • Hybrid model that mixed retail outlets and direct sales • Value-based 'well-being' • Eco-friendly Brazilian roots	• Eco-friendly products • Country-rooted branding
PETROBRAS (Oil & Gas, Brazil)	• Market liberalization: competition at home and privatization • Expansion necessary to replace depleted resources • High commodity prices (Chinese demand)	• Learn to compete • Strengthen its downstream position in Latin America • Risk reduction	• Opportunistic asset purchases from Western companies in retreat from Latin America • Greenfield operations in worldwide exploration	• Experts in deep-water drilling • 'National champion' • Semi-public status and successful privatization • Excellence in ethanol technology

	Drivers	Motives	Strategies	Sources of competitive advantage
(continued)	• Ethanol boom • Economic crisis in the region		• Joint ventures • Bidding for drilling rights • Acquisitions	• Own delivery global model • Iris-recognition technology • 'Near-shoring' • Banking technology
POLITEC *(Technology, Brazil)*	• Brazilian industrial policy • Creation of Brasscom	• Drive revenue growth • Market, technology and knowledge-seeking • Risk reduction • Gain competitive advantage	• Alliances • Tailor its product and service portfolio • Acquisitions • Global diversity within a client-driven mindset • Opening branches in countries with cheaper costs	
POLLO CAMPERO *(Restaurants, Guatemala)*	• Small home market in Guatemala • Large number of Latin immigrants opened new markets	• Respond to foreign competition in domestic market • Market-seeking • Risk reduction • Value chain integration and parenting advantage • Looking for competitive advantage	• Franchise system • Alliances with established market participants and experience investor groups • Natural markets • Differentiation strategy	• Superior flavoring adapted to a specific customer base • Country-rooted branding • Franchise model • Tropicalization • Leadership/entrepreneurship • Family business

TABLE A.3 (Continued)

	External drivers (*macro level*)	Internal drivers (*company level*)	Strategic approach	Uniqueness
VALE (*Metals & Mining, Brazil*)	• Market liberalization • Anti-trust concerns in iron ore position • Soaring demand for iron ore (Chinese demand) • High commodity prices	• Diversify revenue base • Risk reduction • Scale advantages • Expansion in its alumina refining business	• Geographic roll-up to keep foreign competition out of Brazil • Securing markets abroad • Securing resources through M&A, greenfield and brownfield investments • Securing customers through joint ventures and co-investments	• Integrated business model as one stop shop for the global steel industry • High quality reserves with lower production cost • Customized pelletizing operations • 'National champion'

Source: Lourdes Casanova, Henning Hoeber and Samantha Rullán.

TABLE A.4 Selected Global Latinas: International Presence and Financial Data (December 2007)

	Global Latinas: Presence in regions (number of countries/region) / Financial data										
	América Móvil	Astrid & Gastón	Bimbo	Cemex	Concha y Toro	Vale	Embraer	Natura	Petrobras	Politec	Pollo Campero
Latin America	14	6	14	9	12	4	–	4	11	–	7
Europe	–	1	1	14	5	5	1	1	2	4	1
Asia	–	–	1	6	4	9	2	–	5	3	2
North America (US & Canada)	1	1	1	1	2	2	1	–	1	1	1
Africa	–	–	–	1	3	5	–	–	6	–	–
Australia	–	–	–	1	–	2	1	–	–	–	–
Revenues (US$ mm)	28,544.2	30	6,622.9	21,681.5	400	36,562.7	5,636.2	1,732.1	96,300	270	450
Net profit (US$ mm)	5,367	N/A	349.2	2,391.8	400	11,294.3	370.9	260.7	12,144.6	N/A	N/A
Total employees	45,646	N/A	81,000	67,000	2,035	60,405	20,180	5,900	68,931	6,500	7,000
Employees outside home country	N/A	N/A	42,800	29,200	N/A	12,000	3,100	500	6,800	N/A	N/A
Countries active in	15	7	17	32	26	27	5	5	25	8	11
International sales/exports as % of total	50%	65%	32%	82%	95%	84%	96.4%	4%	5%	5%	N/A
Listed stock exchanges	AMX NYSE (2000) Nasdaq Latibex	Not listed	AMX (1980)	AMX (1976) NYSE (1999)	NYSE (1994)	Bovespa (1943) NYSE (2000) Latibex (2000)	Bovespa NYSE (2000)	Bovespa (2004)	Bovespa NYSE BCBA Latibex Dow Jones Sustainability Indexes	Not listed	Not listed

Source: Lourdes Casanova, Henning Hoeber and Samantha Rullán based on 2008 *América Economía* data, company reports and personal interviews with companies.
Note: N/A – figure not available.

175

TABLE A.5 **Latin American Companies in** *Fortune Global 500* **(1987 versus 2008)**

Latin American companies in the *Fortune Global 500*

1987			2008		
Rank	Company	Country	Rank	Company	Country
26	Petrobras	Brazil			
40	Pemex	Mexico	42	Pemex	Mexico
49	Petróleos de Venezuela	Venezuela			
			63	Petrobras	Brazil
138	Yacimientos Petrolíferos	Argentina			
			204	Bradesco	Brazil
			235	Vale (formerly CVRD)	Brazil
			273	Itaúsa-Investimentos	Brazil
			282	Banco do Brasil	Brazil
			283	América Móvil	Mexico
335	CVRD (now Vale)	Brazil			
340	Codelco	Chile			
362	Empresa Colombiana de Petróleo	Colombia			
			389	Cemex	Mexico
405	Sidor	Venezuela			
408	Ford Brasil	Brazil	408	Comisión Federal de Electricidad	Mexico
409	Industrias Votorantim	Brazil			
436	General Motors do Brasil	Brazil			
456	Grupo Alfa	Mexico			
			464	Carso Global Telecom	Mexico
485	Chrysler de Mexico	Mexico			
500	Siderúrgica Nacional	Brazil			

Source: Lourdes Casanova, Henning Hoeber and Samantha Rullán based on data from *Fortune Global 500* of 1987 and 2008.

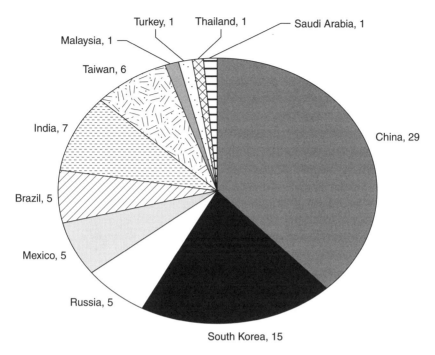

Figure A.2 **Breakdown by country of the 78 Multinationals from Emerging Countries in** *Fortune Global 500* **(2008).**
(Source: Lourdes Casanova and Henning Hoeber based on data from *Fortune Global 500* 2008.)

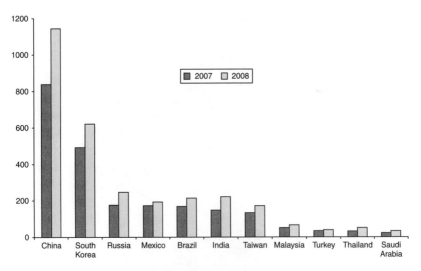

Figure A.3 **Multinationals from Emerging Countries in** *Fortune Global 500* **in 2007 and 2008 (based on revenues in US$ million).**
(Source: Lourdes Casanova and Henning Hoeber based on data from *Fortune Global 500* 2008.)

ACKNOWLEDGMENT

The support of Xavier Cózar from Universidad Veracruzana in Mexico in the preparation of the charts and tables of this appendix is gratefully acknowledged.

NOTES

INTRODUCTION

1 Wilson, D. and Purushothaman, R. (2003), *Global Economics Paper No. 99: Dreaming with BRICs: The Path to 2050*. New York: Goldman Sachs.

2 Wolf, M. (2007), 'Globalisation's Future is the Big Long-term Question', *Financial Times*, 9 January.

3 Wheatley, J. and Lapper, R. (2008), 'Surfing a Big Wave of Confidence', *Financial Times*, 8 July.

4 Zeng, M. and Williamson, P.J. (2007), *Dragons at Your Door: How Chinese Cost Innovation is Disrupting the Rules of Global Competition*. Boston, Mass: Harvard Business School Press.

5 Prahalad, C.K. (2004), *The Fortune at the Bottom of the Pyramid: Eradicating Poverty Through Profits*. Upper Saddle River, NJ: Wharton School Publishing.

6 *Fortune* (2008) 'Fortune Global 500'. See Appendix for more data.

7 Aguiar, M., Bhattacharya, A., de Vitton, L. et al. (2007), *The 2008 BCG 100 New Global Challengers – How Top Companies Are Changing the World*. The Boston Consulting Group, December.

8 Accenture (2008), *Multi-Polar World 2: The Rise of the Emerging-market Multinational*. Accenture.

9 Aldunate, F. and Díaz, R. (2007), 'Bigger than Ever', *América Economía*, September.

10 Economic Commission for Latin America and the Caribbean (ECLAC) (May 2007), *Foreign Direct Investment in Latin America and the Caribbean, 2006*. Santiago, Chile: United Nations, p. 15.

11 Case Study: Cemex, in Casanova, L. and Fraser, M., et al. (2009), 'From Multi-latinas to Global Latinas – The Latin American Multinationals (Compilation Case Studies)' Inter-American Development Bank Working Paper. January 2009. Washington DC: IDB.

12 *The Economist* (1997), 'Inside Story: Family Firms Still Rule', 4 December.

13 Sinha, J. (2005), 'Global Champions from Emerging Markets', *McKinsey Quarterly*, No. 2, May, 27–35.

179

14 ECLAC defines 'Trans-Latins' as 'emerging Latin American transnationals that have made direct investments outside their home countries, including those which have not gone outside Latin America'. Economic Commission for Latin America and the Caribbean (ECLAC) (2006), *Foreign Direct Investment in Latin America and the Caribbean, 2005*, Santiago, Chile: United Nations.

15 Economic Commission for Latin America and the Caribbean (ECLAC) (May 2007), *Foreign Direct Investment in Latin America and the Caribbean, 2006*. Santiago, Chile: United Nations, ch. III.

16 Casanova, L. (2002), 'Lazos de Familia: Las Inversiones Españolas en Iberoamérica', *Foreign Affairs* (Spanish version), Vol. 2, No. 2, May; and Casanova, L. (2004), 'East Asian, European, and North American Multinational Firm Strategies in Latin America', *Business and Politics*, Vol. 6, No. 1, Article 6.

17 The term 'Washington Consensus' was coined in 1989 by J. Williamson of the Institute of International Economics, an advisor to the IMF. It entailed broad policy objectives such as fiscal discipline, competitive exchange rates, trade liberalization, privatization of state-owned assets, deregulation and secure property rights.

18 Martinez, A., De Souza, I. and Liu, F. (2003), 'Multinationals vs Multilatinas: Latin America's Great Race', *Strategy + Business*, 11 September.

19 Ocampo, J.A. (ECLAC's Executive Secretary) (2002), *ECLAC Notes*, no. 24, September.

20 United Nations Conference on Trade and Development (UNCTAD) (2006), *World Investment Report 2006 – FDI from Developing and Transition Economies: Implications for Development*. (United Nations Publication No. E.06.II.D.11.) New York and Geneva: United Nations, p. 73.

21 Economic Commission for Latin America and the Caribbean (ECLAC) (2007), *Foreign Direct Investment in Latin America and the Caribbean, 2006*. Santiago, Chile: United Nations, p. 13.

22 Gerchunoff, P. (2007), 'Latin America's Era of Milk and Honey', *Latin Business Chronicle*, August. For a detailed economic study of economic growth in Latin America, see ECLAC (2007), 'Economic Growth in Latin America and the Caribbean: Multiple Growth Transitions in the Absence of Steady States', *Economic Survey of Latin America and the Caribbean 2006–2007*, United Nations, July.

23 Economic Commission for Latin America and the Caribbean (ECLAC) (2007), *Foreign Direct Investment in Latin America and the Caribbean, 2006*. Santiago, Chile: United Nations. ECLAC reported that the average growth in emerging countries was 6.5 percent.

24 *The Economist* (2007), 'Latin America's Middle Class: Adiós to Poverty, Hola to Consumption', 16 August.

25 Kroll, L. (ed.) (2008), 'The World's Billionaires', *Forbes*, 3 May, available at: http://www.forbes.com; *Business Week* (2007), 'Carlos Slim's Fat Fortune', 4 July; *International Herald Tribune* (2007), 'Mexico's Carlos Slim now World's Richest Person', 3 July; *Fortune* (2007), 'Carlos Slim, the Richest Man in the World', 20 August; and *Forbes* (2007), 'The World's Billionaires', 3 August.

26 United Nations Conference on Trade and Development (UNCTAD) (2007), *World Investment Report 2007 – Transnational Corporations, Extractive Industries and Development.* New York and Geneva: United Nations.

27 For more on 'South–South' flows, see United Nations Conference on Trade and Development (UNCTAD) (2006), *World Investment Report 2006 – FDI from Developing and Transition Economies: Implications for Development.* (United Nations Publication No. E.06.II.D.11.) New York and Geneva: United Nations; see also Aykut, D. and Goldstein, A. (2006), OECD Working Paper no. 257: 'Developing Country Multinationals: South-South Investment Comes of Age', OECD Development Centre, December.

28 Economic Commission for Latin America and the Caribbean (ECLAC) (2007), *Foreign Direct Investment in Latin America and the Caribbean, 2006.* Santiago, Chile: United Nations.

29 World Economic Forum (2006), 'Assessing Latin American Competitiveness: Challenges and Opportunities', *The Latin American Competitiveness Review 2006.* Davos: World Economic Forum.

30 *Latin Trade* (2007), 'Top 500 Companies in Latin America', July.

31 This is one less than the previous year, because Venezuelan nationalized oil company PVDSA, the largest corporation in Latin America with more than US$100 billion in revenues, did not submit data on time. If it had done so, PVDSA would have ranked 31st in the 'Fortune Global 500' (2007).

32 *Fortune Magazine* (1987 and 2007), 'Fortune Global 500'.

33 Sinha, J. (2005), 'Global Champions from Emerging Markets', *McKinsey Quarterly*, No. 2, May, 27–35.

34 Interview with author, August 2007; see also Haberer, P. and Kohan, A.F. (2007), 'Building Global Champions in Latin America', *McKinsey Quarterly*, in special edition, March: Shaping a New Agenda for Latin America.

35 Khanna, T. and Palepu, K. (2006), 'Emerging Giants: Building World-class Companies from Emerging Countries', *Harvard Business Review*, Vol. 84, October, 60–69.

36 Dawar, N. and Frost, T. (1999), 'Competing with Giants: Survival Strategies for Local Companies in Emerging Markets', *Harvard Business Review*, Vol. 77, No. 2 (March–April), 119–129, 187.

37 Goldstein, A. (2007), *Multinational Companies from Emerging Economies: Composition, Conceptualization and Direction in the Global Economy.* New York, NY: Palgrave, ch. 5.

38 World Economic Forum (2006), 'Assessing Latin American Competitiveness: Challenges and Opportunities', *The Latin American Competitiveness Review 2006*. Davos: World Economic Forum, p. 21.

39 Dunning, J.H. (1993), *Multinational Enterprises and the Global Economy*. Reading, Mass: Addison-Wesley.

40 Economic Commission for Latin America and the Caribbean (ECLAC) (2006), *Foreign Direct Investment in Latin America and the Caribbean, 2005*. Santiago, Chile: United Nations, ch. IV.

41 On *maquilas*, see Casanova, L. (2005), 'Latin America: Economic and Business Context', *International Journal of Human Resource Management*, Vol. 16, No. 12, December, 2173–2188.

42 United Nations Conference on Trade and Development (UNCTAD) (2006), *World Investment Report 2006 – FDI from Developing and Transition Economies: Implications for Development*. (United Nations Publication No. E.06.II.D.11.) New York and Geneva: United Nations, p. 173.

43 Casanova, L. and Fraser, M., et al. (2009), 'From Multi-latinas to Global Latinas – The Latin American Multinationals (Compilation Case Studies)' Inter-American Development Bank Working Paper. January 2009. Washington, DC: IDB.

44 Investment grade is given by rating agencies such as Moody's or Standard and Poor's to countries that are likely enough to meet payment obligations.

45 As the book is going to press in December 2008, this context of high liquidity is declining.

46 Deutsche Bank Research (2007), *The Emergence of Latin Multinationals*, March, 14.

47 Haberer, P. and Kohan, A.F. (2007), 'Building Global Champions in Latin America', *McKinsey Quarterly*, in special edition, March, Shaping a New Agenda for Latin America, p. 44.

48 On 'natural markets', see Casanova, L. (2002), 'Lazos de Familia: Las Inversiones Españolas en Iberoamérica', *Foreign Affairs* (Spanish version), Vol. 2, No. 2, May.

49 Hamel, G. (2006), 'The Why, What and How of Management Innovation', *Harvard Business Review*, February, 1.

CHAPTER 1 – THE LEADERS OF GLOBAL LATINAS: LONG-TERM PLANNERS AND FLEXIBLE VISIONARIES

1 Thomson, A. (2007), 'Transcript: Interview with Carlos Slim', *Financial Times*, 27 September.

2 Kroll, L. (ed.) (2008), 'The World's Billionaires', *Forbes*, 3 May. Available at: http://www.forbes.com.

3   Thomson, A. (2007), 'Transcript: Interview with Carlos Slim', *Financial Times*, 27 September.

4   Mehta, S.N. (2007), 'Carlos Slim, the Richest Man in the World', *Fortune*, 20 August, p. 2. Available at: http://money.cnn.com/2007/08/03/news/international/carlosslim.fortune/

5   Slim, C., 'Carlos Slim Helú: Biography', p. 2. Available at: http://www.carlosslim.com.

6   See www.carlosslim.com.

7   Thomson, A. (2007), 'About to Hang Up?', *Financial Times*, 25 September.

8   Mehta, S.N. (2007), 'Carlos Slim, the Richest Man in the World', *Fortune*, 20 August. Available at: http://money.cnn.com/2007/08/03/news/international/carlosslim.fortune/

9   Ibid.

10 *The Economist* (2005), 'The Master Builder', 13 October.

11 Van Agtmael, A. (2007), *The Emerging Markets Century*. New York: Free Press, p. 158.

12 Ibid., p. 156.

13 Ibid., p. 158.

14 *The Economist* (2005), 'The Master Builder', 13 October.

15 Wheatley, J. (2007), 'Consensus Builder with Discipline', *Financial Times*, 10 January.

16 Wheatley, J. and Mahtani, D. (2008), 'Investors Uneasy Over Vale Strategy', *Financial Times*, 21 January.

17 Van Agtmael, A. (2007), *The Emerging Markets Century*. New York: Free Press, p. 195.

18 Ibid.

19 Ibid., p. 196.

20 *The Guardian* (2008), 'Meet the New Breed', 14 March.

21 Schneyer, J. (2008), 'Brazil's Iron Giant Reaches for the Top', *Business Week*, 21 February.

22 Van Agtmael, A. (2007), *The Emerging Markets Century*. New York: Free Press, p. 177.

23 Ibid., p. 181.

24 Ibid., p. 178.

25 Ibid., p. 179.

26 Ibid., p. 181.

27 *The Guardian* (2008), 'Meet the New Breed', 14 March.

28 Crooks, E. (2007), 'Ten Top Powers to be Reckoned With', *Financial Times*, 9 November.

29 *The Guardian* (2008), 'Meet the New Breed', 14 March.

30 The speech is available at: http://www.up.edu.pe/agenda//noticiasdatos.php?fecha=2006&mes=04&id=1138&area=2800. An English translation of the speech is available at: http://www.perufoodblogspot.com, posted on 16 May 2007.

31 Ibid.

32 Schexnayder, C.J. (2006), 'An Interview with Peruvian Chef Gastón Acurio', 7 November. Available at: http://www.livinginperu.com.

CHAPTER 2 – BRAZIL'S 'NATIONAL CHAMPIONS': BEYOND PRIVATIZATION

1 Casanova, L. and Fraser, M., et al. (2009), 'From Multi-latinas to Global Latinas – The Latin American Multinationals (Compilation Case Studies)' Inter-American Development Bank Working Paper. January 2009. Washington, DC: IDB.

2 On 23 June 2008, Embraer's market capitalization was US$5.5 billion; Vale's US$168.2 billion; and Petrobras' US$286.3 billion, according to finance.google.com.

3 Aldunate, F. (2008), 'Las Más Globales de América Latina', *América Economía*, Especial Multilatinas, 1 April.

4 Ibid.

5 *Fortune* (2008), 'Fortune Global 500', 30 July.

6 *América Economía* (2008), 'Las 500 Mayores Empresas de América Latina', July; and *Exame* (2007), 'A Embraer na encruzilhada', 23 May.

7 *Fortune* (2008), 'Fortune Global 500', 30 July.

8 *América Economía* (2008), 'Las 500 Mayores Empresas de América Latina', July.

9 Casanova, L. (2005), 'Latin America: Economic and Business Context', *International Journal of Human Resource Management, Management*, Vol. 16, No. 12, December, 2173–2188.

10 Ibid.

11 Ibid.

12 The contribution of Henning Hoeber, visiting researcher at INSEAD, to this section is gratefully acknowledged.

13 The process of pelletizing produces a higher grade of iron ore concentrated in a special manufacturing process in which small and fine particles are aggregated into larger and consistent iron ore fragments.

14 Vale case study in Casanova, L. and Fraser, M., et al. (2009), 'From Multi-latinas to Global Latinas – The Latin American Multinationals (Compilation Case Studies)' Inter-American Development Bank Working Paper. January 2009. Washington, DC: IDB.

15 Ibid.

16 Ibid.

17 Ibid., p. 10; see also Wheatley, J. (2007), 'CVRD Leads Brazil's Move Further Afield', *Financial Times*, 11 January.

18 Campbell, K. (2007), 'Brazilian Group to Build Coal Mine in Mozambique', *Mining Weekly*, 22 June.

19 Ibid.

20 Author's interview with Keith Martin, general manager, international public affairs, Vale and Andre Huber, communications analyst, Vale, Rio de Janeiro, 9 May 2008.

21 Kinch, D. (2006), 'With Eyes on No. 1, CVRD Plans US$15.3 Billion Bid for Inco', *American Metal Market*, 11 August; and *Canada NewsWire* (2006), 'CVRD Announces Proposed All-cash Offer to Acquire Inco', 11 August. Both retrieved October 2007 from Factiva database.

22 Vale case study in Casanova, L. and Fraser, M., et al. (2009), 'From Multi-latinas to Global Latinas – The Latin American Multinationals (Compilation Case Studies)' Inter-American Development Bank Working Paper. January 2009. Washington, DC: IDB; see also *Reuters News* (2007), 'Brazil's CVRD Buys Australia Coal Project', 23 July. Retrieved October 2007 from Factiva database.

23 Chaddad, F.R. (2003), *CVRD Mining by 2010: Redrawing Firm Boundaries for 3x Market Cap*, Accenture Case Study no. 303-003-1. São Paulo, Brazil: Accenture.

24 The contribution of Henning Hoeber, visiting researcher at INSEAD, to this section is gratefully acknowledged.

25 Hoyos, C. (2007), 'The New Seven Sisters: Oil and Gas Giants that Dwarf the West's Top Producers', *Financial Times*, 19 June. The *FT* identified the 'New Seven Sisters' as: Saudi Arabia's Saudi Aramco, Russia's JSC Gazprom, CNPC of China, Iran's NIOC, Venezuela's PDVSA, Petronas of Malaysia and Brazil's Petrobras.

26 Crooks, E. (2007), 'Ten Top Powers to be Reckoned With', *Financial Times*, 9 November.

27 BBC News Channel (2008), 'Oil Price "May Hit $200 a Barrel"', 7 May, http://www.bbc.co.uk.

28 Petrobras case study in Casanova, L. and Fraser, M., et al. (2009), 'From Multi-latinas to Global Latinas – The Latin American Multinationals (Compilation Case Studies)' Inter-American Development Bank Working Paper. January 2009. Washington, DC: IDB, p. 6.

29 J. Kerr, *Petrobras and the PT Government in Brazil*, Industry Report, Global Insight, 2003. Retrieved on October 2007 from Global Insight database; see also Petrobras case study in Casanova, L. and Fraser, M., et al. (2009), 'From Multi-latinas to Global Latinas – The Latin American Multinationals (Compilation Case Studies)' Inter-American Development Bank Working Paper. January 2009. Washington, DC: IDB.

30 Author's interview with Petrobras executives.

31 Global Markets Direct (2007), *Petroleo Brasileiro S.A. Company Profile*, Analyst Report no. GMDGE0880P.

32 Petrobras teleconference, 17 October 2002, on the 'Signing of the Definitive Stock Purchase Agreement to Acquire Controlling Interest in Pérez Companc S.A.' Retrieved in October, 2007 from www.petrobras.com.br.

33 Petrobras case study in Casanova, L. and Fraser, M., et al. (2009), 'From Multi-latinas to Global Latinas – The Latin American Multinationals (Compilation Case Studies)' Inter-American Development Bank Working Paper. January 2009. Washington, DC: IDB; see also Desai, M. and Reisen de Pinho, R. (2003), *Drilling South: Petrobras Evaluates Pecom*. Case Study no. 9-204-043. Boston, US: Harvard Business School Publishing.

34 Ibid.

35 Ibid.

36 Ibid.

37 Ibid.

38 *The Economist* (2006), 'Now it's the People's Gas', 6 June; see also Petrobras case study in Casanova, L. and Fraser, M., et al. (2009), 'From Multi-latinas to Global Latinas – The Latin American Multinationals (Compilation Case Studies)' Inter-American Development Bank Working Paper. January 2009. Washington, DC: IDB, p. 12.

39 Capital IQ, at www.capitaliq.com, accessed October 2007; see also Petrobras case study in Casanova, L. and Fraser, M., et al. (2009), 'From Multi-latinas to Global Latinas – The Latin American Multinationals (Compilation Case Studies)' Inter-American Development Bank Working Paper. January 2009. Washington, DC: IDB, p.12.

40 Ibid., pp. 12–13.

41 Ibid.

42 Busch, A. (2007), 'Petrobras: Tupi or not Tupi', *Handelsblatt*, 15 November. Retrieved February 2008 at: http://www.handelsblatt.com/News/Vorsorge-Anlage/Bulle-Baer/_pv/_p/203978/_t/ft/_b/1352297/default.aspx/petrobras-tupi-or-not-tupi.html.

43 Bloomberg News (2007), 'Petrobras' Tupi Oil Field May Hold 8 Billion Barrels (Update6)' November 8, available: http://www.bloomberg.com/apps/news?pid=20601086&refer=news&sid=arYFojM6udEl.

44 The contribution of Andrea Goldstein, Senior Economist, OECD, to this section is gratefully acknowledged.

45 Embraer case study in Casanova, L. and Fraser, M., et al. (2009), 'From Multi-latinas to Global Latinas – The Latin American Multinationals (Compilation Case Studies)' Inter-American Development Bank Working Paper. January 2009. Washington, DC: IDB.

46 Ibid.

47 Ibid.

48 Ibid.

49 Van Agtmael, A. (2007), *The Emerging Markets Century*. New York: Free Press, p. 178.

50 Cabin pressurization is the means by which air is pumped into the aircraft to increase air pressure and thereby provide sufficient oxygen for the passengers when the plane flies at high altitudes of 3000 meters and over.

51 Van Agtmael, A. (2007), *The Emerging Markets Century*. New York: Free Press, pp. 176–182.

52 Embraer (2003), 'Jet Blue Airway Orders 100 Embraer 190', company press release, 10 June. Available at: http://investor.jetblue.com.

53 Embraer case study in Casanova, L. and Fraser, M., et al. (2009), 'From Multi-latinas to Global Latinas – The Latin American Multinationals (Compilation Case Studies)' Inter-American Development Bank Working Paper. January 2009. Washington, DC: IDB.

54 Ibid.

55 Ibid.

56 Economic Commission for Latin America and the Caribbean (ECLAC) (2007), *Foreign Direct Investment in Latin America and the Caribbean, 2006*. Santiago, Chile: United Nations, p. 71.

57 Nuttall, W.J. and Manz, D.L. (2008), *A New Energy Security Paradigm for the Twenty-first Century*, EPRG Working Paper. Cambridge, Judge Business School. Cambridge, UK: University of Cambridge.

CHAPTER 3 – THE GLOBAL MEXICANS: BETTING ON THE US?

1 This chapter draws on Casanova, L. and Fraser, M., et al. (2009), 'From Multi-latinas to Global Latinas – The Latin American Multinationals (Compilation Case Studies)' Inter-American Development Bank Working Paper. January 2009. Washington, DC: IDB.

2 *América Economía* (2008), 'Las 500 Mayores Empresas de América Latina', July.

3 Kose, M.A., Meredith, G.M. and Towe, C.M. (2004), *How Has NAFTA Affected the Mexican Economy? Review and Evidence, IMF Working Paper*, IMF, April, p. 7.

4 Ibid., p. 10.

5 Ibid.

6 Ibid., p. 12.

7 Ibid., p. 16.

8 Ibid., p. 17.

9 Ibid., p. 25.

10 Ibid., p. 28.

11 Economic Commission for Latin America and the Caribbean (ECLAC) (2007), *Foreign Direct Investment in Latin America and the Caribbean, 2006.* Santiago, Chile: United Nations, p. 78; see also UNCTAD World Investment Report (2007), *Country Fact Sheet: Mexico.* Available at: http://www.unctad.org/wir.

12 US Census Bureau, *Foreign Trade Statistics.* Available at: http://www.census.gov.

13 Casanova, L. (2005), 'Latin America: Economic and Business Context', *International Journal of Human Resource Management*, Vol. 16, No. 12, December, 2173–2188.

14 See Cemex corporate website at: http://www.cemex.com. Viewed in July 2008.

15 *América Economía* (2008), 'Las 500 Mayores Empresas de América Latina', July. These financial numbers do not reflect Cemex's acquisition in 2007 of Australian-based Rinker Group; *Fortune* (2008), 'Fortune Global 500', 30 July.

16 Economic Commission for Latin America and the Caribbean (ECLAC) (2007), *Foreign Direct Investment in Latin America and the Caribbean, 2006.* Santiago, Chile: United Nations, p. 79.

17 Van Agtmael, A. (2007), *The Emerging Markets Century.* New York: Free Press, p. 155.

18 Cemex case study in Casanova, L. and Fraser, M., et al. (2009), 'From Multilatinas to Global Latinas – The Latin American Multinationals (Compilation Case Studies)' Inter-American Development Bank Working Paper. January 2009. Washington, DC: IDB.

19 Ibid.

20 Ibid.

21 Ibid.

22 Poole, C. (1990), 'Cement wars', *Forbes*, 1 October.

23 Van Agtmael, A. (2007), *The Emerging Markets Century*. New York: Free Press, p. 156.

24 Ibid., p. 155.

25 Cemex case study in Casanova, L. and Fraser, M., et al. (2009), 'From Multi-latinas to Global Latinas – The Latin American Multinationals (Compilation Case Studies)' Inter-American Development Bank Working Paper. January 2009. Washington, DC: IDB.

26 Ibid.

27 BBC News (2008), 'Venezuela Cement is Nationalised', 5 April. Available at: http://www.bbc.co.uk.

28 Cemex case study in Casanova, L. and Fraser, M., et al. (2009), 'From Multi-latinas to Global Latinas – The Latin American Multinationals (Compilation Case Studies)' Inter-American Development Bank Working Paper. January 2009. Washington, DC: IDB.

29 Ghemawat, P. (2005), 'Regional Strategies for Global Leadership', *Harvard Business Review*, Vol. 83, No. 12, 98–108.

30 Fink, H. and Mittman, G. (2003), *Cemex's Market Entry into Indonesia*, Unpublished MBA paper, INSEAD.

31 Cemex case study in Casanova, L. and Fraser, M., et al. (2009), 'From Multi-latinas to Global Latinas – The Latin American Multinationals (Compilation Case Studies)' Inter-American Development Bank Working Paper. January 2009. Washington, DC: IDB.

32 Ibid.

33 Deutsche Bank (2004), Analyst Report, *Global Cement Update – Mexican Wave*, 26 November.

34 Cemex case study in Casanova, L. and Fraser, M., et al. (2009), 'From Multi-latinas to Global Latinas – The Latin American Multinationals (Compilation Case Studies)' Inter-American Development Bank Working Paper. January 2009. Washington, DC: IDB.

35 Ibid.

36 Orascom Cement is part of the Orascom Group, a conglomerate with construction and telecoms companies, owned by the Sawiris family, one of Egypt's wealthiest families.

37 *América Economía* (2008), 'Las 500 Mayores Empresas de América Latina', July.

38 *Business Week* (2008), Investment Report, available at: http://investing.business week.com, viewed July 2008.

39 América Móvil case study in Casanova, L. and Fraser, M., et al. (2009), 'From Multi-latinas to Global Latinas – The Latin American Multinationals

(Compilation Case Studies)' Inter-American Development Bank Working Paper. January 2009. Washington, DC: IDB.

40 Buchanan, R. (2007), 'Competition: Beer and Oil Monopolies Head the List of Targets', *Financial Times*, 12 December.

41 Parks, K. (2007), 'Mexico's Iusacell Eyes Expansion Into Latin America', *Dow Jones Newswire*, 28 August.

42 América Móvil case study in Casanova, L. and Fraser, M., et al. (2009), 'From Multi-latinas to Global Latinas – The Latin American Multinationals (Compilation Case Studies)' Inter-American Development Bank Working Paper. January 2009. Washington, DC: IDB.

43 Telmex paid US$628 million for Embratel and MCI had originally paid US$2.3 billion.

44 América Móvil case study in Casanova, L. and Fraser, M., et al. (2009), 'From Multi-latinas to Global Latinas – The Latin American Multinationals (Compilation Case Studies)' Inter-American Development Bank Working Paper. January 2009. Washington, DC: IDB.

45 *International Herald Tribune* (2007), 'Telecom Italia Becomes National Drama', 8 April; and *New York Times* (2007), 'AT&T Drops Offer to Invest in Telecom Italia', 17 April.

46 *Reuters* (2007), 'AT&T, América Móvil Seek Telecom Italia Deal', 1 April.

47 *The Independent* (London) (2007), 'Carlos Slim: The Mexican Tycoon Who Could Soon be the World's Richest Man', 10 March; see also *Financial Times* (2007) ' "About to Hang Up?" His Sons in Charge, Mexico's Slim Now Looks to His Legacy', 25 September.

48 Grupo Bimbo case study in Casanova, L. and Fraser, M., et al. (2009), 'From Multi-latinas to Global Latinas – The Latin American Multinationals (Compilation Case Studies)' Inter-American Development Bank Working Paper. January 2009. Washington, DC: IDB.

49 Ibid.

50 Ibid.

51 Dawar, N. and Frost, T. (1999), 'Competing with Giants: Survival Strategies for Local Companies in Emerging Markets', *Harvard Business Review*, Vol. 77, No. 2 (March–April), 119–129, 187.

52 Goldstein, A. (2007), *Multinational Companies from Emerging Economies: Conceptualization and Direction in the Global Economy.* New York, NY: Palgrave Macmillan, p. 71.

53 Prakash, A. and Hart, J.A. (eds) (2000), *Responding to Globalization.* London: Routledge, p. 195.

54 Grupo Bimbo case study in Casanova, L. and Fraser, M., et al. (2009), 'From Multi-latinas to Global Latinas – The Latin American Multinationals

(Compilation Case Studies)' Inter-American Development Bank Working Paper. January 2009. Washington, DC: IDB.

55 *The Economist* (2002), 'Grupo Bimbo: Pushing North', 20 May.

56 Grupo Bimbo case study in Casanova, L. and Fraser, M., et al. (2009), 'From Multi-latinas to Global Latinas – The Latin American Multinationals (Compilation Case Studies)' Inter-American Development Bank Working Paper. January 2009. Washington, DC: IDB.

CHAPTER 4 – BUSINESS MODEL INNOVATION IN LATIN AMERICA: MAKING THE UNUSUAL USUAL

1 Chung, R., Marchand, D. and Kettinger, W. (2005), *The Cemex Way: The Right Balance Between Local Business Flexibility and Global Standardization.* Case Study No. IMD-3-1341. Lausanne, Switzerland: IMD – International Institute for Management Development.

2 Dutta, S. (2001), *Technology Excellence in the Developing World: Mission Impossible?* INSEAD Working Paper. Research in Information Systems Excellence. 2001/66/TM/RISE.

3 Ghemawat, P. and Matthews, J.H. (2000), *The Globalization of Cemex*, Case Study No. 9-701-017. Boston, USA: Harvard Business School Publishing.

4 Miller, S. (2002), 'Emerging Titans', *Foreign Direct Investment*, December 2002/ January 2003. Retrieved October 2007 from http://www.fdimagazine.com.

5 For a detailed description of the post-merger integration approach of Cemex, see Austin, M. (2004), 'Global Integration the Cemex way', *Corporate Dealmaker*, 1 March.

6 *The Economist* (2001), 'The Cemex Way', 14 June.

7 Bear Stearns (2007), *Cemex S.A. de C.V. – The Cash King*, Analyst Report, 22 March.

8 Kim, W.C. and Mauborgne, R. (2005), *Blue Ocean Strategy: How to Create Uncontested Market Space and Make the Competition Irrelevant.* Boston, USA: Harvard Business School Press.

9 Rekha, R., Iyengar, H. and Venkatesh, T. (2005), *Cemex, Mexico – Revolutionizing Low-cost Housing.* Case Study No. 505-081-1. Bangalore, India: ICFAI Business School, Bangalore.

10 See United Nations Centre for Human Settlements (2001), *Cities in a Globalizing World.* London: Earthscan. Free preview at: http://books.google.co.uk/books.

11 Bear Stearns (2007), *Cemex S.A. de C.V. – The Cash King*, Analyst Report, 22 March.

12 Van Agtmael, A. (2007), *The Emerging Markets Century.* New York: Free Press, 176–182.

13 Fraser, I. (2006), 'Natura's Back-to-Nature Success', *World Business*, July–August, 32–33.

14 Ibid., p. 34.

15 The 2007 figures were reported in Brazilian *reais* (millions) on www.finance.google.com as follows: annual revenue, BRL 3,072.70 and net income (profit), BRL 462.25. The figures were converted into US dollars by the author and rounded up on 8 July 2008.

16 Fraser, I. (2006), 'Natura's Back-to-nature Success', *World Business*, July–August, 32–33.

17 Chattopadhyay, A., Tanure, B. and Paavola, N. (2006), *Natura: Expanding beyond Latin America*, INSEAD Case Study, No. 06/2007-5635, Fontainebleau; see also Sull, D., Ruelas-Gossi, A. and Escobari, M. (2003), 'Innovating Around Obstacles', *Strategy & Innovation*, Harvard Business School, November–December.

18 The contribution to this section of Ramón Molina and his team at Universidad Adolfo Ibáñez in Chile is gratefully acknowledged.

19 Corporate website at: http://www.conchaytoro.com.

20 Concha y Toro *Annual Report, 2007*, available at: http://www.conchaytoro.com.

21 Van Agtmael, A. (2007), *The Emerging Markets Century*. New York: Free Press, pp. 75–81.

22 Concha y Toro, *Annual Report, 2007*, available at: http://www.conchaytoro.com.

23 Ibid.; see also Van Agtmael, A. (2007), *The Emerging Markets Century*. New York: Free Press, pp. 75–81.

24 Information taken from the corporate website on February 2008. Available at: http://www.grupo.bimbo.com.

25 Goldstein, A. (2007), *Multinational Companies from Emerging Companies: Composition, Conceptualization and Direction in the Global Economy*. New York: Palgrave Macmillan, p. 71.

26 Grupo Bimbo case study in Casanova, L. and Fraser, M., et al. (2009), 'From Multi-latinas to Global Latinas – The Latin American Multinationals (Compilation Case Studies)' Inter-American Development Bank Working Paper. January 2009. Washington, DC: IDB.

27 The contribution to this section of Carlos Arruda and André Almeida at Fundação Dom Cabral in Brazil is gratefully acknowledged. The financial support of Orkestra, the competitiveness institute of the Basque Country for the research in this section is gratefully acknowledged.

28 Information on Politec is drawn from the case study in Casanova, L. and Fraser, M. (2009), *From Multilatinas to Global Latinas: The New Latin American Multinationals*, Washington, DC: Inter-American Development Bank.

29 Aguiar, M., Bhattacharya, A., de Vitton, L. et al. (2007), *The 2008 BCG 100 New Global Challengers – How Top Companies Are Changing the World*. The Boston Consulting Group, December, pp. 7–10.

30 Ibid., pp. 18–27.

31 Van Agtmael, A. (2007), *The Emerging Markets Century*. New York: Free Press, p. 222.

32 Aguiar, M., Bhattacharya, A., de Vitton, L. et al. (2007), *The 2008 BCG 100 New Global Challengers – How Top Companies Are Changing the World*. The Boston Consulting Group, December, p. 19.

33 Ibid., p. 22.

34 Haberer, P. and Kohan, A.F. (2007), 'Building Global Champions in Latin America', *McKinsey Quarterly*, in special edition, March: Shaping a New Agenda for Latin America, pp. 46–47.

35 Available from corporate website at: http://www.tenaris.com.

36 Aguiar, M., Bhattacharya, A., de Vitton, L. et al. (2007), *The 2008 BCG 100 New Global Challengers – How Top Companies Are Changing the World*. The Boston Consulting Group, December, p. 23.

37 Van Agtmael, A. (2007), *The Emerging Markets Century*. New York: Free Press, pp. 220–221.

38 Ibid., p. 224.

39 Ibid.

40 Goldstein, A. (2007), *Multinational Companies from Emerging Economies: Conceptualization and Direction in the Global Economy*. New York, NY: Palgrave Macmillan, p. 121; Toulan, O. (2002), 'The Impact of Market Liberalization on Vertical Scope: The Case of Argentina', *Strategic Management Journal*, 23, 551–560.

41 Van Agtmael, A. (2007), *The Emerging Markets Century*. New York: Free Press, p. 225.

42 Goldstein, A. (2007), *Multinational Companies from Emerging Economies: Composition, Conceptualization and Direction in the Global Economy*. New York, NY: Palgrave, p. 121.

43 Corporate website and Annual Report 2007, available at: http://www.tenaris. com.

44 Aguiar, M., Bhattacharya, A., de Vitton, L. et al. (2007), *The 2008 BCG 100 New Global Challengers – How Top Companies Are Changing the World*. The Boston Consulting Group, December, p. 22.

45 Figures obtained from Grupo Modelo Annual Report 2007 relate to the value of the Mexican *peso* as of December 2007. Available at: http://www.gmodelo.com.mx.

46 Ibid., p. 19.

47 Ibid., p. 18.

48 Van Agtmael, A. (2007), *The Emerging Markets Century*. New York: Free Press, pp. 93–95.

49 Ibid., pp. 94–95.

50 Ibid., p. 95.

51 Corporate website, Grupo Modelo. Available at: http://gmodelo.com.mx.

52 Natura Cosméticos case study in Casanova, L. and Fraser, M., et al. (2009), 'From Multi-latinas to Global Latinas – The Latin American Multinationals (Compilation Case Studies)' Inter-American Development Bank Working Paper. January 2009. Washington, DC: IDB.

53 Corporate website. Available at: http://www2.natura.net.

CHAPTER 5 – LATIN AMERICA AS A BRAND: HARD SELL AND SOFT SELL

1 'Fuels for friendship', *The Economist*, 1 March 2007.

2 The crisis started in October 1973, when the Organization of Arab Petroleum Exporting Countries (OAPEC) announced during the Yom Kippur War that it would not send oil to countries supporting Israel.

3 BBC News (2007), 'US-Brazil deal to boost bio-fuels', 10 March. Available at: http://www.bbc.co.uk.

4 *Latin America-Asia Review* (2007), 'Biofuels: What the Trend Means', April, p. 5.

5 Rideg, T. and Smith, M. (2007), 'Big Upside Potential for Brazil's Ethanol Industry', *Tendencias InfoAmericas*, Latin American Market Report, p. 4.

6 Ibid., p. 3.

7 Ibid., p. 4.

8 Petrobras' research and development center (CENPES) is working on 'second generation' biofuels, derived from different types of biomass. In this case, CENPES is intensifying its work on creating ethanol from sugarcane bagasse and straw, with the aim of producing quantities on a semi-industrial scale by 2010. It is continuing to develop its H-Bio technology, which produces a high-quality diesel that generates lower levels of sulfur. Petrobras has well-developed plans to export biofuel products to markets in Japan, India and South Africa. *Petrobras Magazine* (2007), 'Corporate strategy', 53rd edition. Available at corporate website: http:// www2.petrobras.com.br.

9 Rideg, T. and Smith, M. (2007), 'Big Upside Potential for Brazil's Ethanol Industry', *Tendencias InfoAmericas*, Latin American Market Report, p. 10.

10 *Reuters* (2008), 'RPT-Brazil Cellulosic Ethanol Plant Possible in 5 Yrs', 5 June. Available at: http://uk.reuters.com.

11 BBC News (2007), 'US-Brazil Deal to Boost Bio-fuels', 10 March. Available at: http://www.bbc.co.uk.

12 Rideg, T. and Smith, M. (2007), 'Big Upside Potential for Brazil's Ethanol Industry', *Tendencias InfoAmericas*, Latin American Market Report, p. 3.

13 Riveras, I. (2008), 'Brazil Ethanol, Sugar Mills Miss the Commodity Boom', *Reuters*, 7 July. Available at: http://uk.reuters.com.

14 *Reuters* (2008), 24 April. Available at: http://uk.reuters.com/article/environment News/idUKN2434962420080424.

15 Riveras, I. and Khalip, A. (2008), 'Ethanol Consolidation to Increase in Brazil', *Reuters*, 24 April. Available at: http://uk.reuters.com.

16 Luna, D. (2008), 'Petrobras' 1st Ethanol Pipeline, Mill Ready in '09', *Reuters*, 12 June. Available at: http://uk.reuters.com.

17 'Ethanol On the Rise', *Petrobras Magazine*, 52nd edition. Available at corporate website: http:// www2.petrobras.com.br.

18 *The Economist* (2008), 'Grow Your Own: The Biofuels of the Future Will be Tailor-made', in A Special Report on the Future of Energy, 21–27 June, 15–17.

19 Ibid., p. 17.

20 Ibid.

21 *Petrobras Magazine* (2007), 'Corporate strategy', 53rd edition. Available at corporate website: http:// www2.petrobras.com.br.

22 'Ethanol On the Rise', *Petrobras Magazine*, 52nd edition. Available at corporate website: http:// www2.petrobras.com.br.

23 Ibid.

24 Bound, K. (2008), 'Brazil – the Natural Knowledge Economy', *The Atlas of Ideas*. London: Demos. Further information available at http://www.demos. co.uk.

25 Demerjian, D. (2008), *Wired Blog Network*, 23 April. Available at: http://blog.wired.com.

26 Bound, K. (2008), 'Brazil – the Natural Knowledge Economy', *The Atlas of Ideas*. London: Demos, p. 75. Further information available at http://www.demos.co.uk.

27 Ibid.

28 Schexnayder, C.J. (2006), 'Have Fish, will Travel', *Latin Trade*, 1 August. Retrieved on Factiva database in October 2007.

29 Harman, D. (2006), 'Incan Fusion at a *Cevichería* Near You', *The Christian Science Monitor*, 20 April. Retrieved on Factiva database in October 2007.

30 *The Economist* (2004), 'Just Add Spice', 29 January.

31 Astrid and Gastón case study in Casanova, L. and Fraser, M., et al. (2009), 'From Multi-latinas to Global Latinas – The Latin American Multinationals

(Compilation Case Studies)' Inter-American Development Bank Working Paper. January 2009. Washington, DC: IDB.

32 Schexnayder, C.J. (2006), 'Have Fish, will Travel', *Latin Trade*, 1 August.

33 Miliken, M. (2006), 'Chef Prepares Peruvian Cuisine to Conquer the World', *Reuters News*, 1 March. Retrieved from Factiva database in October 2007.

34 *América Economia* (2007), 'Banquete Latino', 8 October.

35 Astrid and Gastón case study in Casanova, L. and Fraser, M., et al. (2009), 'From Multi-latinas to Global Latinas – The Latin American Multinationals (Compilation Case Studies)' Inter-American Development Bank Working Paper. January 2009. Washington, DC: IDB.

36 Pollo Campero case study in Casanova, L. and Fraser, M., et al. (2009), 'From Multi-latinas to Global Latinas – The Latin American Multinationals (Compilation Case Studies)' Inter-American Development Bank Working Paper. January 2009. Washington, DC: IDB.

37 Ibid.

38 *El Periódico de Guatemala* (2007), 'Un Pollo Al Que Le Quedó Chiquita Centroamérica', 12 February.

39 Corporate website – http://www.campero.com.

40 Pollo Campero case study in Casanova, L. and Fraser, M., et al. (2009), 'From Multi-latinas to Global Latinas – The Latin American Multinationals (Compilation Case Studies)' Inter-American Development Bank Working Paper. January 2009. Washington, DC: IDB.

41 *Expansión* (2006), 'El socio Americano de Telepizza llega a España en plena puja la cadena', 15 July.

42 *América Economía* (2007), 'Pollo Oriental', 12 March.

43 Politec case study in Casanova, L. and Fraser, M., et al. (2009), 'From Multi-latinas to Global Latinas – The Latin American Multinationals (Compilation Case Studies)' Inter-American Development Bank Working Paper. January 2009. Washington, DC: IDB.

44 Farrell, D., Laboissière, M. and Pietracci, B. (2007), 'Assessing Brazil's Off-shoring Prospects', *The McKinsey Quarterly*, Special edition, March: *Shaping a New Agenda for Latin America*.

45 Politec case study in Casanova, L. and Fraser, M., et al. (2009), 'From Multi-latinas to Global Latinas – The Latin American Multinationals (Compilation Case Studies)' Inter-American Development Bank Working Paper. January 2009. Washington, DC: IDB.

46 Gisoldi, R. (2008), 'The country plans to export US$5 billion in information technology', 28 May, Brasscom's website (http://www.brasscom.com.br).

47 Politec case study in Casanova, L. and Fraser, M., et al. (2009), 'From Multi-latinas to Global Latinas – The Latin American Multinationals (Compilation Case Studies)' Inter-American Development Bank Working Paper. January 2009. Washington, DC: IDB.

48 BBC News (2008), 'G8 Vows to Halve Greenhouse Gases', 8 July. Available at: http://www.bbc.co.uk.

CHAPTER 6 – ASIA'S CHALLENGE TO LATIN AMERICA: COOPERATION AND COMPETITION

1 Casanova, L. (2004), 'East Asian, European, and North American Multinational Firm Strategies in Latin America', *Business and Politics*, Vol. 6, No. 1, Article 6. http://www.bepress.com/bap/vol6/iss1/art6.

2 Pacek, N. and Thorniley, D. (2007), *Emerging Markets: Lessons for Business Success and the Outlook for Different Markets* (2nd ed). London: Profile Books, p. 216.

3 Economist Intelligence Unit, in association with the Columbia Program on International Investment (2007), *World Investment Prospects to 2011: Foreign Direct Investment and the Challenge of Political Risk*, p. 37.

4 Also of interest, by 2006, the Eastern Europe region had replaced Latin America as the second most important emerging market for FDI, even though the total FDI flow into Latin America still exceeded US$100 billion. On the positive side, FDI flows into Latin America doubled during 2004–2005, after plummeting to US$47 billion in 2003.

5 The Maquila Portal. http://www.maquilaportal.com.

6 'Zorba', 'Maquila Labor Trends' at http://www.maquilaportal.com/public/artic/artic20.htm.

7 The Maquila Portal. http://www.maquilaportal.com.

8 Nissan Marubeni Website. http://www.nissanmarubeni.cl/fempresa.html.

9 Sukehiro, H. (1975), *Japanese Foreign Aid: Policy and Practice*. New York: Praeger.

10 Usiminas. http://eng.usiminas.com.br.

11 Companhia Siderúrgica Tubarão at http://www.cst.com.br.

12 As for Japanese expatriates, Brazil has the highest number (72,000) after the United States (316,000), *International Herald Tribune*, 25–26 October 2003.

13 The Maquila Portal. http://www.maquilaportal.com.

14 *Latin Business Chronicle* (2007), 'China Undermines US in Latin America', 4 June, p. 1. Available online at: www.latinbusinesschronicle.com.

15 Caspary, G. (2008), 'China Eyes Latin American Commodities', *Latin Business Chronicle*, 21 January (republished with the permission of the Yale Center for the Study of Globalization).

16 *Latin Business Chronicle* (2007), 'China Undermines US in Latin America', 4 June, p. 2. Available online at: www.latinbusinesschronicle.com.

17 Ibid., p. 8.

18 *Latin America-Asia Review* (2006), 'China's Changing Relationship with Latin America', September, p. 1.

19 Ministry of Commerce: The People's Republic of China, available at: http://english.mofcom.gov.cn/. Accessed 11 April 2007.

20 *Latin America-Asia Review* (2006), 'China's Changing Relationship with Latin America', September, p. 1.

21 *Latin Business Chronicle* (2007), 'China Undermines US in Latin America', 4 June, p. 9.

22 Ibid.

23 Ibid.

24 Lederman, D., Olarreaga, M. and Perry, G. (2006), *Latin America and the Caribbean's Response to the Growth of China and India: Overview of Research Findings and Policy Implications*. Washington, DC: The World Bank: Office of the Chief Economist – Latin America and the Caribbean Region, p. 14. Paper prepared for the program of seminars at the World Bank and IMF annual meetings held in Singapore, August.

25 Ibid., pp. 16–17.

26 Ibid., pp. 37–38.

27 In September 2007, China launched a US$200 billion investment sovereign fund called the China Investment Corporation (CIC) to get greater returns for its foreign exchange reserves.

28 Arroba, A.A., Avendaño, R. and Estrada, J. (2008), *Adapting to the Rise of China: How can Latin American Companies Succeed?* World Economic Forum and the OECD Development Centre, p. 15.

29 Ibid., p. 15.

30 Ibid., p. 17.

31 Ibid., p. 19.

32 Cevallos, D. (2008), 'Science: Latin America Lags in Innovation and Technology', *Tierramérica News Service*, p. 1.

33 Ibid., p. 2.

34 Arroba, A.A., Avendaño, R. and Estrada, J. (2008), *Adapting to the Rise of China: How can Latin American Companies Succeed?* World Economic Forum and the OECD Development Centre, p. 20.

35 Ibid., p. 21.

CHAPTER 7 – FROM GLOBAL LATINA TO A CORPORATE CITIZEN: ARE POVERTY AND INEQUALITY BUSINESS ISSUES?

1 Corporate social responsibility in Latin America: Interview of Marcelo Linguitte from Ethos; document included in the Digital Library of the Inter-American Initiative on Social Capital, Ethics and Development of the Inter-American Development Bank (IDB). www.iadb.org/ethics accessed as of 24 June 2008.

2 Economic Commission for Latin America and the Caribbean (ECLAC) (2007), *Social Panorama of Latin America.* Santiago, Chile: United Nations.

3 Prahalad, C.K. (2004), *The Fortune at the Bottom of the Pyramid: Eradicating Poverty Through Profits.* Upper Saddle River, NJ: Wharton School Publishing.

4 OECD (2008), *Latin American Economic Outlook.*

5 Rioseco, M.J. (2004), 'La Gran Mano de los Más Grandes', Americaeconomica.com; 4 April.

6 Guevara, M. (2004), 'Best Corporate Citizens 2004', *Latin Trade,* May.

7 Ayub, Arturo Elías (general manager, Telmex Foundation) (2004), quoted in Guevara, M. (2004), 'Best Corporate Citizens 2004', *Latin Trade,* May.

8 Porter, M.E. and Kramer, M.R. (2006), 'Strategy and Society: The Link Between Competitive Advantage and Corporate Social Responsibility', *Harvard Business Review,* December.

9 2007 Edition of the sustainability guide published by the Brazilian business magazine *Exame: Guia Exame 2007 de Sustentabilidade,* December 2007.

10 Schwab, K. (2008), 'Global Corporate Citizenship: Working with Governments and Civil Society', *Foreign Affairs,* January/February.

11 Ayub, Arturo Elías (general manager, Telmex Foundation) (2004), *Latin Trade,* May.

12 Benchmarking created by the magazine *Latin Trade* and the Spanish consulting firm 'Management and excellence', based on the responses of 258 companies, big and small. May 2005.

13 Prada, P. and Rueda, M. (2005), 'The Good-deed Column', *Latin Trade,* May.

14 See www.management-rating.com.

15 The term 'remittances' refers to the money sent back by emigrants to their home country to support their families. For Mexico, remittance payments from the United States are the second biggest source of foreign currency after oil export revenues.

16 Mexico is the second biggest world producer of silver and the fifth biggest producer of lead and oil; Venezuela is the fifth exporter of oil, while Chile is the top exporter of copper. Peru is the third producer of lead and the ninth producer of gold.

17 Cardenas-Moller, M. and Bianco, A. (2006), *Sustainable Development of the Latin American Mining Industry.* Sinclair Knight Merz: SKM Technical Papers, 25 January.

18 The *maquila* program of Mexico provided in-bond assembly for re-export, and permitted US-based firms to export tax-free parts manufactured in the United States for assembly in Mexico. Re-exports to the United States faced a tariff on the overseas value-added component.

19 OECD (2008), *Latin America Economic Outlook 2008.*

20 Ross, J. (2006), 'Brazil Makes Headway in Bid for "Zero Hunger"', *Christian Science Monitor*, 11 September.

CONCLUSION: GLOBAL LATINAS AND GLOBALIZATION 3.0

1 Thomson, A. (2007), 'Richer, More Confident, But Still Looking to the US', *Financial Times*, 12 December.

2 Ibid.

3 Wheatley, J. and Lapper, R. (2008), 'Surfing a Big Wave of Confidence', *Financial Times*, 8 July.

4 Wheatley, J. (2008), 'Byzantine Taxes Sap Brazil's Business Spirit', *Financial Times*, 25 February.

5 Wheatley, J. and Lapper, R. (2008), 'Surfing a Big Wave of Confidence', *Financial Times*, 8 July.

6 PricewaterhouseCoopers (2008), 'Competing And Collaborating: What Is Success in a Connected World?', 11th Annual Global CEO Survey 2008, p. 4. Available at: http://www.pwc.com/ceosurvey.

BIBLIOGRAPHY

Accenture (2008), *Multi-Polar World 2: The Rise of the Emerging-Market Multinational*. Accenture.

Aguiar, M., Bhattacharya, A., Bradtke, T., Cotte, P., Dertnig, S., Meyer, M., Michael, D.C., and Sirkin, H.L. (2006), *The New Global Challengers – How 100 Top Companies from Rapidly Developing Economies are Changing the World*. Boston, MA: The Boston Consulting Group.

Aguiar, M., Bhattacharya, A., de Vitton, L., Hemerling, J., Wee Koh, K., Michael, D.C., Sirkin, H.L., Waddell, K., and Waltermann, B. (2007), *The 2008 BCG 100 New Global Challengers – How Top Companies Are Changing the World*. Boston, MA: The Boston Consulting Group.

Arroba, A.A., Avendaño, R., and Estrada, J. (2008), *Adapting to the Rise of China: How can Latin American Companies Succeed?* World Economic Forum and the OECD Development Centre.

Austin, J., Reficco, E., Berger, G., Fischer, R.M., Gutiérrez, R., Koljatic, M., Lozano, G., Ogliastri, E. and the Social Enterprise Knowledge Network Research Team (2004), *Social Partnering in Latin America: Lessons Drawn from Collaborations of Business and Civil Society Organizations*. Cambridge, MA: Harvard University Press.

Aykut, D. and Goldstein, A. (2006), *Developing Country Multinationals: South-South Investment Comes of Age*, Industrial Development for the 21st Century: Sustainable Development Perspectives, OECD.

Bear Stearns (2007), *Cemex S.A. de C.V. – The Cash King*. Analyst Report, 22 March.

Bound, K. (2008), 'Brazil – The Natural Knowledge Economy', *The Atlas of Ideas*. London: Demos.

Brandão, F. (1998), *The Petrobras Monopoly and the Regulation of Oil Prices in Brazil*. Oxford: Oxford Institute for Energy Studies.

Business Insights Limited (2006), *The Top Ten Oil & Gas Companies – Growth Strategies, Consolidation and Convergence in the Leading Players*. Industry Report, Business Insights Limited.

Cardenas-Moller, M. and Bianco, A. (2006), *Sustainable Development of the Latin American Mining Industry*. Sinclair Knight Merz Technical Papers, 25 January.

Casanova, L. (2002), 'Lazos de Familia: Las Inversiones Españolas en Iberoamérica', *Foreign Affairs* (Spanish version), Vol. 2, No. 2, May.

Casanova, L. (2004), 'East Asian, European, and North American Multinational Firm Strategies in Latin America', *Business and Politics*, Vol. 6, No. 1, Article 6.

Casanova, L. (2005), 'Latin America: Economic and Business Context', *International Journal of Human Resource Management*, Vol. 16, No. 12, December, 2173–2188.

Casanova, L. and Fraser, M., et al. (2009), 'From Multi-latinas to Global Latinas – The Latin American Multinationals (Compilation Case Studies)' Inter-American Development Bank Working Paper. January 2009. Washington, DC: IDB.

Casanova, L., Gradillas, M., Abouchakra, R. and Somani, D. (2005), *América Móvil: Building a Wireless Leader in Latin America (A & B)*. Fontainebleau: INSEAD.

Cemex, S.A.B. de C.V. (ed.) (2006), *Cemex – The Centennial Book* (1st ed.). México: Editorial Clío, Libros y Videos, S.A. de C.V.

Chaddad, F.R. (2003), *CVRD Mining by 2010: Redrawing Firm Boundaries for 3x Market Cap*. Case Study No. 303-003-1. São Paulo, Brazil: Accenture.

Chattopadhyay, A., Tanure, B. and Paavola, N. (2006), *Natura: Expanding beyond Latin America*, INSEAD case study, No. 06/2007-5635 Fontainebleau: INSEAD.

Chung, R., Marchand, D., and Kettinger, W. (2005), *The Cemex Way: The Right Balance between Local Business Flexibility and Global Standardization*. Case Study No. IMD-3-1341. Lausanne, Switzerland: IMD – International Institute for Management Development.

Cirera, X., McCullock, N., and Winters, A.L. (2001), *Trade Liberalization and Poverty: A Handbook*. London: Center for Economic Policy Research. Department for International Development.

Citigroup Smith Barney (2005), *Cemex S.A. de C.V. (CX) – Concrete Punch!* Analyst Report, 3 March.

Credit Suisse First Boston (1995), *Companhia Vale do Rio Doce – Riding on the Strength of Brazil's Natural Resources*. Analyst Report, 9 October.

Cuervo-Cazurra, A. (2007), 'Liberalización Económica y Multilatinas', Revista Globalización, Competitividad y Gobernabilidad, Georgetown University / Universia, Vol. 1. No. 1, 66–87, 2007.

Datamonitor (2007), *Companhia Vale do Rio Doce*. Company Profile No. C9952AB1-8493-4737-9A36-703B59C381C2.

Dawar, N. and Frost, T. (1999), 'Competing with Giants: Survival Strategies for Local Companies in Emerging Markets', *Harvard Business Review*, Vol. 77, No. 2, 119–129, 187.

Desai, M. and Reisen de Pinho, R. (2003), *Drilling South: Petrobras Evaluates Pecom.* Case Study No. 9-204-043. Boston, US: Harvard Business School Publishing.

Deutsche Bank (2004), *Global Cement Update – Mexican Wave.* Analyst Report, 26 November.

Devlin, R., Estevadeordal, A., and Rodriguez, A. (2004), *The Emergence of China: Opportunities and Challenges for Latin America and the Caribbean.* Washington: Inter-American Development Bank. Integration and Regional Programs Research Department.

Diniz, C.C. and Razavi, M. (1999), 'São José dos Campos and Campinas: State-anchored Dynamos', in Markusen, A., Lee, Y.S. and Digiovanna, S. (eds) *Second Tier Cities: Rapid Growth Beyond the Metropolis.* Minneapolis: University of Minnesota, 97–126.

Dosi, G., Nelson, R., and Winter, S. (2000), *The Nature and Dynamics of Organizational Capabilities.* Oxford: Oxford University Press.

Dunning, J.H. (1993), *Multinational Enterprises and the Global Economy.* Reading, MA: Addison-Wesley.

Dutta, S. (2001), *Technology Excellence in the Developing World: Mission Impossible?* INSEAD Working Paper. Research in Information Systems Excellence. 2001/66/TM/RISE.

Economic Commission for Latin America and the Caribbean (ECLAC) (2006), *Foreign Investment in Latin America and the Caribbean, 2005.* Santiago, Chile: United Nations.

Economic Commission for Latin America and the Caribbean (ECLAC) (2007), *Foreign Direct Investment in Latin America and the Caribbean, 2006.* Santiago, Chile: United Nations.

Economic Commission for Latin America and the Caribbean (ECLAC) (2007), *Social Panorama of Latin America.* Santiago, Chile: United Nations.

Economic Commission for Latin America and the Caribbean (ECLAC) (2007), *Economic Growth in Latin America and the Caribbean: Multiple Growth Transitions in the Absence of Steady States*, Economic Survey of Latin America and the Caribbean 2006–2007. Santiago, Chile: United Nations.

Economist Intelligence Unit (2007), *World Investment Prospects to 2011: Foreign Direct Investment and the Challenge of Political Risk*, Economist Intelligence Unit written with the Columbia Program on International Investment.

Euromoney Institutional Investor (1998), *Corporate Dialogue: Cemex. Institutional Investor – International Edition*, Vol. 23, No. 12. Retrieved October 2007, from Business Source Premier database.

Evans, P.B. (1979), *Dependent Development: The Alliance of Multinational, State, and Local Capital in Brazil.* Princeton, N.J.: Princeton University Press.

Farrell, D., Laboissière, M. and Pietracci, B. (2007), 'Assessing Brazil's Offshoring Prospects', *The McKinsey Quarterly*, special edition, March, Shaping a New Agenda for Latin America.

Fink, H. and Mittman, G. (2003), *Cemex's Market Entry into Indonesia*. MBA paper, INSEAD.

Forteza, J.H. and Neilson, G.L. (1999), *Toward the Next Generation Multinationals in Latin America*. USA: Booz Allen and Hamilton.

Friedman, M. (1962), *Capitalism and Freedom*. Chicago: University of Chicago Press.

Fuentes-Bérain, R. (2007), *Oro Gris. Zambrano, la Gesta de Cemex y la Globalización en México* (1st ed.), Mexico City, Mexico: Santilla Ediciones Generales, S.A. de C.V.

Ghemawat, P. (2005), 'Regional Strategies for Global Leadership', *Harvard Business Review*, Vol. 83, No. 12.

Ghemawat, P. (2007), *Redefining Global Strategy*. Boston: Harvard Business School Press.

Ghemawat, P. and Matthews, J.L. (2000), *The Globalization of Cemex*. Case Study No. 9-701-017. Boston, USA: Harvard Business School Publishing.

Ghemawat, P., Herrero, G., and Monteiro, L. (2000), *Embraer: The Global Leader in Regional Jets*. Harvard Business School Case Studies, 701-006.

Goldberg, R.A., Knoop, C., and Sunder, S.R. (1998), *Grupo Industrial Bimbo S.A.* Boston, MA: Harvard Business School Publishing, 4 December.

Goldstein, A. (2007), *Multinational Companies from Emerging Economies: Composition, Conceptualization and Direction in the Global Economy*. New York, NY: Palgrave Macmillan.

Goldstein, A. and McGuire, S. (2004), 'The Political Economy of Strategic Trade Policy: Explaining the Brazil-Canada WTO Export Subsidies Saga', *The World Economy*, Vol. 27, No. 4, 541–566.

González, R.A. and Viana, H. (2006), 'Cruzsalud. Prepaid Health Care for Low Income Consumers', in *ReVista: Harvard Review of Latin America*. Fall 2006 issue on *Social Enterprise, Making a Difference*. Cambridge, MA: David Rockefeller Center for Latin American Studies.

Grosse, R. and Mesquita, L.F. (eds.) (2007), *Can Latin American Firms Compete?* Oxford: Oxford University Press.

Haberer, P. and Kohan, A.F. (2007), 'Building Global Champions in Latin America', *McKinsey Quarterly*, special edition, March, Shaping a New Agenda for Latin America.

Hamel, G. (2006), 'The Why, What and How of Management Innovation', *Harvard Business Review*, February, 1.

Inter-American Development Bank (2008), *Social Capital, Ethics and Development Fund.* http://condc05.iadb.org/iadbtrustfunds/funds/FundDetails.aspx? FundId = 174&DonorId = NO&FundName = Social%20Capital,%20Ethics%20and%20 Development %20Fund. Accessed as of June 2008.

Jenkins, R. (2005), 'Globalization, Corporate Social Responsibility and Poverty', *International Affairs*, Vol. 81, 525–540.

Jones, G.G. and Reisen de Pinho, R. (2006), *Natura: Global Beauty Made in Brazil*, *Harvard Business School Case Studies, 9-807-029.*

Kerr, J. (2003), *Petrobras and the PT Government in Brazil.* Industry Report, Global Insight. Retrieved October 2007 from Global Insight database.

Kerr, J. (2005), *Lessons from Brazil's Proalcool Ethanol Programme.* Industry Report. Global Insight. Retrieved October 2007 from Global Insight database.

Khanna, T. and Palepu, K. (2002), *Emerging Markets Giants: Building World Class Companies in Emerging Markets.* Case Study No. 703–431. Boston: Harvard Business School.

Khanna, T. and Palepu, K. (2006), 'Emerging Giants: Building World-Class Companies in Emerging Markets', *Harvard Business Review*, Vol. 84, October, 60–69.

Kim, W.C. and Mauborgne, R. (2005), *Blue Ocean Strategy: How to Create Uncontested Market Space and Make the Competition Irrelevant.* Boston, USA: Harvard Business School Press.

Kose, M.A., Meredith, G.M., and Towe, C.M. (2004), *How Has NAFTA Affected the Mexican Economy? Review and Evidence*, IMF Working Paper, IMF, April.

Lasserre, P. and Picoto, J. (2007), *Cemex: Cementing a Global Strategy.* Case Study No. 307-233-1. Fontainebleau, France: INSEAD.

Latin American and Caribbean Institute for Economic and Social Planning (ILPES) / Economic Commission for Latin America and the Caribbean (ECLAC) (2008).

Lederman, D., Olarreaga, M., and Perry, G. (2006), *Latin America and the Caribbean's Response to the Growth of China and India: Overview of Research Findings and Policy Implications.* Washington: The World Bank – Office of the Chief Economist, Latin America and the Caribbean Region.

Lee, H. and Hoyt, D. (2005), *Cemex: Transforming a Basic Industry Company.* Case Study No. GS33. Stanford, USA: Stanford University.

López-Claros, A. and Klaus, S. (2006), *Latin American Competitiveness Review: Paving the Way for Regional Prosperity.* Geneva, Switzerland: World Economic Forum.

Mariscal, J. and Rivera, E. (2007), 'Mobile Communications in Mexico in the Latin American context', *Information Technologies and International Development*, Vol. 3, No. 2, 41–55.

Martínez, J. (2002), *Carlos Slim: Retrato Inédito.* México: Editorial Océano.

Martinez, A., De Souza, I., and Liu, F. (2003), 'Multinationals vs Multilatinas: Latin America's Great Race', *Strategy + Business*, 11 September.

Mergent (2007), *Mining – Latin America*. Industry Report No. 618. Retrieved October 2007 from Factiva database.

Moreno, L.A. (2006), '*Unlocking Opportunity. For a Neglected Majority*', in *ReVista: Harvard Review of Latin America*. Fall 2006 issues on *Social Enterprise, Making a Difference*. Cambridge, MA: David Rockefeller Center for Latin American Studies.

Network for Interchanging and Disseminating Excellent Experiences for Achieving the Millenium Development Goals. http://ideea.cepal.org/ideea/ideea.htm. Santiago de Chile: United Nations.

Nuttall, W.J. and Manz, D.L. (2008), *A New Energy Security Paradigm for the Twenty-first Century*, EPRG Working Paper, Judge Business School. Cambridge, UK: University of Cambridge.

Pacek, N. and Thorniley, D. (2007), *Emerging Markets: Lessons for Business Success and the Outlook for Different Markets* (2nd ed.), London: Profile Books.

Plunkert, P.A. (2002), 'Bauxite and Alumina'. In United States Geological Survey (ed.), *U.S. Geological Survey Minerals Yearbook – 2002*. Retrieved October 2007 from: http://minerals.usgs.gov/minerals/pubs/commodity/bauxite/index.html#pubs.

Porter, M.E. and Kramer, M.R. (2006), 'Strategy and Society: The Link Between Competitive Advantage and Corporate Social Responsibility', *Harvard Business Review*, December.

Prahalad, C.K. (2005), *The Fortune at the Bottom of the Pyramid: Eradicating Poverty Through Profits*. Upper Saddle River, NJ: Wharton School Publishing.

Prakash, A. and Hart, J.A. (2000), *Responding to Globalization*. New York: Routledge.

PricewaterhouseCoopers (2008), *Competing and Collaborating – What is Success in a Connected World?* 11th Annual Global CEO Survey. London.

Prudential Securities (1995), *Concha y Toro: Small Cap Research*, 22 December.

Rekha, R., Iyengar, H., and Venkatesh, T. (2005), *Cemex, Mexico – Revolutionizing Low-Cost Housing*. Case Study No. 505-081-1. Bangalore, India: ICFAI Business School, Bangalore.

RING Alliance (2003), *The Development Dimensions of the UN Global Compact*. July www.ring-alliance.org/documents/global_compact.pdf.

Roberts, J. and Podolny, J. (1998), *The Global Oil Industry*. Technical Note No. S-IB-15. Stanford, US: Stanford University.

Robles, F., Simon, F., and Haar, J. (2003), *Winning Strategies for the New Latin Markets*. New Jersey: Financial Times Prentice Hall Books.

Sanborn, C. and Delgado, A. (2006), 'Palmas del Espino. Harvesting Hope in the Upper Huallaga', in *ReVista: Harvard Review of Latin America*. Fall 2006 issue on *Social Enterprise, Making a Difference*. Fall. Cambridge, MA. David Rockefeller Center for Latin American Studies.

Sanborn, C. and Portocarrero, F. (eds) (2005), *Philanthropy and Social Change in Latin America*. Cambridge, MA: Harvard University Press. David Rockefeller Center for Latin American Studies.

Sánchez, G. (2006), *El Potencial Competitivo de Guatemala – Casos de Éxito de Empresas Guatemaltecas Competitivas*. Guatemala: INCAE Business School.

Santiso, J. (2007), *The Emergence of Latin Multinationals*. Frankfurt am Main: Deutsche Bank Research.

Sarathy, R. and Wesley, D. (2003), *Cemex – The Southdown Offer*. Case Study No. 8B03M013. London, Ontario, Canada: Richard Ivey School of Business.

Sauvant, K.P. (ed.), (2008), *The Rise of Transnational Corporations from Emerging Markets: Threat or Opportunity?* Northampton, UK: Edward Elgar Publishing.

Schwab, K. (2008), 'Global Corporate Citizenship: Working with Governments and Civil Society', *Foreign Affairs*, January/February 2008.

Segel, A., Chu, M., and Herrero, G. (2004), *Patrimonio Hoy*. Case Study No. 9-805-064. Boston, MA: Harvard Business School Publishing.

Siegel, J. (2007), *Grupo Bimbo*. Boston, MA: Harvard Business School Publishing.

Sikkink, K. (1992), *Ideas and Institutions: Developmentalism in Brazil and Argentina*. Cornell University Press.

Sinha, J. (2005), 'Global Champions from Emerging Markets', *McKinsey Quarterly*, No. 2, May 2005, 27–35.

Sukehiro, H. (1975), *Japanese Foreign Aid: Policy and Practice*. New York: Praeger.

Sull, D., Ruelas-Gossi, A., and Escobari, M. (2003), *Innovating Around Obstacles'*, *Strategy & Innovation*, Harvard Business School, November–December.

Sull, D.N. and Ruelas-Gossi, A. (2006), 'Orquestación Estratégica: La Clave Para la Agilidad en el Escenario Global', *Harvard Business Review América Latina*, Vol. 84, No. 11, 42–52.

United Nations Centre for Human Settlements (2001), *Cities in a Globalizing World*. London: Earthscan.

United Nations Conference on Trade and Development (UNCTAD). (2006), *World Investment Report 2006 – FDI from Developing and Transition Economies: Implications for Development* (United Nations publication no. E.06.II.D.11). New York and Geneva: United Nations.

United Nations Conference on Trade and Development (UNCTAD). (2007), *World Investment Report 2007: Transnational Corporations, Extractive Industries and Development*. New York and Geneva: United Nations.

Van Agtmael, A. (2007), *The Emerging Markets Century: How a New Breed of World-Class Companies is Overtaking the World*. New York: Free Press.

Vedpuriswar, A.V. and Krishna, T. (2003), *Cemex – Mexico's Global Giant*. Case Study No. 303-095-1. Hyderabad, India: ICFAI Knowledge Center.

Williamson, P. and Butler, C. (2001), *Cemex in Asia*. INSEAD Case Study No. 301-078-1. Fontainebleau, France: INSEAD.

Wilson, D. and Purushothaman, R. (2003), *Dreaming with BRICs: The Path to 2050*. Goldman Sachs Global Economics Paper No. 99. New York: Goldman Sachs.

World Economic Forum (2006), *Assessing Latin American Competitiveness: Challenges and Opportunities*, The Latin American Competitiveness Review 2006. Davos: World Economic Forum.

Yamada, G. and Chacaltana, J. (2007), *Generación de Empleo en el Perú: Seis Casos Recientes de Éxito*. Lima, Perú: Centro de Investigación de la Universidad del Pacífico.

Zeng, M. and Williamson, P.J. (2007), *Dragons at Your Door: How Chinese Cost Innovation is Disrupting the Rules of Global Competition*. Boston, MA: Harvard Business School Press.

INDEX